Darkness Over Europe

Darkness Over Europe

First-Person Accounts
of Life in Europe
During the War Years 1939–1945

Edited by Tony March
For Army Times Publishing Company

Rand McNally & Company Chicago New York San Francisco

Preface

Evil, as old as mankind itself, is distinguished from generation to generation and from era to era only by minor variations, although they are intensified by the mass possibilities of scientific methods of obliteration.

The hate and oppression of World War I merely ebbed after the Armistice in 1918 to return with vastly magnified virulence as World War II. By the time of VJ Day, in September, 1945, this global conflict had claimed the lives of nearly thirty-eight million civilians and military.

It was and still remains difficult to comprehend the misery and slaughter of those six terrible years. It is perhaps no easier to appreciate the conditions under which occupied Europe existed or to understand how so many people were in fact able to survive. Murky in the distancing years is the chronicle of day-to-day living, the events which are a part of being under abject tyranny.

The object of this book is to probe behind the front lines. It is not a history of armies and battles, but rather the life and times of the average man—drama and tragedy on a large scale, as well as in lesser vignettes. Some of the accounts are translated and published here for the first time.

The authors, with few exceptions, are not professional writers but people who themselves lived to tell about World War II at home.

Of all the persons who made this collection possible, the editor wishes to thank in particular H. R. Baukhage; Mrs. Margarete Buber-Faust of Stockholm, Sweden; Mrs. Ruth Chenault; Carlo Christensen, Cultural Attaché of the Royal Danish Embassy in Washington; Mrs. Kate Cohn (Catherine Klein) of London; Bjoern Heimar, Washington correspondent for the Oslo *Aftenposten;* Georgi I. Isachenko, Counselor, Embassy of the Union of Soviet Socialist Republics in Washington; Lieutenant Colonel Donald B. Stewart (United States Army, ret) of San Antonio, Texas; Emil Trinka of Lidgerwood, North Dakota; and Miss Lena A. Yovitchitch of Edinburgh, Scotland.

Table of Contents

Darkness Over Europe

Darkness Over Europe

Introduction

*On March 12, 1938, a raw spring Saturday, Germany's armies oc-
cupied the Austrian Republic and foreshadowed World War II in
Europe.*

The Nazi entry into Vienna was observed by the London Daily
Mail's *veteran correspondent, G. Ward Price, whose report in the
newspaper's March 13 issue was almost immediately relayed to
Hitler. Price wrote:*

I watched Herr Hitler throughout his triumphal drive today
through 120 miles of the Austrian countryside from Linz to the
capital, where a tremendous welcome awaited him.

"Have you ever known anything like this?" he asked me,
during the halt his long column of crowded open gray cars made
at St. Pölten for luncheon.

"And remember that if I had not come, there would have
been bloodshed instead of this rejoicing, and bitter tears instead
of joy."

From the outskirts of Vienna to its heart, the procession
drove for five miles at the slowest pace through solid banks of
people, packed forty, fifty, and—in the public squares and at the
openings of side streets—several hundreds deep.

Countless thousands could not even see Herr Hitler as he
stood, in his belted brown greatcoat and uniform peaked cap,
upright in the front seat of his car. But all could cheer him, and
they made a deafening tumult.

The whole way across upper and lower Austria, it had been
the same—even in formerly Red towns like Amstetten and in
strong Catholic centers like Melk, where the deep chimes of the

richest abbey in Austria, which stands on a high rock above the silver Danube, were ringing out a welcome.

I saw smiling nuns grouped at the doors of convents giving the Nazi salute as he went by; there were workmen—certainly socialists till two days ago—leaning over the wall of their factory, waving swastika flags. The whole population was on the roadside, shouting "Heil Hitler," and that slogan which has settled the fate of Austria—"One folk, one state, one leader."

That constantly repeated chorus has changed the course of Austrian history. When Herr Hitler crossed the frontier of this country on Saturday, he had no intention of proclaiming the immediate *Anschluss* [political union].

I was near him on the balcony of the Linz Town Hall when he made his speech, and saw how instantly he responded to that cry, "One folk, one state, one leader."

This was the moment, as he told me afterward, when the resolution to unite the two nations without more delay was suddenly formed in his mind, and it was swiftly carried out.

Flowers were hurled into his car at every stopping place. At one village a company of officer cadets of the Austrian army was drawn up by the roadside.

That morning they had taken the oath of allegiance to their new commander in chief and the head of their state, Adolf Hitler.

In their enthusiasm three young men broke their ranks and swarmed round the Führer's car, cheering and holding their arms upraised in salute.

Sometimes we found detachments of the former Austrian army—now the German Eighth Army—drawn up to salute Herr Hitler with colors and bands that had learned to play the hitherto forbidden "Horst Wessel" anthem overnight.

More than twenty-five thousand German gendarmes and security police are on duty in Austrian territory. When Herr Hitler entered the capital, German infantry were standing with clasped hands by the roadside holding back the pressure of the vast crowds. They did not carry arms.

So Hitler entered in triumph the city in whose streets he had once shoveled snow, and where he had lived for three years in a workman's refuge.

A year later Hitler entered Prague, capital of his latest "protectorate," Czechoslovakia, where he got a very different reception. The March 15, 1939, Manchester Guardian Weekly carried the following account from its Central European correspondent:

This morning at six o'clock the march of German troops into Bohemia and Moravia started. A motorized column hurried from Reichenberg toward Prague, and at 8:30 the first German patrols reached the city. An hour later the motorized column entered and passed through the main thoroughfares.

As the Germans drove on the right side of the road and the Czechs continued to keep to the left [then the rule of the road in Czechoslovakia], there soon was traffic chaos on the narrow streets of Prague. The ministerial buildings and the president's palace were occupied by German troops.

The Germans in Prague put out swastika flags and received the Germans with cheers. But the Czechs watched the sorrowful spectacle with shaking fists and boos, and many with tears. Many others sang the Czech national anthem—mingled with the "heils" of the Germans. At some points the crowd got out of control, but there were no major incidents.

The Gestapo was at first mainly occupied with guarding the Führer, but immediately after he left for Brno, the wholesale roundup of enemies of the Nazis began. SS [*Schutzstaffel,* the Nazi protection unit] and SA [Sturmabteilung, the attack unit] men in motorcars and lorries have since been visiting the working-class districts, as well as have the Gestapo, searching for arms. Many communists and socialists have been arrested and it seems that the estimation of five thousand arrests has already been exceeded. The prisoners are being taken to the main police station and to other jails, as well as to the newly established concentration camps, the biggest of which is in one of the barracks.

The anti-Jewish campaign was begun almost immediately. The Czechs may theoretically be anti-Semitic but they have never felt disposed toward an actively anti-Semitic policy. Now an atmosphere has been created by the Germans which reminds one of the first days of the entry into Vienna.

The German airplanes which could not fly over Prague Wednesday because of the snow have now arrived in hundreds.

Just as in Vienna last year, these bombers are swarming low over the town as a way of intimidating the population.

By this conquest the Third Reich had acquired seven million more people and one of the richest and most efficient economic areas in Europe. Some hundred thousand Jews had also fallen into the hands of Germany. And with the annexation of Czecho-slovakia, a new phase in German expansion had begun.

Soon afterward Nazi leaders began planning the invasion of Poland. When unable to provoke Warsaw into committing an act of aggression, Germany invaded that nation on September 1, 1939.

Initially, the spirit of the people was one of optimism. "Poland was calm, determined, and almost ready on Thursday night. The country was bracing itself for a hard struggle, prepared to make the greatest sacrifices, but still confident in surviving the war as a state." So wrote Professor Karel Estreicher of the University of Kraków. He continued:

The night was black and clouded. Men and women, weary after a busy day, went to sleep and carefully blacked out their windows for the first time. They switched off their receivers after the announcer wished them good night in his smooth, steady voice.

Kraków was just beginning to wake up. The sun was rising beyond the river amid rosy mists and its first rays sparkled on the golden spire of St. Mary's Church and the old Market Square.

The workmen were already getting up to go to their factories, the peasants to carry their products to town, for Friday had been from time immemorial the market day for Kraków. In the churches, still dark except for an occasional ray of light filtering through the stained glass, priests were celebrating the dawn mass, attended by only a few of the faithful.

When the trumpeter sounded his call ending on the broken note from the tall tower of St. Mary's, as he had done for the last five hundred years at every hour of the day, he did not know that two hundred miles away pilots were boarding their bombers, intoxicated with the lust of destruction. From the south, the west, and the north, squadrons flew over Poland, leaving a trail of fire and death. They flew high, mistrusting the reports of the German staff, according to which Polish antiaircraft batteries were supposed to be placed in the hills southwest of Kraków, some five miles from the town.

The pilots had orders to keep to the right bank of the Vistula River, after crossing the Carpathians, and then to make a circle to the right and attack Kraków from the south. Avoiding the positions of our antiaircraft defenses, they were to swoop down and attack the airfield at the northern extremity of the town, destroying the hangars and the Polish fighters.

Kraków suddenly heard the roar of bombers at full speed. The pilots recognized the town easily and compared it with their plans, tracing at once the large Market Square at the river, the station, and, on the outskirts, the airfield.

The attack was quite unexpected. Heavy explosions were heard near the town, and they became like a steady roll of thunder.

The hangars were smashed and the aircraft buried under their ruins. Both the civil airport and the Air Force Station were instantly on fire, while fresh bombs were being dropped every few seconds. There was confusion and terrific noise, while the flames of burning oil shot high and swathed the entire place in thick black smoke.

"To the guns! Take off! Get at them!" Orders rang out one after another, but the surprise made defense difficult.

Most of the buildings were already on fire when the antiaircraft artillery and machine guns went into action. The German bombers were just disappearing in the sky. It was six in the morning.

But there was more convincing proof to come. A drone was heard overhead, soon growing in volume to a deafening roar, and a German airplane, flying low over the houses—too fast to be a target for either artillery or machine guns—rained incendiary and explosive bombs on the town. The windowpanes were blown out by the blast of the explosions. Some houses were torn to pieces and flames appeared here and there. German planes flew between the houses on the wider streets, aiming their fire on the windows on both sides.

On the first day a German bomber flew low over the police barracks in Siemircedzi Street and sprayed the building with machine-gun fire. It then turned toward the Vistula and tried to attack the bridge, but was eventually driven off by the defense.

I was just driving into Kraków, and I found it a scene of terror. The air-raid sirens, the railway engine whistles, the car horns, and the loudspeakers were sounding alarm. People were running toward doorways in the streets, but they stayed under the porches instead of going in, kept there by curiosity.

Many disbelieved the radio and could not bring themselves to realize that war had started. At six in the morning, many who heard noise and shooting and sirens on the outskirts of the town could not draw any grave conclusions. If anyone shouted in the street that it was only a rehearsal, he was instantly believed.

Everybody rushed to buy newspapers. The press reported vaguely that a number of Polish towns had been bombed. The radio repeated the same news. Poland considered the air raids to be a declaration of war, especially as the German motorized divisions at the same time attacked Silesia, southern Poland, and Pomerania. The first war communiqué reported contact with the enemy.

At 10:00 A.M. sirens screamed again. The second air raid of that day, not as heavy as the first, was directed mainly against the bridges on the Vistula. The neighboring houses lost their windowpanes and had some damaged roofs, but the bridges were not hit.

Red Cross ambulances with wounded soldiers from the front appeared in the streets of Kraków. The available public buildings were turned into military hospitals and first-aid posts for the civilian population.

The first day of the war was hectic but free from panic. The radio played military tunes, national songs, and mazurkas; everybody worked hard to make himself useful to the country, and there was still hope in our hearts. Men were eager to join up as volunteers, to get rifles and to shoot Germans. Unfortunately, volunteers were not enlisted.

The evening came and welcome darkness enveloped the city at last. The blackout was complete, but traffic continued without accidents.

Polish troops began to pass through the town, going southward and westward. We saw mechanized units, artillery, and infantry. The soldiers looked well; they were thoroughly trained and equipped with modern weapons. The general feeling was one of optimism and of hope of stopping the invasion.

It was a vain hope. World War II blazed into being two days later when England and France, somewhat to the surprise of Hitler, honored their obligations by declaring war on the Third Reich. And much more of Europe would lie in the tideway of Nazi conquest.

Prologue

"Death roves mercilessly through town and country; mercilessly it preys upon men, women, and children. Villages are razed to the ground, the prisons are overflowing, and hundreds of people throughout the country face firing squads every day.

"The Czechs pass to and fro in the streets, silent and grim; all signs of laughter or lightheartedness have disappeared. You notice that people are constantly feeling in their pockets or handbags to make sure that their identification card or pass is safe, for if they are caught in the street without these papers after eight o'clock in the evening they are shot.

"The same fate befalls a man who may happen to have expressed himself without sufficient care, and with him his wife and children, brothers and sisters. These Czechs must be wiped out—that is the system upon which the Germans act.

"Then there are domiciliary visits, when houses, offices, and shops are completely ransacked. Movies and restaurants are raided and everybody inside must produce his identification card, which somebody or other is almost sure to have forgotten—and, if so, he is doomed."

The time was July, 1942. The place Czechoslovakia. But with only slightly altered shadings, this could have been a report about almost any other occupied country in Europe during the course of World War II.

18

Part 1
In the Path of the Invaders

Chapter 1

"Where are the English?"

In April, 1940, Hitler's army invaded Norway. Robert W. Bean was an American studying in Oslo from the beginning of the war in September, 1939, until May 9, 1940, one month after the arrival of the Nazi troops. Much of his account was written day by day during the invasion.

First Day—Tuesday, April 9.

Someone pounded at my door, then ran down the corridor. It was 5:00 A.M. I pulled on my slippers and robe, but the corridor was already empty. I lighted my way with matches to the basement we used as a bomb shelter. No one was there. Outdoors I found the students talking excitedly in the cold morning light. Air-raid claxons had sounded. No one yet knew why.

We saw the first German planes at 7:30 A.M. Far off to the south over the fjord we could see two, then three, then more planes coming out of the white cloud edges. Professor Mowinckel pushed us into the cellar, but we ran to the other end, up to the balconies at the front of the building. From there we could see the city and harbor lying in front of us, the ridges of Nordmarka to the right, Östmarka to the left. Across an inlet of the harbor and beyond Bydgö lay Fornebu, the new passenger airfield. We had top-row seats in the amphitheater.

German planes were over the city and flying low along the harbor. The first were large bombers. More were coming in the distance. Norwegian guns opened fire. The Germans climbed higher, flying in and out of clouds to protect themselves. From Fornebu, Norwegian pursuit planes rose to chase them off. We counted thirty bombers; others continued to come.

The first bombs fell at Fornebu, scoring hits and starting fires on the field. Evidently they weren't going to bomb the city. Black smoke from antiaircraft guns popped out in the clouds and drifted away. Always the smoke puffs were far below and behind the German planes.

No air battles took place; the heavy German bombers were faster than Norway's small fighting ships. We saw no planes shot down. Continuous fire from the Oslo batteries apparently didn't disturb the Germans. Heavy shells were interrupted by frequent rapid fire from mitrailleuses. None of it was effective. The German planes flew right through the fire and ignored it.

Telephone and subway service had stopped, so I walked to the American Legation. The Norwegian government had fled to Hamar early in the morning and Mrs. Harriman [Mrs. F. Borden "Daisy" Harriman, Minister from the United States to Norway] had gone with them. British and French legations left hastily, after assigning their duties to the American staff. There was no other news.

Back at the *Studenterhjem* [dormitory] I learned that Oslo had surrendered. German ships had been fighting their way past Oscarsberg in the narrowest part of Oslofjord. One had got through early in the morning, but had run aground. Others managed to land troops, which were coming to the city in trucks and buses requisitioned along the way. The New Zealander, Mason, had been whisked out of town by an Englishman who lectured at the university. They headed for Hamar with the British Legation staff.

At Akershus [the old fort which overlooks the Oslo harbor], Sörensen and I found crowds of people flowing through the gates to see shell holes and damaged buildings. A small Norwegian boy, obviously enthusiastic, asked to stand beside one of the German guards while I photographed him. Although Germans were in possession, Norway's flag still flew over Akershus. Later, when Norway's decision to resist was made public, it was replaced by the swastika flag.

On every building German proclamations read *"til det norske Volk."* ["Attention, Norwegian people!"] The message was written in Danish, all nouns capitalized. Only the German word *Volk* made it clear where the proclamation had been set in type.

German guards with hand grenades and rifles were posted at Oslo Bourse, at every important pier, at the East railway station. In the station, long lines of people wearing ski clothes and carrying knapsacks waited to take any train anywhere. The Storting [Norwegian parliament] and university were occupied by German troops, with all entrances guarded. Oslo's newest hotel, the Continental, was taken for officers' quarters. Troops were barracked in the National Theater; behind it the subway station was filled with persons who had been sitting in the tunnel since the previous night. At every gate and every hill of the Palace Park, German soldiers were stationed with machine guns. The royal guard had mobilized and gone. The royal family was at Elverum [near Hamar, about seventy miles northeast of Oslo].

Second Day—Wednesday, April 10.

Electric power was switched on during the night, and radios worked again. The morning news was that Norway had a Nazi government organized under Vidkun Quisling. Among members of the new government was named one respected citizen, Jonas Lie. He later announced that he had received no notice of his appointment and refused to serve.

At dinner everyone supposed all Norway had surrendered, as Denmark had done. That meant there was nothing to do but take what came. We could only guess what that would be. Everyone's question was: "Where are the English?" This was their war. Norway couldn't fight it for them. German speed and efficiency had impressed us all. The English would need to act quickly. And we all thought they would.

Then for a moment we thought they had. A flight of bombing planes roared over, and we heard and felt a succession of explosions. Not the Germans this time, we thought. The city had already surrendered.

But they were Germans, and they let go twenty to thirty bombs in the area between Blindern and Steinerud, on the Holmenkoll railroad. Most of these fell in an empty field a few hundred meters from the Studenterhjem. They were small, perhaps only hand grenades, and did little more than shatter windows.

On Tuesday *Aftenposten* had managed to get out a four-page extra edition announcing the invasion, the government's flight, orders for general mobilization, and plans for complete evacuation of Oslo and Aker. That was the last of Oslo's free press. Wednesday's papers and radio announcements were in German hands.

The new government, guided by the German high command, immediately issued orders counter to those of the Nygaardsvold government. There was to be no mobilization, no evacuation of Oslo.

Wednesday was to be The Day. We were expecting a battle. Tuesday night had been quiet, but no one thought it would last. When no news came, we made news. Wednesday was a day of rumors.

Like Tuesday, it was warm and clear. Planes were flying over the city as they had all the day before, but we looked up less often. At 11:00 A.M. Sörensen, Kverndal, and I started for town, stopping along Apalveien to look again at the bombed field and gardens. Kverndal was nervous, and when a Heinkel bomber flew over us he was all for running back. Excited students coming from town met us and announced that there was an order for Oslo to be evacuated by twelve o'clock noon—British planes were coming to bomb the city. It was then a quarter to twelve. That settled it for Kverndal; he hurried back. Sörensen and I decided to go on. We didn't go far. In five minutes the street was flooded with trucks, cars, bicycles, and people rushing from the city. Everyone had heard the order, and everyone was obeying, but no one knew who had given it. Sörensen and I turned back toward the Studenterhjem.

Crossing Blindernveien was like crossing Times Square at 5:00 P.M. Trucks and cars and people on foot were all hurrying in one direction. No slow, tedious procession—it went like mad. They carried suitcases, sleeping bags, whatever they could take.

At Blindern students were fast disappearing. Most of them took ski clothes and packs; some took skis. All headed for Nordmarka. It looked like the wildest of Holmenkoll days. Kverndal was already out of sight. Rasmussen was on his way. Sörensen and I decided to sit in the sun and watch. If there was a good reason for evacuating, there was certainly no good reason for going to Nordmarka, where several batteries of antiaircraft guns lay concealed in the forest. In less than two hours some came straggling back again, announcing that a counterorder had been given not to leave Oslo.

Those who went to Nordmarka said it was worse than Holmenkoll Day, when no one takes a car because it's useless. During the evacuation panic Nordmarka was jammed with autos, trucks, motorcycles, bicycles, skiers. The earliest of those who took skis had been able to reach distant cabins. Kikut, Lörenseteren, and Ulevaalseteren were packed. The rest were squashed together at Holmenkollen and in Maridal.

Dozens of injured persons were taken to hospitals and first-aid stations, many with broken arms and legs. Newspaper reports claimed that four persons over middle age were killed, not by blows or trampling, but by shock. While we sat on the steps at Blindern, a lame man appeared and demanded to be carried to a hospital. We made a kind of stretcher and packed him into the shelves of a bread truck which someone had overlooked.

Not many cars or trucks were overlooked. They were taken wherever found. New cars without license numbers were driven from salesrooms and warehouses. Everything was used that would roll.

Newspapers, under German editorship, claimed that the evacuation order was panic-inspired rumor. The counterorder obviously came from the Germans. Later we knew that Norwegians had purposely started the rumor in order to get men of military age, particularly officers, out of the city where they were effectively imprisoned by German orders. Once outside, they would be able to find their way north and join Norwegian troops. But at that time we still did not know there were Norwegian forces defending Norway. We thought the entire country was given over to the Germans.

Newspapers claimed that King Haakon was negotiating with the German minister for a settlement. Radio reports, under German control, were the same. Broadcasting stations in other parts of Norway had been cut off. A great many evacuees came back to the city, not knowing why they had been ordered to leave.

All during the day we heard new rumors. Persons who claimed to have heard reports from Swedish stations said that

King Haakon had broken off negotiations with the German minister and refused to recognize Quisling's government. They said Norwegians were fighting near Hamar and Elverum, where the Nygaardsvold government had gone later Tuesday. They said the British and Germans were fighting a terrific sea battle up and down the western coast, with hundreds of ships and over a thousand planes. They said both Sweden and America had declared war on Germany. The last rumor was too much. I began to doubt all reports, including those of Norwegian resistance outside Oslo.

The now-German press and radio did everything to encourage our doubts. Afternoon papers denounced all reports from Sweden's broadcasting stations. Few in Oslo knew the real situation.

Third Day—Thursday, April 11.

At 1:00 A.M. I was awakened by rapping at the door. In the common rooms the students were holding a tense meeting. At 11:00 P.M. radio news had come from an English station confirming rumors that King Haakon refused to recognize the new government, that Norwegian troops were fighting north of Oslo and on the west coast, that English and Germans were engaged in a heavy sea battle from Narvik to Skagerrak.

It was the first time we knew for certain that German reports of surrender were false. Since eleven o'clock the students had talked over that news; few had gone to bed. All of them came from towns in other parts of Norway. They had heard nothing from their families since the invasion began.

Sörensen knew only that Kristiansand, where he lived, had resisted and had been bombed, that his house was but a short distance from a church which had been reported destroyed, that the town had evacuated to unknown places. He and others felt helpless and desperate in Oslo. Men of military age seen leaving the city would be shot on sight. Yet if Norway were fighting, they should be fighting. The order had been given to mobilize; only the Germans had countermanded it. If they remained any longer at the Studenterhjem, the Germans might come there to intern them. Shouldn't they take skis and packs and go to Nordmarka at once, in the night, and try the next day to reach Elverum and Hamar where there was fighting? There was hot dispute. The leaders commanded, "Dress and go to Nordmarka now—or go back to bed."

I, being neutral and sleepy, went back to bed. At breakfast it was clear that many had gone to Nordmarka.

I went to town, intending to withdraw my funds from the banks. Outside was a queue of persons which would be there for two hours. All banks were the same; long lines of depositors stood outside until closing time. I decided to wait another day. The next morning all banks were locked.

The Days that Followed—April 12–May 9.

British broadcasts called on Norwegians in occupied zones to obstruct the Germans by sabotage and private resistance, but these zones were filled so quickly with well-armed troops that resistance was useless. So the Norwegians took it calmly. Rumors began that two or three hundred persons in Oslo had been shot for resisting, but I heard no proof of even one case.

Many people left the city against threat of death and joined Norwegian forces in the north. The Studenterhjem dwindled from two hundred fifty students to about forty. For those who remained in Oslo, there was no course but submission.

German military regulations were not severe, except with regard to resistance. All foreigners were required to register with the Oslo [Norwegian] police. French and British men of military age were sent to Germany for internment. No one was permitted to leave the city without a military pass. No one was permitted to carry arms or wear Norwegian uniforms. Blackout regulations were strictly enforced. Notices posted on every building began *Skutt blir han som* . . . ["Shot will be he who . . ."] and there followed a list of offenses which could endanger German success.

The invaders conducted themselves well. Goods taken from shops were paid for. Lodging and meals for troops were paid for. In town, schoolhouses were used to quarter troops. Near Fornebu, where there were few public buildings, houseowners were asked to give lodgings to soldiers if they had extra beds available. None of the horror stories which have come out of Poland could be repeated about Norway. On the streets, Norwegians who muttered audible insults in German were ignored by soldiers who pretended not to hear.

One day a troop of SA officers marched to the Studenterhjem after sending notice that lodgings should be prepared for one hundred men. There was ample space because so many students had left Oslo to fight. The officers reached the house and tried to form a cramped line in the driveway before the door. They looked very unhappy until one of them discovered the sports field behind the house, where they joyfully formed ranks, counted off, and drilled for half an hour before going to their quarters. From then on life at the Studenterhjem was easier for the students; food rations improved and hot water ran all day—a convenience few people in Oslo enjoyed after the invasion.

Chapter 2

"It was a blessing the child did not cry . . . "

On May 10, 1940, it was Belgium's turn, and Holland's. In four days, the center of Rotterdam was bombed to rubble by Stukas. As many as forty thousand civilians died. The Dutch army, which had sustained nearly a hundred thousand casualties, surrendered on May 14.

This is the story of one who escaped, Liesje van Someren, the wife of a British diplomat who lived in The Hague:

We were awakened on May 10, 1940, to the sound of big guns, as the onslaught of the Low Countries began. We jumped up to see and noticed how strange it was that three planes were proceeding in spite of the guns. I thought, Surely the planes would soon realize they were over neutral territory and go away.

Soon people dressed in all types of odd garments began to appear in their windows, on the streets, everywhere, and all of a sudden the sky was black with bombers almost touching the roofs of the houses. I can still hear Alick [her husband] saying, "Here they are—it's all up now."

We had most of our money in the banks in Amsterdam How foolish we were not to have taken precautions before now, but who could foresee total collapse? It was the end of our life in Holland.

People rushed out into the streets and even then one could pick out the fifth columnists, as they wore looks of keen satisfaction. As I passed one, I heard him say, "I cannot help thinking we would be better off under German rule."

All modes of transportation had been forbidden to civilians since 3:00 A.M. that morning. It was then 5:00 A.M. The planes were making swoops over the city to frighten the people. They soared in again and again. Everybody was talking and staring at the planes, without realizing they were exposing themselves to great danger.

A friend came to our house and told of his brother who had tried to reach Amsterdam and was stopped on the road by German parachutists. His car was taken from him and he thought he was lucky to have escaped at all. The order had been given for no one to leave town and many innocent people were shot in the first rush to leave.

A strange thing was that it was not until 8:00 A.M. that it was officially announced that the Germans had invaded Holland. Finally the sirens sounded, and the Dutch thought it meant for them to take shelter. Dutch air-raid wardens helped to clear the streets and doorways.

In spite of this air activity, life had to come and go. Shops opened, and one of them was run by Jews. One would have expected them to be indignant. I was surprised when the only comment the Jewish woman made about the situation was: "Yes, Madam, there is a war on."

It was pathetic to see the long lines form in front of banks. People wanted to save their money at all costs, in spite of the danger to their lives. The banks paid as long as they had cash, since they did not want to disappoint customers, but finally had to stop when they ran out of money. Most of their customers took it very well. One woman was crying and cursing the Germans; she was convinced she had lost her last cent.

The streets were heavy with soldiers. Germans did not have enough soldiers to keep civilians in line and were fighting with the Dutch soldiers. It was an extraordinary sight to see a procession made up of our men and one captured German moving along the streets, the German walking arrogantly and a lot of people cursing and shouting at him. Dutch soldiers had a hard time protecting their German prisoners from the mobs.

Sights like these appeared throughout the day in The Hague. Streets were machine-gunned by German planes as they came in low to shoot civilians. First-aiders had much to do. There was little damage to The Hague the first day, as the Germans had planned to enter and take the royal family and all government leaders alive. But it did not work. The people did not know this nor did they know how badly equipped our soldiers were.

Finally, Alick decided he should try to reach the British Legation, which was in the center of the city, even though he would have to walk most of the way. We had to figure out what to pack to take with us so that we could travel as lightly as possible. Everything was so dear.

A servant came running upstairs, where I was packing, and she was trembling. A bomb hit our house then and the ceiling came tumbling down in the top-floor bedroom. It missed us by inches. A propeller fell on our roof. We rushed to get ready and get out.

German soldiers were dropping in front of our house in parachutes. I will never forget that day as long as I live. Our soldiers had to protect themselves by pointing rifles out of windows. Dutch soldiers took up positions and tried to surround the paratroops. About a hundred meters away, some forty Dutch soldiers tried to join their units. A Dutch officer in command ordered his soldiers to fire on those trying to join them. The sergeant said he could not fire on his own countrymen.

The officer said, "They are not Dutch soldiers. They are Germans."

His men opened fire and the others were mowed down like corn. The officer was proven right because, upon inspection, it was learned they were Germans dressed as Dutch. We asked the officer how he knew they were Germans.

"By the way they march," he said.

It was about May 13 when we decided we had best try to reach Amsterdam, where we learned from the British consulate that a boat would be leaving the next evening. We must get there by 6:00 P.M. to get aboard. So we set out with all the clothes we could wear on our backs and pack into our suitcase. We jumped into our car with our baby, to try making our way along the streets, but we were stopped every hundred meters by soldiers who always searched the car.

Finally we reached the outskirts of The Hague, and from then on driving became really dangerous. Roads were narrow and they were blocked at regular intervals by barricades, so we had to zigzag in and out and at the same time try to avoid the water-filled areas of the roads. Therefore we could travel at only about ten miles an hour; it seemed ages before we reached Leiden, but it was actually only an hour.

A car passed us on that road going only slightly faster than we were. In it was a colonel, with a soldier driving him. As we approached a filling station ahead of us, we noticed two soldiers in Dutch uniforms standing in front of the building, who shot into the colonel's car as it drove up. The colonel was killed instantly. The driver jumped out and fired at two soldiers in front of the pumps, and they dropped dead. Some paratroopers appeared on the scene and we just had time to pull up behind the colonel's car and take shelter by dropping to the floor. We were in the middle of the battle. Bullets flew all around us, but luckily we were not hit. Dutch soldiers arrived in time, and when they finished, dead bodies were strewn all over the road. It was a ghastly sight, but the Dutch won. While the first group had been dressed in Dutch uniforms, they were really German soldiers who had been dropped in.

We were taken by the Dutch soldiers to nearby headquarters and were severely cross-examined. This took a long time and they finally forbade us to continue our journey, because the roads ahead were filled with German troops which made traveling extremely dangerous.

We set out for our home, one driving the car and the other sitting on the floor with our daughter. We took turns doing this and soon were the target of a plane that came low overhead and began machine-gunning us. Our car was ripped by the bullets, but fortunately we were not hurt. We were left stranded in enemy territory with a useless car, and at any moment we might have been fired on by the enemy ambush.

Alick took our daughter and I struggled with the suitcase and food, following behind them along the road. Shortly a car pulled up beside us. Fearing the worst, we were very surprised when it turned out to be two of our own soldiers, who told us that they had observed the incident and had orders to get us off the road at once. We got in their car and drove off toward The Hague. We were returned to our home and went to bed.

We were not asleep long when there was a loud knocking on the door. Dutch soldiers told us that German tanks were approaching and everyone must help dig ditches at once. We got out of bed, and all the men, women, and children in the area went to their attics and storehouses to bring articles for making barricades.

We dug and dug without taking the slightest rest, and we realized then more than any other time that we were truly fighting a last-ditch stand. By then Rotterdam—which was badly damaged by bombings—was supposed to be in German hands, and it was said that the northern part of the country was already occupied. However, it was difficult to find out the truth.

In about three hours I had to get back to attend to my child and try to find milk for her. I went to the nearest shop and, as at all other shops, I had to stand in line and wait my turn. After obtaining some milk, I started home. On the way, a Dutch soldier stopped me to see my papers; when he saw that I was Dutch, as well as a British subject, he said to get home quickly because if the Germans found me, they would shoot me immediately.

We emptied our suitcases and made bundles which we could fit into the baby's pram. The servants put bottles filled with hot water into the pram and we put on as many clothes as we possibly could. We filled our pockets with things we thought we would need for the long journey on foot, and set out.

We pushed the pram past sentries, who asked where we were going. They thought we were completely mad, because no one knew what part of our country was in German hands. But the soldiers wished us a safe journey on our terrible gamble.

As soon as it was dark, we changed our light coats for dark ones, left the pram behind, and started for the road. Alick carried our daughter and I took the food and bundle.

Our progress was very slow and we could hear the machine guns in the distance. We dropped to the ground and crouched as close down as possible, moving a little, stopping to listen, and then Alick going ahead a bit. Shortly we were stopped by: "Halt!"

We showed our own passports and the military passports which the officer had given us at the last stop. The soldier said,

"One thousand meters ahead Germans have captured a position, so don't stay on the road; go through the dunes."

It was dark and the moon was rising. It was such a beautiful night. It was unthinkable that so much death and fear was all around us. We went about five hundred meters and then I tied our daughter on Alick's back with a napkin. It was a blessing that the child did not cry at this juncture, and we held our breath, hoping that she would not make a sound to give us away.

We proceeded on hands and knees for a bit; then all of a sudden a light came on and lit up the night. We could hear voices but could not tell if they were German. We lay very still and were glad the officer had told us to put on dark coats.

After taking a short rest, we crawled past what we thought was the danger zone and finally got up and stretched, only to find that our hands and knees were bleeding. We hastened to get to the nearest house in the area, keeping as close to the buildings as possible to escape detection. We were trying to get to a little inn that Alick knew, near the harbor where the underground had contacts with a small fisherman.

At last we found it, and when we rang the bell, a woman appeared.

"What do you want?" she whispered.

We showed her our daughter and made signs for her to let us in. After hearing our story, she said that she did not know of anyone who could help us get to England, but she would get her son, Kreles. The presence of our daughter probably convinced her that we were not German spies.

"A pal of mine is due to sail at 2:00 A.M.—about forty-five minutes from now, but of course he will be taking great risk and I feel that he will charge a lot. Perhaps a thousand guilders a head is his fee," Kreles finally told us, after determining that we were all right.

We looked at each other in shock. Certainly we had expected to have to pay, but not such an exorbitant sum. It would amount to three thousand florin altogether, an amount we did not possess. It had been difficult to get two thousand florin.

"That is an exorbitant sum. We only have two thousand, and the child will not take much room. Two thousand florin is all I can pay."

But time was growing short and we had to agree to go with him. We stepped out into the dark and he led us to the harbor where a great number of ships were lying, like a lot of trees without leaves. Kreles took us to the small fishing boat that belonged to his pal. I felt terrified just thinking of crossing the channel in such a small craft.

Kreles gave a low whistle which was scarcely audible. Finally, a voice: "Is that you, Kreles?"

"Bertus," murmured Kreles, "put up the gangway. Here are some customers for you."

We finally got aboard and into the small dingy cabin, where we sat at a table to begin negotiations.

"You are just in time," Bertus said. "I was about to set sail. My price is one thousand florin per head."

"What about the child?" we asked.

"She can come for nothing!" he said.

We tried to persuade him to accept half then and half later, on arrival. But he said, "Pay now or not at all."

When we paid, we were left entirely penniless. How anyone can behave this way at a time like this is more than a human being can comprehend, I thought.

We were told to go below, that we were going to weigh anchor. As we entered, we saw women sitting on seats, children crawling on the floor, men pacing the floor. They were dressed in a variety of garments and everyone seemed to be staring at us. Alick tried to start a conversation with one of the men, who said he was a Jew and had been put in a concentration camp but had managed to escape to Holland. Now, he noted sadly, they have conquered this country, so we have nothing but misery all around us.

There was a girl sitting next to me who was very young. She was Dutch and had married an Englishman who was now serving in the war. She was trying to get to England before she had her baby, and it looked as if she would do so at any minute.

The boat left and soon the rocking began to make us ill. But we had waited a long time for this opportunity and felt fortunate to be on our way.

No one seemed inclined to sleep. In one corner sat a Jew

and his daughter. He told us how successful he had been in getting his money out. The moment England and Germany declared war, he got all of his cash and went to bed every night with it under his mattress. Consequently, when the Germans entered, he only had to stuff his pockets and clear out.

There was another German Jewish family, who stuffed their tummies with food as soon as the boat left; first they ate thick sandwiches of meat, then another slice of meat with apples and bananas. But when the woman asked for a gherkin—which she ate with great relish and obvious delight—there was a smile of gentle amusement on the faces of many in the crowd who realized that these two were perhaps eating to quell their fears.

We all eventually fell asleep, after spreading the bundles of straw around on the floor for a communal bed. For the next four days we would share the bed on our way to English shores, through two bombings and machine gunning.

The boat's crew steered a zigzag course which brought us through enemy fire. A few casualties were accounted for, but none were serious.

The expectant Dutch mother in this crowded boat gave birth to a boy during the final aerial attack. Liesje and other female passengers doubled as midwives. The next morning, the white cliffs of Dover and salvation greeted the haggard, hungry refugees.

Chapter 3

"The French flag
is taken down . . . "

*France fell in six weeks. On June 14, 1940, Paris was occupied
by General Georg von Kuechler's Eighteenth Army.*

*A week later, a provisional French government—the Vichy state
—led by Marshal Henri Philippe Pétain, hero of another world
war, signed a truce and France as a nation was out of the war.*

*Roger Langeron, prefect of police for seven and a half years
(until he was imprisoned by the Gestapo in February, 1941) tells
the story of the arrival of the German troops in Paris:*

Paris awakened this morning—Tuesday, June 11—in a sort of
dense cloud of black smoke. It is now nearly impossible to see in
the streets. The crowds have gathered to ask questions of one
another. Did the French troops burn their supplies before their
retreat, or did the Germans destroy them as they advanced?
The most severe problem for everyone is the mental anguish.
What has happened to our armies? Where are they? The black
sky only augments the uncertainty, the doubts.

We have just learned that the oil storage tanks, located quite
close to the city, were set afire during the night by the German
bombardment. The exodus has increased considerably.

From my windows on the Boulevard du Palais, I watch a sad
and uninterrupted stream of horsecars, cattle, wagons, bicyclists,
pedestrians, dogs, and farm animals. Mattresses are tied to the
tops of cars, bags tied on behind, and the vehicles are filled with
people and their most precious possessions, gathered hurriedly.

At last, on Friday, the atrocious thing has come to pass. German troops have occupied Paris. Their headquarters have been set up at the Hotel Crillon.

We wonder when and how they will confront us. Will they be cruel and violent? It seems to me most likely that I will be arrested right away and taken to Germany. I have a bad record with them, the Cagoulard, the fifth column.

For me, it is a solution. But I worry about what will happen to my officers, to whom I feel so attached, to whom I have promised my protection.

At 7:45 A.M., it was reported that four German automobiles had penetrated the heart of the city. Not long afterward the four officers pulled up in front of my office and stepped out. They were announced a few minutes later—a colonel and another superior officer.

They appeared in the doorway, but stopped on the threshold and saluted me correctly. I wondered why I should rate such respect. Perhaps they were survivors of the other war? Hardly; they seemed much too young. Country boys who did not know any better, perhaps? Or was this an omen of things to come?

They asked me, in French, to report to Crillon at 11:00, in order to meet with the commander of the Army of Occupation.

After their departure, I learned that an immense, interminable procession of motorized troops had begun to travel through Paris beginning at 8:00 A.M. They came from Saint-Denis and from the northern suburbs toward Montrouge. At first, there were leather-jacketed motorcyclists on cycles with sidecars. Then came a wave of automobiles and tanks.

The streets were nearly deserted, and most of the houses were shuttered. The procession would continue, uninterrupted. I awaited the hour of the rendezvous in my office.

Numerous intelligence reports were arriving from all corners of Paris and from the suburbs. There seemed to be no hindrance to the freedom and rapidity of communications, nor to the activity of my informers.

They brought me a note, quite moving in its administrative

In the Path of the Invaders 39

dryness, which recapitulated the events of the morning:

3:40—A German motorcyclist crosses the Place Voltaire.

5:20—Three vehicles carrying German soldiers arrive in front of the Saint-Denis barracks.

5:30—Two carts loaded with German soldiers and five or six motorcyclists pass the Villette Gate.

5:35—German troops move down Rue de Flandre in the direction of the North and East railroad stations.

5:50—Thirty policemen are taken prisoner at Bondy. They are disarmed by the Germans.

6:10—Five or six cars covered with blinds move toward Aubervilliers.

7:00—The passage of German detachments is signaled at different points throughout Paris. German troops arrive at the Saint-Denis barracks and disarm a policeman.

7:15—Several German motorcycle couriers and an automobile pass the Quai des Grands-Augustins.

7:50—German units patrol the Boulevard Saint-Michel.

7:55—Several German officers arrive at the Hotel Crillon.

8:05—A German column spreads through Saint-Denis, headed for the East Fort.

8:10—German soldiers establish contact with French soldiers at the Orleans Gate. The French are allowed to continue their way freely.

8:15—A German column passes Saint-Ouen on the way to the Maillot Gate.

8:30—About twenty German motorcyclists start up the Champs-Elysées. German vehicles equipped with loudspeakers pass Rue de Lafayette. Over the loudspeakers is broadcast an order to stay in our homes for forty-eight hours until the German troops have passed. They announce that looters will be shot. The French flag is raised at the Naval Ministry.

8:50—Flags are also raised at the corner of the Place de l'Etoile and the Champs-Elysées.

9:00—A French soldier opens fire on a group of German soldiers, killing one and wounding another. The Germans respond with machine-gun fire, killing the French soldier and a woman. Following this incident, several machine guns are installed at the Croix de Berny, creating an area off limits to everyone. The Foreign Affairs Ministry is occupied and the French flag is taken down. A sentry, stationed at the gate, holds a sign written in German which indicates that the Ministry is under the protection of the German army.

9:10—German soldiers patrol the Avenue de Versailles. The PTT [Paris Telephone and Telegraph] central office on the Rue des Archives is occupied by the Germans. Small German units march past the Avenue de Wagram in the direction of the Place de l'Etoile.

9:25—German soldiers move through the Rue du Faubourg–Saint-Honoré.

9:27—The German flag is hoisted over the Air Ministry.

9:45—The Germans raise the flag of the swastika over the Arc de Triomphe as they play a triumphal march. Motorized troops move into the Place de l'Etoile and onto the Champs-Elysées. A cannon is leveled at the Avenue MacMahon.

10:00—On the Boulevard de Sébastopol, people line up to get gasoline. The flag of the swastika flies over the Hotel de Ville [City Hall].

10:15—In the Belleville section, the following announcement is made to the people over German loudspeakers: "No demonstrations will be allowed during the passing of the German troops. Weapons in private hands must be turned in. The services of the Paris police department continue to function. The other principal services continue to function. All hostile acts will be punished by death."

10:20—A German officer, following a detachment of troops in a car, stops at the Place du Châtelet to make a hateful speech to some one hundred persons. He repeats the Hitler propaganda in French, saying in particular that the French are poorly governed, that he cannot possibly understand why France started the war with Germany, and that Germany's war is with England alone. In finishing, he affirms that no harm will come to anyone.

At eleven o'clock, I went to Crillon. The prefect of the Seine arrived at the same time. General von Studnitz received us immediately in one of the large salons on the first floor. He wore a monocle and a little mustache, and displayed a manner rather unlike that of a cavalry officer. I wondered if the Nazi army might be similar to the Kaiser's old army. However, Von Studnitz was undoubtedly an exception. Next to the general was an officer whom he introduced to us as Oberleutnant Speitel.

The general then turned to me, saying, "Can you guarantee the maintenance of order?"

I replied sharply, "I can guarantee it if I am left alone to do my work."

He thought for a moment, then quickly retorted, "If order is maintained, if I can count on the security of my troops, you will not hear anything from me."

I gave him my accord, and we did not pursue the matter any further. The population will be able to circulate freely. The new order has set a curfew at 9:00 P.M. Every day a conference will be held at headquarters, where the two prefects will see a director. The conversation ended. We exchanged salutes and I departed.

A motorized German column passes Montreuil on its way to Paris. A German lieutenant, accompanied by a representative of the Swedish Legation, opens the German Consulate but stays only a few moments. Movie cameras are installed on the Place de la Concorde to film the passage of German troops. Two German officers have just arrived at the Hotel Crillon, where the German headquarters will be established permanently. Very important patrols move through the Place de la Concorde. The swastika flies over the Naval Ministry. The German infantry marches through the Rue de Belleville in front of a crowd that remains amazingly calm.

12:15—A French soldier and a civilian are found dead on the Quai Gallieni, at Suresnes. Information gathered at the scene reveals that a French military man opened fire on a German motorized machine gun passing by. A German soldier responded with a burst of machine-gun fire, killing the soldier and a civilian. An inquest is begun.

12:50—In the crossroads at the Croix de Berny, a French

soldier fires on a German detachment, killing a German soldier. The detachment returns the fire. Two deaths are counted on our side.

In the afternoon, I conferred at the Hotel de Ville. We did not make any pretense about our distrust of the announced German intentions to maintain the status quo. We are sure this is only a front for worse things to come. I mentioned that the Gestapo would not waste any time in arriving and that the atmosphere would change then. As I left, I encountered M. de Fontenay, a municipal counsel and a man of great distinction in whom, I am sure, the two government representatives will find support and friendship.

The solicitor-general and the solicitor of the Republic have been complaining that they lack a sufficient number of personnel to assure the proper functioning of their services, and that they have received contradictory instructions regarding special charges. Nevertheless, they will organize two courts, two tribunals and four information offices. The police will assume the duties of the prison guards.

I took a leisurely tour through the Latin Quarter. Then I made several jaunts through different areas of Paris. The city was calm, silent, and drawn completely tight within itself. Paris is waiting. . . .

I returned to the prefecture and found a telephone message from [United States Ambassador William C.] Bullitt. I returned his call. He wanted the French government representatives to feel that they were not alone, that the ambassador of the great republic was very close to them. I thanked him with a feeling of strong emotion and true friendship.

They have brought me a copy of a tract which has been distributed to the public in several quarters, especially near the Lyon station, by the passengers of a German army automobile.

FRANÇAIS
Italy is now at war against France!
This is the consequence of the blind politics of your government. Your incapable politicians have bungled Franco-Italian relations

just as they spurned the hand that England extended to France.
Now you must choose between immediate peace or abandoning all hope of peace.
Think of the plight of Poland, who was pushed into a war against Germany by England.
Eighteen days later, she no longer existed.
And your allies?
The Low Countries capitulated after five days. The Dutch soldiers have already been forced back.
The Belgians gave up their arms after eighteen days of useless combat. They did not want to shed their blood for England.
Countless numbers of the British Expeditionary Force in France have been killed, wounded, and imprisoned; hundreds have fled. Their war supplies are in our possession.
Do not forget that the First, the Seventh, and the Ninth French Armies have already been defeated and their generals captured. The secret documents that have fallen into our hands have given us the opportunity to study your military situation thoroughly.
You are most certainly deceived!
The Maginot Line has no more value. You have paid excessive taxes for nothing.
There is no longer an effective resistance to oppose the German-Italian superiority.
It is useless to continue the battle. There would be no other result but to augment the suffering and misery of France and the French people. And when the ship goes down, those who are responsible will abandon it to its destiny and seek shelter for themselves.
French citizens, think of your poor children, of your unfortunate wives. Save France from total disaster. Make your government end this struggle which has no hope of success.

The tract was a good omen. They seemed to fear that the battle would continue.

At 2:00 P.M., a new but similar incident. An open vehicle carrying two German officers pulled up across from the Hotel de Ville. Glancing up at the swastika flying over the hotel, the two officers stepped out of the car. Their arrival caused a small crowd to assemble, and one of the officers addressed the people in excellent French.

"You are free. You can move about as you wish. We do not wish you any harm. The English have engaged you in a war that you lost before you began. Ladies, you want your husbands to return, don't you?"

"Yes."

"Well, my wife wants hers, too. After the peace has been signed between us, we will take care of the English in fifteen days."

The two officers returned to their vehicle, smiling, then drove off toward the Seine. At the same time, two German airplanes appeared over the Place de la Concorde.

At 4:40 P.M. a column of German artillery moved toward Saint-Denis on the Rue de Flandre. A German soldier, speaking excellent French, declared, "The war will be over in fifteen days at the latest. We do not wish it on the poor workingmen who are our friends. We want to fight our war with the big man." He accompanied these words with a significant gesture of the hand, adding, "It is the English who are our enemies; but since their entry into the war, I have not met one."

It is 7:00 P.M., and innumerable wagons and cars are traveling through the city. There is a continuous wave of troops and war matériel. This military fracas, this invasion of green uniforms that continues through all the main streets of the capital as if many immense floodgates had been opened suddenly—those who have had this atrocious vision, can they ever forget it? Motorized machine guns have been placed in every corner of Paris, especially the Place de la Concorde. There are four surrounding the police prefecture. I have not yet seen anyone inconvenienced—on the contrary. All would be going well for them except for an affectation of confidence, an excess of politeness.

I made a new tour through several areas today and visited the commissariats. I want my men to have a feeling of strong and vital liaison. All of them assured me, above all, of the calm of the city and the emptiness of the streets.

Upon my return, I learned that Jacques Simon, my Director of General Information, had been summoned hastily to a German office.

I went immediately to the United States Embassy. It was impossible to permit this first and inadmissible violation of the assurances given to me just this morning. I asked Bullitt for advice and help. He did not hesitate for a second. He sent the counselor of the embassy to the Hotel Crillon with the message that the security of Paris could no longer be guaranteed.

The encounter was a short one. Simon returned at 11:00 P.M. and repeated to me countless questions that had been asked of him.

Alas! We know nothing of what is happening on the other side. What are our armies doing? What is the government doing?

The next morning, before breakfast, Langeron opened the door of his apartment for a caller from the Gestapo who said he regretted to inform him that "France is fallen."

The Parisian police official had no reason to doubt his visitor and now could himself speculate in anguish: "What will be the conditions of the armistice? What will become of France?"

Chapter 4

"You Greeks
are in Paradise . . . "

Greece fought back ferociously when the Italians staged a surprise invasion of their homeland on October 28, 1940.

The wretched performance of Benito Mussolini, Hitler's fat, boastful Axis partner, not only enraged the Führer; it also delayed his secret attack, under the code name "Barbarossa," against Russia. Moreover, unexpected refusal from Yugoslavia for the transit of German troops slowed Hitler's attempt to come to Mussolini's aid. But the German Wehrmacht [army] cowed Yugoslavia in just ten days.

The swastika flag was unfurled over the Acropolis on April 27, 1941, three weeks after hostilities had commenced. The Greek government fled to Crete. The following account tells of the experiences of the newest Nazi-Fascist victims in the months immediately preceding the fall of Greece. Co-authors were Dr. Ruth Parmelee, Director, and Emilie Willms, Chief of the Nursing Division, of the American Women's Hospital in Athens.

On October 28, 1940, the sirens which wakened us were different. We had been trained to the sound for a year in practice air alarms, but this time, from the long-continued piercing shrieks, accompanied by the clanging of church bells, we instinctively knew that Greece was at war. At the same time, news flashed from the Athens broadcasting station. It told of how the Italian minister had wakened the Greek prime minister, John Metaxas, in the night, to present the ultimatum of the Italian government, to which he gave the famous reply, "No!" that was heard by all the world.

The blackout, too, had been practiced for over a year, but with this day it became so rigid a police regulation that only the moon dared to defy it. This defiance on the part of the moon brought little comfort, however, to the people having business out at night, in view of the easily accessible targets it offered to the enemy bombers.

What did this war cry do to the people of the country? Just this: With the shriek of the sirens and the tolling of the church bells, the people became instantly as one man, with the sole purpose of defending their country, regardless of cost. All government departments and civil organizations coordinated effectively, and for a period of six months this national unity was the sole secret of the Greek army's success in conquering the Italians in the Pindus Mountains (a nation of eight million against forty-five million), and resisting for several weeks on the Macedonian front the massive forces of Germany (a nation of one hundred million).

The invasion of Greece by Italy found us on the staff of the Children's Hospital, St. Sophia, under the leadership of Greek Crown Princess Frederika. On October 31, it was decided to evacuate the hospital from the city immediately; therefore, our first bit of war work was the transfer on November 2 (the sixth day of the war) of the equipment, patients, and staff to the slopes of Penteli. By putting into effect the evacuation plan we had worked out some five months before, the moving was completed in four hours. A trail was blazed, and day after day the Athens streets were cluttered with the trucks that were loaded with equipment of civilian hospitals being evacuated to the suburbs.

No sooner had the work of settling the Children's Hospital in new quarters been accomplished than opportunities were offered to us for service in other fields. Miss Willms responded to the call of the crown princess, who was sponsoring all the military hospitals, to return to the city to take charge of the nursing of the Seventh Military Hospital of Athens. She immediately received her official appointment as Directress of Nurses from the Greek Red Cross Nursing Division and the Ministry of War. In the meantime, Dr. Parmelee's field of activity developed along the line of civilian relief.

The Seventh Military Hospital was opened in the building recently vacated by the Children's Hospital and the wards, which previously accommodated two hundred fifty sick children and infants, were now used to house seven hundred wounded soldiers. The wounded came pouring in from the Albanian front before the buildings were adequately equipped, nor was there anywhere enough linen, instruments, or surgical supplies. However, this shortage only served as a stimulus to work the harder toward getting the needed things, as we came face to face every day with the heroism and courageous spirit of the soldiers as they arrived at the hospital.

With the exception of two graduate nurses and a few practical nurses, the nursing staff consisted of volunteers who had been trained by the Greek Red Cross. The tireless devotion shown by these Greek nurses in war service, assisting physicians with fifteen hundred surgical dressings daily, special treatments, and routine care of the patients, is now remembered in never-to-be-forgotten scenes that have made a lasting impression.

Two hidden factors aided in the speedy recovery made by the average wounded soldiers: their original sound physical condition and their mental attitude that no price was too great to pay for the freedom and independence of their country. These men, with their maimed and infected bodies, many legless or with frostbitten feet, others with backs full of shrapnel wounds, were physically exhausted from the long and uncomfortable journey from the battlefield to Athens. However, their spirit was commendable. It was not surprising to hear men of such caliber expressing as their sole aim the desire to return to the front. Even legless Spiro had the courage to dream of returning when he learned of a ship on the high seas bringing material for permanent artificial legs from the United States.

As the hospital filled with patients, it soon took on the atmosphere of one large family. Often brother would meet brother, or neighbor meet neighbor. Each was unconscious of the other's nearness until he had had that first long sleep of exhaustion and could exhibit interest about who his ward comrades might be. It wasn't long before the wards reverberated with the exchange of war stories of their regiments, while music and songs were pealing from radio sets brought in by the recreational group.

Scattered throughout the wards, too, were the figures of attractive young women in uniforms of blue or khaki, bending over the more helpless, getting information to write to their families and distributing cigarettes or reading matter. And always, always quietly and with dignity in the midst of the hubbub, the surgical dressing carriage was rolled from bed to bed.

In this atmosphere of skilled and tireless service and with the aid of good food, wounds soon healed; before long, convalescent soldiers appeared everywhere about the hospital and premises—sharing in the lighter duties in the wards.

Many soldiers' families of the laboring class had been in dire need since their supporters had been called to the colors. The number of bombardment victims was increasing as time went on. Although Athens proper was not being bombed, there were many houses destroyed and people wounded in the region of the Piraeus harbor, and many families had fled from Greek towns that had suffered severe bombardments.

Within a few weeks of the outbreak of war, Archbishop Chrysanthos of Athens called a meeting of representatives from all the churches and organized them for relief work, with the parish as a unit. In the beginning, the fourteen hundred volunteer parish workers supported their work by dipping into their own pockets, or by soliciting from friends. The rapidly increasing needs of the people made it necessary, however, to apply to the Athens Committee of the Greek War Relief Association, which made appropriations to the archbishop's organization to meet these needs.

In the center opened by the American Women's Hospital for giving medical relief to soldiers' families and bombardment victims, we came into close contact with many fine women who, as parish visitors for the archbishop's organization, brought patients to us and gave their special attention to carrying out the examination or treatment advised. Some of our most satisfactory work was done in the fourteen parishes that were receiving help through Princess Alice, who was in constant personal touch with her parish visitors and the families themselves. Being centrally located in the Municipal Hospital of Athens, the American Women's Hospital Center was able to reach people coming from all directions. Among those we helped was a family whose father was wounded at the time their house in Preveza was destroyed; then, as refugees near Piraeus, they lost their home a second time from the bombing. Another of our bombed-out mothers was receiving milk from the center for her baby who had been born in an air-raid shelter in Thessaloniki.

On one of the survey trips made to the front by members of the Athens relief committee, we observed an illustration of the way in which the soldiers accepted the shortage of food that was due to the great difficulty of transporting supplies to the front lines. When driving through the snow, down the steep mountain towards Koritsa, we overtook two cold, weary soldiers with bloodshot eyes and gave them a lift. With what joy they settled back in the car and munched the sweet chocolate we gave them! In telling of their experiences, one of them remarked, "We were shouting, 'Long live the eighth!' Do you know what that meant? Our daily portion of bread, an eighth of a loaf."

March 25, 1941, Independence Day. A day celebrated annually to honor the patriots who fought and won independence for Greece, over one hundred years ago. It was a sober celebration. In and around Athens all looked grave, and all were wondering anxiously whether the country was on the eve of losing its independence. And rightly so, for black clouds hung over Greece. That very day a group of ministers representing Yugoslavia were signing the Axis Pact and German troops were massed on the Bulgarian frontier.

On April 6, King George II of the Hellenes announced to his people that Germany had attacked Greece. The prime minister called his cabinet for a council of war, and so the second "no" was proclaimed. A brave fight was put up, but on April 19 Thessaloniki was taken, and on April 27 the enemy rolled down from the north into Athens; now Greece was to experience the "friendly" occupation of Germany.

Memories were still fresh of the three weeks' terrible struggle in the battle against the German forces, and the horrors of the Jannina Hospital bombardment on Good Friday. At that time doctors, nurses, and patients in the operating room were blown to pieces. Not forgotten were the dive-bombing and sinking of all the Greek hospital ships, the sinking of ships that carried British and Greek evacuees, and the direct attacks by Stukas on groups of demobilized, stranded soldiers struggling to get to their homes on foot. With these memories still so vivid before our eyes, it was not hard to understand the feeling of the Greek people. When the news spread of the German high command's saying to the mayor, on arrival in Athens, "We have brought you peace and quiet, and come as friends," it fell on deaf ears and heavy hearts.

In view of the ground they had covered and the countries—beginning with Czechoslovakia—that they had occupied, ruthless looting, confiscation, and billeting must have become second nature to the German army by the time they reached Greece. At least, that is the impression we gathered from personal observation. Within two weeks after the occupation of Athens, children of the neighborhood were coming into the hospital grounds and scraping the garbage cans.

Our patients who had made splendid recovery soon became listless, hollow-cheeked, and heavy-eyed, and their wounds reopened. Daily some commodity was dropped from the diet list—milk, butter, cheese, macaroni, olives, lemons, oranges, tomatoes, sugar, coffee. Bread was rationed to less than seven ounces (one quarter of the normal amount) per person.

When the mayor remonstrated with the German authorities for taking all the rice and begged them to leave some for the sick people and infants, the reply was: "You Greeks are in Paradise. No one is falling in the streets from hunger. In Poland one and a half million people are starving to death." And this was in the first weeks of the occupation!

The ever increasing scarcity of food commodities was due to the Germans' systematic seizure of all kinds of supplies to be used by their army and to be shipped home by airplane. Each soldier was permitted to send packages weighing up to fifty kilos, containing food, clothing, and other supplies. They confiscated truckloads en route from farms into town, or emptied the shops before the eyes of the housewives standing in line to purchase vegetables for their families. Often a woman went to market at dawn, to return hours later with nothing but a bit of parsley. We found only shoestrings for sale at the fish market and, on the grocery shelves, pickles and mustard as the sole display.

Produce was taken right from the ground—the potatoes as they were dug, the grapes as they were gathered. Tomatoes were canned and shipped, potatoes were fried before sending. In a few weeks it was a serious problem to find anything to eat, let alone meat, eggs, oil, butter, or coffee, of which there were none to be had. One day a man brought nice green peppers to our door to sell. We purchased a double quantity and sent some to a friend, who later told us, "You saved our lives. I had nothing in the house to give my family to eat."

There was neither rich nor poor; all were in the same condition. As we were leaving Athens, one of Miss Willm's nurses, a young woman of culture and education, came to say good-bye and brought her most valued possession as a farewell gift—her day's ration of bread. The remark of a friend of ours illustrates the speed with which food supplies were disappearing from the market: "We have always said that no matter what happened, we could live on bread and olives; but now even they are not available."

Raw materials also came in for confiscation, and milliners, seamstresses, and shoemakers were sorely put to carry on their work—to say nothing of the large industries. When one manufacturer of cloth had his whole stock of raw cotton seized, he said to the Germans, "What shall I do about my 750 employees?" To which they replied, "That is your responsibility."

During the war, Princess Helen took upon herself the tremendous task of supplying military hospitals with linen, pillows, and pajamas. Imagine our shocked surprise when one day we saw a German truck driver and his companions sitting on familiar-looking pillows, their truck loaded with linen; following it came another truck loaded with bedside tables. We said nothing; there was nothing to say. Our eyes followed the truck for a moment and then we went silently on our way. We knew that the looting of hospitals had begun.

It was a common thing to see army trucks loaded with tins of gasoline and Shell oil, oriental rugs, furniture from private homes (including pianos), and cows (of which Greece had so few). Taxis and private cars (which were confiscated and re-painted a dark army gray) soon disappeared from the streets, and all that could be seen was a constant procession of somber German cars of all kinds. The swastika and Italian flags flaunted themselves from buildings where once the Greek colors of blue and white had waved gracefully in the wind.

For a time we were puzzled as to why the streetcar con-ductors and storekeepers had such difficulty in making change and their customers often had to accept stamps instead. The puzzle was solved when eyewitnesses of an accident reported the collision of two trucks, one Greek and one German. The boxes that crashed to the ground from the German car broke open, and out rolled nickel coins of five-, two-, and one-drachma denominations.

One of the most painful sights to which we had to accustom ourselves was that of the German soldiers strutting the streets in their English khaki uniforms and the Italians in their chic blue-grays and plumes, while the Greek convalescent soldiers had to discard their uniforms on pain of death. Since most of them came from the provinces and the islands, they roamed the streets of Athens in pajamas.

It was a common sight, long after the German occupation had taken place, to see stray lone soldiers arriving from the front, careworn and footsore. While in the business district of Athens one day with a Greek friend, we noticed such a figure, still in his forbidden uniform. His toes were sticking out of his shoes and the uniform was torn and shabby, as it had not been off his back for days. His face was swollen and unshaven, his lips parched, his eyes bleary.

We accosted him gently, since he appeared dazed, offering to give him help and food and to take him to his destination.

Gradually and with great effort he succeeded in straighten-ing himself to a soldierly height and spoke in a barely audible voice, saying, "No, thank you. You have your laws and we have ours."

For a moment we were unable to understand his meaning. Then it dawned on us that he had taken us for German women.

Our Greek friend explained that we were Americans and wanted to help him. The scene that followed was pathetic. It was hard for him to realize that Americans were still in Greece. Finally he accepted some help, but refused food and walked away mumbling, "God bless America."

Part 2
Resistance Fighters

Chapter 5

"They fell strangely,
like sacks of potatoes . . . "

*Resistance cells came into being surprisingly fast within the con-
quered countries. Although the Nazis moved in counterintelli-
gence operatives, patriots persisted in their efforts to thwart the
conqueror.*

*Summary executions, torture, and the worst means of intimida-
tion failed to extinguish the underground. Guerrillas succeeded
in tying down dozens of Wehrmacht divisions, from Scandinavia
to the Ionian Sea. While many of the resistance fighters had been
members of their respective countries' armed forces, countless
civilians—men, women, and children—also joined in underground
activities.*

*One young man, Chris Jecchinis of Athens, watched the Italians
enter his city in October, 1940. Two years later, on his twentieth
birthday, Jecchinis became a private in the British army. Soon
afterward he spent four months in central Macedonia with Force
113, a group of officers and men in the Allied Military Mission
that was attached to every major guerrilla unit. How the members of a group respected and depended on each other is illus-
trated by the young Greek soldier's care of the desperately ill
Major McAdams (Mac), the twenty-five-year-old Scotsman who
led his Lapworth group.*

There was not much respite. After only one day of rest, we were
ready for another attack. Colonel West, who was in charge of
all OSS [Office of Strategic Services] troops in Greece, paid a
visit to Chuma's group with his regional commander, a Captain
Blanas. This time we were to strike again near Dhion, but with
different objectives and a different method.

Mac was looking very pale and sick again. He said he thought he could stand the strain of another maneuver, but he asked me to stay close to him before, during, and after the attack, in case he collapsed. He was really in no fit state to carry on, but he did not want anybody, particularly Colonel West, to know this before the big day.

We left our hiding place late in the afternoon, and reached the shepherds' hut near the village of Koundouriotissa, where we prepared the charges. Mac was looking and feeling worse every hour. Without his horse, which he had managed to get over from Ano Melia, he could never have made the journey. He must have had to fight hard against his sickness while he planned these final operations. Taking all the responsibility, working on the explosives, and arguing with guerrilla leaders was no occupation for any but the strongest of men.

We had been informed that a big trainload of troops and ammunition would be leaving the Dhion station at 2400 hours (12:00 P.M.). We left the huts at 2230 and walked through the fields in silence, avoiding the paths. It took longer but was safer, since we had begun to stir up so much trouble in the area. I was walking beside Mac's horse when I heard Mac muttering to himself in a mild delirium. I pulled his horse away from the others, not wanting them to know how ill he was. He leaned over and took my hand to ask if all was going well. I told him not to worry, that soon we were going to stop as we had almost reached our destination.

He rode the rest of the way silent and slumped in the saddle. About midnight we stopped under a clump of trees behind a field of bamboos, from which we could see the line of telegraph poles beside the railway five hundred yards away. I helped Mac to dismount and mopped his sweating head with my handkerchief soaked in water. He pulled himself together and gave his final orders. Colonel West was with us, but he politely put himself under Mac's orders for the operation, and I noticed that the rest of the Americans had by now taken a liking to Mac and enjoyed working under him.

We were expecting trouble. The Germans would be on the alert after our recent attacks, and word must have been sent out from all parts of Greece that their big withdrawal would be coming under heavy and constant attack.

We took more than the usual precautions. The Americans and guerrillas were deployed to cover a small party placing the charges under the rails. Angy was sent farther to the south to blow up the rails after the train had passed and to prevent any armored cars from getting through. He was also to cut the telegraph and telephone lines along the railway, in order to hinder German communications. Fotis and Captain Carver were to do exactly the same thing a little distance to the north. One American, with a machine gun, and some guerrillas were left to guard the mules and cover our rear in case of trouble.

This time we used the long primer-cord, which had to be ignited by hand. We no longer had faith in the "fog-signal" method of detonating. The charges were laid. Everything was ready. Everyone was waiting.

An hour passed and we were still waiting, silent. It was chilly; the earth was damp and smelled of moldy leaves. Legions of mosquitoes buzzed around us, biting our hands and faces. After all our big preparations, the waiting became an unbearable anticlimax. The longer we waited, the more nervous I became, and from the sounds around me, so were the others. Mac started talking to himself again.

All was in readiness for what was to become a real pitched battle—almost static warfare for a time. The sound of the train interrupted my conversation with the delirious Mac. He was suddenly in full command of himself as it rushed onward, and I pulled out my box of special fuse matches.

"Light up," he shouted at me, for the train was almost upon the spot where we had laid the charges.

I struck the match, applied it. The fuse burned for a moment, and then, simultaneously, primer-cord and charges exploded. The engine jolted off the rails.

The scene was indescribable. No sooner had the blast of the derailing explosion rolled over us than we saw and heard the wood and metal of the engine erupting and the shearing groan of telescoped carriages. An ammunition wagon on the train blasted open, and the onrush of air struck me like a blow in the face from an open palm. Showers of wood and other debris were falling on us from extraordinary heights, when Mac ordered us to open fire on the shouting, bewildered troops.

We had enormous firing power. We of Lapworth were in the center of a 320-yard line along the train track. On either side of us the guerrilla detachments opened up with their two heavy German mortars, three heavy machine guns (one German and two British), bren guns, and automatic rifles. From the center of the line the American OSS gave us support with two bazookas and two machine guns. The Germans were getting some of their own medicine from an unexpected quarter.

But the Germans—and I will never know how they managed it—sorted themselves out with amazing speed. A number of troops from the train escaped. They now ranged themselves quickly in line, facing us, and returned our fire.

As we ripped fire and flame into the broken train and the Germans reorganized, explosions to the north and south signaled that the line had been blown on two other places. We were so close to the line that we could hear the German officers ordering their men to fight back, and the Americans, with Colonel West leading, were trying to get in even closer.

Now the Germans had swung the wagons around and were entrenched behind these solid barricades. Machine guns started spitting from the windows of the carriages, and then came the "pom-pom" of antiaircraft and antitank guns, which were mounted on open flats on the train and heavily protected by sandbags.

The pom-poms wrought havoc in our line. They were much heavier than anything we had. I saw a whole line of guerrillas to one side of me. They were intent on their firing when a shell landed among them, and they fell. They fell strangely, like sacks of potatoes or scarecrows. I ran to see if I could help, and smelled the blood. It was the first time I had really smelled blood, although we had killed two Huns on a previous train attack. Probably, I can remember thinking, it was because there was so much spilled. Great patches of it were spreading in dirty stains.

There was one boy who had been hit but not killed outright. A terrible wound was somewhere close to his heart. *"Ay, Mana mou!"* he cried. *"Mana mou!"* My mother! He was in agony for a few minutes; he looked at his friends without seeing them as they carried him toward some trees. He fell and they dragged him the last few yards, but he was dead when they reached the trees. *"Mana mou!"* I ran back to our line. I was choking with impotent rage.

I opened my sten gun against the train, raked it, and got in really close. The heavy guns were outlined by the flames of the fire, and I aimed in the general direction of the manning positions and pressed the trigger with all my might. The Americans were also concentrating their fire on the big guns, and soon one of the guns stopped firing. I think they ran out of ammunition.

At the height of the battle, when things were starting to go well for us, heavy machine-gun fire opened up on our line from a German pillbox about a thousand yards away. We were caught in a kind of enfiladed fire now, just when we had them pinned down with the most accurate and concentrated attack we had yet mustered.

The Americans were still working close to the train, and one of them came within 120 yards of the train engine and potted it with a bazooka, trying to put it right out of commission.

He must have hit the engine's boiler, and the water hissed into the fire almost immediately. Anyway, it was quite spectacular. There was a terrific flash underneath the boiler and the whole engine seemed to burst in two. The train buried its nose in the disintegrated track in front of it, and a geyser of hot water spouted in all directions. We could feel the warm shower from the ruptured boiler as we started to reverse-crawl out of it. In the confusion the Germans lost our position and were shooting to the left of us as we inched to safety.

The only unfortunate thing about this incident was that it provided the train defenders with a perfect cloud screen. But it really did the job. The train was a complete wreck and would never be used again for anything but scrap metal.

Mac had already decided to withdraw when we got back to the line. He was getting anxious; he thought the German garrison might come up on left and right to seal off our escape. The particular section of the line we had attacked had been the scene of two other ambushes, and the Germans would undoubtedly have studied the surrounding area to plan the best means of stopping a retreat. Mac feared that if the Germans could ring us round, they would be able to hold us there until daylight, when their superior numbers would give them the last grim laugh.

Only one of our men had been wounded—an American had picked up a few scratches from flying shrapnel—and the only dead were from the guerrillas I had seen killed so quickly and finally as they stood in line. The operation had been a success, although we had not exploded more than one of the ammunition wagons. The Germans had cunningly placed their ammunition carriers at the end of the train, and they had escaped the worst of the explosion and the subsequent attack.

Mac was feeling better, so he planned the retreat clearly. But before we moved back, we had one additional casualty.

As one of the Americans was bending over to pick up a bazooka rocket, the bombardier fired the weapon and the bending American received the full force of the rocket explosion near the seat of his pants.

The top of his trousers, his wallet, and his underwear disappeared, leaving his lily-white derrière shining in the dark. The victim hopped about yelling, more in concern for his lost wallet than his sore backside. He retreated with the rest of us, his exposed bottom discreetly covered by a pullover, with the sleeves tied around his waist.

We struggled back through the fields and woods to avoid the paths, which were now getting an accurate pasting from the German guns. It was early light before Mac considered it safe to halt and rest.

On the way we passed through a field of melons; I had pilfered one, which I now cut and shared with Mac. The feeling of relief after the operation and the belief that it had been a success overcame his illness for a while, and he was in high spirits.

"You thieving rascal!" he said, accepting his half of the melon.

Before we lay down for a short sleep, I heard Colonel West congratulating Mac and expressing his admiration for the efficiency of the mission. I closed my eyes and imagined I was walking about our rented villa in New Kifissia after breakfast with my mother, uncle, and aunt. It was summer and the one-story red house on the mountainside near Athens was cool in the morning shade of the pine trees.

Mac was asleep beside me, and the big moon slid through the clouds, its face bland, innocent, and timeless.

Chapter 6

"Obedience meant death . . ."

Many nationalities and creeds characterized the individuals who worked together against a common enemy. Eugene Weinstock, a Hungarian Jew who fled persecution in his own country only to find similar oppression threatening the people of Antwerp, joined the Belgian underground.

The Nazis declared all organizations except their own illegal. Before their occupation, the Belgian government had jailed the leaders of the [Léon] Degrelle Belgian Nazi organization. Now these jackals returned with a great hue and cry to feed on the leavings of the lion. They tried to popularize Nazi ideology. They agitated far and wide, greeting the Germans as the saviors of Belgium who were about to liberate all Europe from bolshevism.

The Nazis graciously freed most of the Belgian-Flemish prisoners of war and permitted them to return home. The Walloons, however, a more solidly anti-Nazi group, remained in prison until their final liberation by the Allies.

Not many weeks passed before Belgian and foreign democrats and left-wingers began to organize. First they attempted to counter Nazi propaganda. We Hungarians also gathered again, meeting in apartments in great secrecy, and decided to aid the Belgian movement against the invaders.

Our first action was to organize an illegal Hungarian paper, mimeographed on one sheet. We based the paper on English radio reports, to which we listened despite the law prohibiting it. Once we were engaged in the active illegal fight, we were all happier.

The movement grew. The unfolding of the inhuman policies of the Nazis drove the most disparate elements together in the resistance.

In March, 1942, the Germans sent a summons commanding all Jews in Antwerp between the ages of sixteen and twenty-two to report immediately at local Nazi offices, bringing a three-day supply of food and a change of clothing. The conqueror needed labor power in occupied France. Parents were warned that they too would be deported if they encouraged their children to disobey the order.

The Nazis promised the children easy work and good pay. The order netted them sixteen thousand Antwerp boys and girls. Then they extended the decree to all of Belgium.

Only a few months after this deportation order, another followed. This time the German machine called for all men from the ages of twenty-two to forty. But now the resistance took a hand on the basis of past experience and issued a manifesto, calling upon the Jewish people to disobey the order. At first many were afraid to take our advice, but they gradually realized that obedience meant death. The only hope of survival lay in resistance.

This manifesto created a tremendous organizational task for the underground. Those who did not report had to live in hiding. We who were now leading the underground had to supply them and their families with food or food tickets.

Food, even for those living legally, grew scarcer. The Belgians became more dissatisfied, particularly when they saw the National Socialist Flemish, who were hand in glove with the invaders, receiving double rations and living high while the rest of the people were half-starved. Consequently, the resistance grew and fought more boldly on two fronts: against the invader and against native traitors.

In Antwerp, Flemish collaborationists had taken control of the city administration. In Brussels, however, the Walloons had held on to most of the city offices. In almost all Brussels city departments there were decent officials, and we knew friend from foe. For this reason we took most of those who disobeyed the deportation order to the vicinity of Brussels, where we could find homes for them and even register them at appropriate city bureaus.

By the summer of 1942 the resistance was moving ahead with great energy. Every oppressive measure of the Nazis filled our ranks. However, Rexist informers did their work, and the Germans discovered that there were Belgians who were hiding Jews. The Germans decreed that if the Jews did not present themselves for deportation, they would take young Belgians and send them to Germany rather than to France. Then the Germans began seizing people on the streets. Those who could not prove they were working were sent to concentration camps, to forced labor camps, or to extermination camps.

It was dangerous for any young person or middle-aged man to appear on the streets. Degrelle, Belgium's Quisling (who now enjoyed the hospitality of his fellow jackal, Franco), was strutting about Brussels in his elegant SS uniform. The Nazis exhorted the youth to join the SS and help "exterminate bolshevism." Some, who were Nazi or Rexist sympathizers, joined. All these became cannon fodder on the Eastern front, and the promise of double rations that the Nazis made to their families was soon honored in the breach.

In the fall of 1942 the resistance organized military groups in every Belgian city. We answered terror with terror. We dressed as civilians, but acted under army discipline. We blew up a German military storehouse. We demolished a Nazi movie theater filled with 750 German soldiers enjoying a Hitler film.

Following the explosion of the movie theater, the Germans began the savage practice of taking hostages. It was then that the Walloon mayor of Brussels proved himself a true hero. He issued a declaration to the people, calling upon them to sabotage German decrees and defy the oppressor. He then submitted his resignation and awaited his arrest, which came the following day.

But the declaration had a powerful effect. German troop trains were blown up or derailed. Railway bridges disappeared at night. Fires broke out. The broad Belgian resistance absorbed the foreign-speaking underground groups, and the "Independence Front" appeared under a unified leadership.

The Belgian resistance was now an army.

Etta Kostelnik was a little past thirty, her face somewhat hard, but her eyes clear, kind, and filled with the pain of much bitter struggle. She wore a shabby dress. There were gray threads in her black hair. By day she worked—washing, ironing, and housecleaning in the city of Brussels where she lived with her twelve-year-old son in one room on the Rue de Rivage.

None of us knew how this wife of a Hungarian Catholic worker came to be in Belgium, nor did we ask, although we had heard that Franco's mercenaries had murdered her husband during the invasion of Spain.

Etta was high in the ranks of the heroines of the resistance. In Catholic Belgium, a Catholic workingwoman could live a comparatively peaceful life with her family, especially when that family was only one small boy. Etta, however, rejected such a peaceful life. Driven by concern for her Hungarian anti-Nazi countrymen and for the Jewish people, she entered the Belgian resistance.

As the least likely among us to be suspect, Etta had the job of keeping our most incriminating documents in her apartment, as well as the hand-mimeographing machine with which we published our illegal Hungarian paper. She also distributed the paper to its readers, every one of whose names and addresses she hid in her home. She also managed the money and food tickets which the resistance supplied to those in need of them. (Armed partisans stole these tickets from the distribution center, or received them from patriotic Belgian authorities who were helping those in hiding.)

Etta Kostelnik's hands were full enough. During her working day and at night when her work was done, she came and went tirelessly, particularly to more public places where better-known people could not show themselves without risking their lives. Her little boy was her faithful assistant. He worked in the same spirit as his mother. He delivered papers, took relief to people in hiding, carried messages, and bore the responsibility for hundreds of lives—all with the tragic seriousness and dignity that a child may sometimes attain.

One day Stephen Molnar, leader of the Hungarian partisans in Belgium, rushed into my place. Tersely, he asked whether Etta's son knew my address or anything else about me.

Etta's son? I must have stared at him, because he felt his questions required explanation. I replied that the boy knew nothing about me, since my name was not on Etta's lists.

Stephen Molnar threw himself down on the sofa like one who wishes to extort from life a moment's peace and quiet. Then he gave me the facts.

"The Gestapo have Etta's boy. They're probably beating him. They may get something out of him."

"What happened?"

"Someone betrayed Etta!" (Someone betrayed Etta! Someone sold his dignity and his right to life for the lying promise of a "double ration"!)

Molnar continued. "The Gestapo men went to her flat about five o'clock this afternoon. She usually gets home then, but only the boy was there. They took him and they must be grilling him now. I notified all the others. I left you to the last."

"How did you get to know all this?" I asked.

He hesitated. Then he said quietly, "I was there when it happened."

I stared blankly. Molnar had a reputation for getting out of tight spots, but his statement surprised me nevertheless.

"I got away," he explained. "The neighbors warned Etta when she got near the house. Friends are taking her to the French border now." He rose, stretched, and took his hat. "I'll have to hurry. I've got a lot to do."

Molnar stopped short in the doorway, drew his revolver from his hip pocket, and examined it. Four of the chambers were empty. He took four fresh cartridges from a box and reloaded the weapon. Then he left without another word.

Days later I heard the story of the four empty chambers. Molnar never bragged. He never talked much at all, for that matter. Evidently the secret police, having found no sign of Etta, began bullying her boy. The boy knew nothing. Then the Gestapo men searched every inch of the apartment. They found the lists of names, the illegal mimeo machine, the forged identification papers, addresses of fugitive Jews, names of people who contributed money.

One of the Brownshirts went to the entrance of the house to prevent anyone from warning Etta. The others stayed in the flat, studying the papers and slapping the boy around. It was then that Stephen Molnar arrived. He thought Etta would be home and he was carrying material for her underground work.

Since the Brownshirt at the door was in civilian clothes, Molnar paid no attention to him. He pressed Etta's bell and started toward the stairs. The Nazi moved over to him quickly and pressed his gun into Molnar's back.

"What's your business with that woman?"

"Nothing important. She does housework for us. I want to tell her not to come tomorrow because we won't be home."

"You can talk about it upstairs." The Gestapo man nudged Molnar with the gun.

Molnar walked obediently, with his arms raised, but when they reached the top step, he suddenly gave a violent kick backward. His foot landed full in the German's belly. The German rolled and somersaulted down the stairs, but long before he reached the landing, Molnar had fired twice at his moving target.

The Gestapo man had dropped his gun. Molnar raced for it. He knew that others would immediately rush out to investigate the shots. He took cover behind a pillar in the ground-floor hall. Two Germans appeared on the stairs. Molnar fired one shot at each. (We discovered later that he wounded both.) Then he hurried away through the gathering crowd of neighbors.

Stephen Molnar notified everyone on Etta's lists in time for them to make good their escapes. That night Belgian and Hungarian partisans took Etta across the French border where she immediately joined the French resistance.

Denounced by a Belgian collaborator, Weinstock was arrested and taken to Buchenwald concentration camp.

Chapter 7

"Calm was written on their faces . . . "

Hitler's surprise invasion of Russia in June, 1941, gambled on a rapid, decisive defeat of the Soviet army. At first, Russian civilians seemed friendly toward the van of the German army, but this changed as soon as the "Reich commissars" came along with their rigorous martial rule. All sympathy was alienated and the countryside settled down to the horrors of partisan warfare.

Many years after the war ended, two Russian partisans wrote of their experiences with the resistance. Ivan Ivanovich Isakov, whose story appears first, is now in his early sixties and a plant manager in the small town of Tosno, near Leningrad. He led the Oredezh partisans who, in 1941, operated south and west of Leningrad.

With every new day, the communiqués from the war front grew gloomier and gloomier. We began to form our partisan unit in July, 1941. It consisted of nine groups, a total fighting force of nearly two hundred men.

At that time I was Second Secretary of the Oredezh District Communist Party Committee, and so was appointed commander of this unit. Each candidate was thoroughly interviewed and we took on only people who willingly volunteered for this mission.

The nine partisan groups were named after the various village soviets in whose neighborhoods they were deployed. Each group had its own man for contact. At night lorries loaded with victuals, weapons, and explosives set out for the headquarters of these groups, which were hidden away in the woods. Meanwhile activists prepared and dispatched incendiary bottles to secret storage places in the woods.

73

The Nazis bombed the railway station of Oredezh for the first time in early July. By mid-August they had already entered the territory of the district.

On August 14, the partisan groups marched into the woods. Their commanders were to leave Oredezh after everyone had gone. Next morning I called on the offices of the district Communist Party Committee. My footsteps echoed down the empty halls and corridors. We had put people on duty at the village soviets whose mission was to telephone the district Party Committee when the Nazis arrived and then to set out for their respective groups. We did not have any other means at the time to evaluate the real state of affairs.

The first telephone call came from Polina Kostygova at about eleven o'clock in the morning. She reported from the Kammeno-Polyansky soviet that the Nazis were already near. A few hours later we learned that enemy troops were moving on Terebush. Later the chairman of the Belsky soviet called. The enemy was now only nine kilometers [5.58 miles] away from Oredezh.

An hour later we drove away from the district center into the woods, now to become true partisans. The headquarters of the partisan movement and the underground district Party Committee were stationed at first some five kilometers away from the Novinka railway station. Later, however, they moved to dugouts arranged near the Chashchinsky forests.

We had started our forest life in earnest. At the beginning we sustained heavy losses. On the very first day, we lost the commander of the Novoberezin group. A week later we learned that the Nazis had hanged G. N. Matveyev, head of the Pechkovsky group.

Enemy successes came as a surprise to us. We could not help feeling anxiety and alarm. We knew practically nothing about the situation at the fighting fronts. We were particularly concerned about what was happening at Leningrad, so we sent a man there—P. P. Laptev, manager of the Oredezh district forestry establishment. He returned in mid-September, bringing wireless operators and equipment. Now we had communication with the mainland, and we sent our first wireless message to Leningrad.

By that time the partisans of our unit had conducted more

than one operation. On August 29 we blew up three hundred barrels of fuel at the village of Berezhok on the Oredezh-Lyuban road. Two days later we destroyed a lorry, passenger car, and motorcycle on the Oredezh-Luga road and killed nine Nazi soldiers and two officers. On September 3 we put another motor vehicle out of action on that same road.

We often arranged ambushes on the roads. Little by little we developed our own tactics, which we learned the hard way through experience. Our unit was divided into three groups. The first would let the enemy vehicle pass, in case others were coming up from behind; we would open fire only when the front vehicle had reached the third and last group.

I remember particularly well one of the first ambushes we organized. At the time, the partisans of our unit were still novices at fighting, but we had to feel sure that our woodsmen-fighters would be able to defeat a well-armed enemy.

You cannot imagine what runs through one's head when one lies in ambush. You lie there and wait, cocking an ear to all the noises, to the whispering of the wind and the rustling of the leaves. A partisan in ambush must not betray himself by the slightest sign.

No matter how much you expect it, no matter how intensely you concentrate, the enemy always seems to appear unexpectedly. On that occasion, a heavy lorry rumbled far away beyond the bend in the road, and I looked at my comrades. I daresay every one of them felt as excited as I. However, calm was written on their faces. Their movements were brief and they prepared for battle without any fuss. Probably I looked just as imperturbable to them.

A train of lorries appeared on the road. Mounted on the front vehicle was a six-barreled mortar. On the second vehicle was an armored platform with mines on it. In a covered van were the Nazis themselves.

The whole operation lasted some twenty minutes. Not a Nazi escaped. Then a hush descended, a penetrating stillness that seemed surprising.

As time went by, the partisans of our unit established firmer contact with the local population. We already had quite a number of good helpers, among them Anatoly Agapov, Nikolai

Mazura, and Georgy Muravyev. Especially helpful was the assistance that the forester Mazura gave us. Without arousing suspicion, he could freely ride around the area and collect the information we required.

Little by little we accumulated experience and finally realized that we could cope with major operations.

We received information from the Leningrad headquarters of the partisan movement that the Nazis were establishing a line of communication between Pushkin and Novgorod. Sited on this forty-mile southeasterly route was the vital railway station of Cholovo. Some seventy Nazi soldiers turned up at this station and set up workshops there.

We decided to raid Cholovo. Sasha Borodulin was sent out to reconnoiter the situation.

Borodulin joined our unit in a rather peculiar way. In 1941 he had just finished his seventh school year. When the Germans occupied his village, Sasha told his parents that he was going to join the partisans. His mother wept, but his father nodded. They did not try to detain him. Under the cover of night, the young patriot made his way into the woods.

Some three kilometers away from the village of Ozereshno on an unused haymeadow stood a dilapidated shed with some hay inside, where Sasha spent the night and from where—having carefully camouflaged the lair he had made for himself in the soft, fragrant hay—he set out on his "operations." He soon knocked down a motorcyclist and acquired a tommy gun with some reserve ammunition. For hours he lay in ambush waiting for enemy vehicles to appear. He usually fired two or three bursts, and then, taking advantage of the panic, vanished into the woods.

One day when our partisans were heading for the forester's cottage, where they usually had their rendezvous with the local inhabitants, they unexpectedly bumped into an enemy guard. Several shots were exchanged and the German sentry was killed. The partisans retreated into the woods, meanwhile sending one of their force to reconnoiter the area.

The partisan cautiously made his way toward the cottage. All of a sudden, he noticed something odd. He stole up to a cluster of bushes, and could not contain his surprise when he saw a young chap he knew from the village of Novinka. It seemed that Sasha had also been watching the forester's cottage. When he heard the shots he had decided to approach a little closer to investigate.

Borodulin made a very good scout. The Nazis had not the slightest inkling of the danger they could expect from this innocent-looking boy whose face looked so open and friendly.

When Sasha reported on the situation at Cholovo, he said, "There are sixty-three Nazis at the railway station; the officers are in the stationmaster's room and there are two sentries."

"How did you manage to learn all that?" I asked.

"It's my own secret," Sasha replied, and his boyish, mischievous face spread out into a broad grin.

The partisans divided into two groups. One took up positions behind a stack of firewood, the other deployed on the other side of the railway station. Sasha Borodulin was with this second group.

A few minutes before we had planned to start the operation, we saw a peasant woman coaxing an obstinate nanny goat across the railway track.

Somebody shouted out: "Run for your life, woman, there's going to be some shooting there."

She let go of the goat and scampered off. That same moment shots rang out—the partisans opening fire with rifles and machine guns. In a split second Sasha rushed forward and tossed a couple of hand grenades into the stationmaster's office. There was a terrific explosion.

The fighting was soon over. The surviving Nazis ran for their lives, and the partisans slipped back into the woods.

Sasha Borodulin was killed at a time when our unit was going through incredible hardship. The Nazis had surrounded us and were crowding us toward the middle of a small section of forest, about one square kilometer in area. We resolved to break through. We mustered our unit in one of the clearings and dashed forward, opening up fire. We covered some three kilometers, but the enemy still pursued us.

We paused for respite and I asked:

"Who will volunteer for a covering rear guard?"

Sasha Borodulin was first to volunteer. He and a few others

took up positions behind the trees, and we moved on. I did not see Sasha again.

In the Belsky soviet there was a teacher whose name was Pavel Savin. He was a quiet sort of person, about whom his neighbors knew little. The Nazis decided to appoint him burgomaster.

"Let me think it over," he pleaded.

The Nazis gave him some time to think. The very next day our Belsky contact reported, "Savin approached me and said he knew I was connected with the partisans. He said he wanted me to arrange a rendezvous with the partisan commander."

I was still not quite sure of the man when I went to the rendezvous. The moment we met, he began to beg, "Please take me into your unit. I've got boys in the army. How will I be able to look them in the face afterward? And it's not only a matter of my boys. I'm Russian, after all. And they're suggesting that I serve them."

We had a long talk, and only toward morning did we agree that he would consent to become burgomaster and at the same time would provide us regularly with all information of interest to the unit.

Savin did his best to help us. He was particularly helpful when a punitive detachment arrived in the neighborhood. To fulfill the anti-partisan directives issued by Field Marshal Brauchitsch in November, 1941, the command of the Sixteenth German Army doubled the guard on its lines of communication. A large punitive force was deployed in the Oredezh district. These were grim days for our unit.

On the night of November 15 Savin informed us that a punitive force of twelve hundred men, equipped with tommy guns, submachine guns, machine guns, and mortars, had arrived in Oredezh. We decided not to engage this punitive force unless it was absolutely necessary. We also resolved to keep all the villages in the vicinities of the headquarters of the partisan units under vigilant observation. The punitive force divided into three groups. In the village of Gverezdno they burned several houses to the ground and killed six persons. A partisan and his son fought like heroes to protect these innocent people, managing to kill three Nazi soldiers and wound a Nazi officer before they themselves were shot dead. Further, in the village of Stroino the Nazis demolished the house of another partisan and shot his father and brother.

On November 17 the headquarters of one unit was encircled and destroyed, though the unit itself managed to move elsewhere without any losses. Nevertheless, ten days later they were again surrounded and had to engage in fighting. In this battle five partisans were killed. The Nazis managed to destroy that headquarters as well as one more.

The enemy was jubilant. We had to quit the theater of hostilities. Some of the partisans dispersed among various villages, while others—mostly the sick and wounded, with many suffering from frostbite—moved to Leningrad. I went along to Leningrad with them. We were hungry and worn out and we left our native region with heavy hearts. However, we firmly believed that when we regained our strength, we would take up once more and return.

And that indeed came to pass. A month later, on December 30, 1941, the reorganization of the unit of Oredezh partisans, who had crossed the front lines, was completed. We still had a long war to fight against the invaders. But we were fully prepared for it.

Yelizaveta Stanishevskaya, whose story follows, was a contact for the Bobruysk partisan unit in the Byelorussia region, 300 to 400 miles southwest of Moscow and north of the Ukraine.

The winter of 1942 was a time of alarm and anxiety. Toward the spring, partisans grew more active again, derailing trains that were carrying enemy soldiers and equipment.

To protect the railway the Nazis forced the civilian population, including even thirteen-year-old children, to guard it at night. For every two or three meters of railway track they posted one civilian, and for every kilometer of track one or two of their own men. The first person to spot partisans had to raise the alarm and report them to the Nazis.

This "guard" was rather comical. The partisans freely passed through to the railway track and, in addition, received from the "guard" all the information they required about the deployment of German occupation forces. This initiated regular contact between our collective farmers and the partisans.

The partisans called on our house for the first time in October, 1942. They were from the saboteur group of the First Bobruysk Brigade. The entire family gladly agreed to help them. Now life had taken on new meaning, even though the activity we were engaged in was exceedingly dangerous. I began to work as a contact for the Bobruysk underground district Communist Party Committee while my husband, Konstantin Stanishevsky, agreed to guide the saboteur group.

A few days later partisans again called on us, and my husband took them along to the railway track. We eagerly but anxiously looked forward to the results. All of a sudden there was a fearful explosion and we heard the "ratata" of the machine guns. We understood what had happened and prepared to leave for the woods. However, there was no need for alarm; everybody returned safe and sound. The operation was a complete success—a whole enemy train of men and equipment had been derailed.

After that the partisans called on us almost every night. Other collective farmers also took a hand in helping them, while our young folk flocked to join the partisan units.

Our village actually led a sort of dual life. In the daytime, when the Nazis and police came, the population stayed indoors and there was dead quiet. But at night, when the partisans occupied the village, a life full of dangers began. Meetings were held, Soviet newspapers and leaflets were read, and the partisans were given information as to the location and deployment of the occupation forces in the vicinity.

In January, 1943, the secretary of the Bobruysk underground district Party Committee and M. I. Semisalov, a district Party Committee member, called to discuss further plans for my work. Besides distributing leaflets and proclamations, collecting intelligence, and recruiting contacts, I was supposed to make contact with Bobruysk and arrange for secret addresses there.

For that purpose, I went into town several times with Semisalov, mostly in the guise of peasants going to market. We prominently displayed all sorts of wares for sale and beneath these things, mostly victuals, we had hidden bundles of leaflets and proclamations. On our way out, we took medicines, maps, paper, clothing, and, quite often, weapons too.

On February 15, 1943, Semisalov and I went into Bobruysk and spent two days. I returned alone; Semisalov took another road. About halfway home, my daughter met me and told me that all the men in the village, including my husband and elder son, Lev, had been seized by the Nazis in vengeance for the participation of our villagers in the killing of seventeen German soldiers in a signal booth.

This is what had happened. Every day several of the villagers were assigned to work on the railway near the signal booth by the village of Lyulevo. The Nazi soldiers stationed in this sector already recognized many of our villagers and let them through.

On that particular day, by a previous arrangement, the partisans of a cavalry group joined the people assigned for work and together they approached the booth. Four of our collective farmers also participated in the killing of the guards there.

The Nazis raised an alarm when everything was over. Shots were fired and one farmer was killed. The others escaped, taking their weapons with them.

Our collective farmers, with the exception of two who raced back to the village to tell the people what had happened, left with the partisans. Shortly afterward the village was surrounded by the Nazis and all the remaining men were arrested and taken away. Even those who had been working in the woods at the time and knew nothing about the operation were arrested. Toward dusk my son managed to escape and join a partisan brigade. I asked the underground Party Committee what I was to do and was told to go on living with my children openly for as long as I could.

More than forty of our villagers were arrested. They were all taken to the Yasen railway station. That same night, after savage torture, the two farmers who had returned to the village were shot. The other villagers were sent first to Osipovichi and subsequently to Bobruysk, to the concentration camp there.

For a time the Nazis seemed to have forgotten our village. They knew that the collective farmers, or at least some of them, would return home, and that is what happened.

Then, on the night of February 21, a punitive force surrounded our village. I hid away in a pit that had been dug in a barn. In the collective farmyard, the Nazis shot all the men they were able to capture.

Meanwhile, the women were herded into a house and ordered to betray the families of the men who had participated in killing the Nazis in the signal booth. The wives and small children of two of these men were among this group, but nobody betrayed them. Then the Nazis threatened to shoot all the women. Realizing that the executioners were about to carry out their threat, the two women displayed great courage and gave themselves up. They were pulled roughly out of the crowd and put into a lorry. The others were told to march toward the marsh beyond the village, and a machine gun was fired above their heads to hurry them on.

With great difficulty the miserable women and children rushed, stumbling, into the swamp, helping one another along. From there they finally managed to get away and scattered themselves among nearby villages. My children and I took up lodgings with our contact, V. V. Sidorovich.

Meanwhile the Nazis carried away two more women to the Tatarka peat-briquetting plant and hanged them there.

On March 5, the party secretary came to my new place of residence. He told me to go to Bobruysk to get medicines and other things that the partisan unit needed. Volodya Sidorovich had been sent, but all suspects were beginning to be arrested.

On the morning of March 8, I called on the village of Sychkovo to get some salt for the partisan unit. That day the Nazis raided our village and seized Sidorovich's mother and sister and my daughter as hostages to be detained until Volodya returned.

Volodya returned toward evening. He had been warned on his way home that he would be arrested. At that time two other contacts of ours, who had been waiting for him, also turned up. The three of them decided to leave at once and report back to the unit. However, on the way they were attacked not far from their homes by the Nazis, who had come to see if Volodya had returned.

One of them managed to escape, but Volodya and the other were captured. The evidence was too damaging. In their sleighs were medicines, maps, binoculars, and other things for the partisan fighters.

This was a grim time for us. However, developments took a quite unexpected turn, thanks to Volodya's selfless gallantry. He took full blame on himself, betraying no one and thus saving his mother and sister, my daughter, and his companion, who were all released. Volodya was incarcerated under horrible conditions till June, 1943, when he was taken out and shot.

In that same month, M. P. Samsonik, our collective farm chairman before the war and now commander of a special group, was sent from across the front lines to organize intelligence work in the enemy's rear.

I gladly agreed to work for this special intelligence group. Samsonik asked me to arrange the observation of railway movements of troop trains and also to provide both a hiding place for the wireless operations from Bobruysk and the people to run them. A new chapter of thrilling and dangerous work began. I often went into town to report in person to Samsonik, or sometimes I would relay my information through our contact. We chose for our place of rendezvous a wood not far from the village of Yasen.

By the month of August we had everything ready for setting up a wireless in Bobruysk. We decided to install it in the house of M. I. Levanovich, who lived at 22-A Oktyabrsky Lane.

We recruited a group of staunch comrades to provide information for our wireless operator. They were to keep an eye on the proceedings at railway stations, the movement of troop units, the erection of fortifications in the city, the locations of dumps, and other activities.

In the second half of August, Samsonik specified the day and hour that I would get a wireless operator from him. The night before, our contacts brought in the wireless equipment, complete with batteries, from the woods; they cached everything away in a shed at my house, which luckily enough had remained intact after the Nazis razed the village of Yasen.

We had to bring the wireless operator, a girl, and all the equipment into Bobruysk. I was to do this alone so that no others ran any danger.

Next morning we loaded everything onto a cart and set off

for Bobruysk. I had a permit which had been arranged for in advance. It was a Sunday, as I remember, and on the way we met peasants going to the market in town.

The Germans had posted guards at the railway crossing before the town. Because of the traffic jam at the crossing, the attention of the guards was naturally distracted. I took advantage of this and told the wireless operator to lie down in the cart as if she were sick. I myself climbed down off the cart, took the horse by the reins, and tried to create the impression that I was in a terrible hurry. One of the Nazi soldiers peered under the blanket at the seemingly sick girl and waved me on. However, only when we got to Oktyabrsky Lane did we feel that all danger had passed.

We hid all the equipment in Levanovich's home. With the help of her friends she got the wireless operator registered as a tenant on the pretext that the girl had come to town to enroll in the girl's school which the Germans were trying to open.

The wireless started operating on the second day after our arrival. We were all very, very happy. Now we could talk with our own folk and exchange greetings with them above the enemy's head, so to speak. Only one who has lived through all the horrors of occupation can understand what we felt.

Throughout September our wireless operated in that house without any particular snags. But toward the end of the month, enemy radio stations began to interfere with the work of our set. It was no longer safe to stay there, and a new place had to be found. We moved the equipment out into the suburbs to a place called Krivoi Kryuk and hid it in a barn in the yard of G. S. Privolovich.

Our wireless was in operating order again. Soon, however, the batteries ran out. We had to bring in new ones, but it was getting harder and harder to get into town.

Nevertheless we found a way. My husband made a false bottom in the cart and there we hid the batteries, along with a couple of slow-action mines for wrecking operations in the city. On the cart itself we placed sacks of potatoes, flour, onions, garlic, a bottle of milk, and a couple of chickens.

I had almost reached Privolovich's house safely and was just a few dozen yards away when his wife came walking in my direction and managed to whisper to me that I must drive past, because there was danger.

Trying to keep calm, I drove slowly past the house and turned into town. I did not know what had happened and, perplexed and puzzled, called on Levanovich. On the way the wireless operator caught up with me and told me that many Nazis had arrived in Krivoi Kryuk, had set up a wireless station, and had located our own wireless.

It had happened that our operator had made wireless contact with the Nazis. Normally, after each broadcast she would give the prearranged signal and set up the hour for the next session. However, the Nazis did not know what our signal was and this saved us, for our operator quickly realized with whom she was dealing. She completed the broadcast and agreed to resume contact at the same hour on the following day. The Nazis, hoping to catch our wireless in operation, did not realize that our operator knew what was going on. We decided to move the set out the next morning, come what might.

Levanovich and I did not sleep the entire night. The wireless operator meanwhile went back to Krivoi Kryuk. At this hour of danger she did not want to be too far away from her wireless set, resolving to destroy it and die herself if she could not save it.

At seven o'clock in the morning on an October day it was still dark, but we could stand to wait no longer. We harnessed a horse to a cart, placed various articles on it, took Levanovich's six-year-old boy with us, and drove toward Krivoi Kryuk under the guise of moving to another flat. On the way we stopped at the house of Levanovich's sister in Tolstoi Street. I stayed behind to hold the horse, while my friend went on ahead by foot to Krivoi Kryuk. Though no more than an hour and a half passed, it seemed an eternity to me. At last I saw the wireless operator, carrying a bundle, make her way stealthily through the kitchen gardens at the back.

She was followed by Privolovich's wife, who also carried a basket. A few minutes later our contact turned up also with a bundle, followed by Levanovich. They had carried away all the equipment right under the noses of the Nazis. Our concern now was to find another suitable place for the set. Levanovich's sister noticed how excited we were. She beckoned to us and asked what the matter was and whether she could help.

We went into a huddle, and decided to tell her what we were carrying and how we had to hide it somewhere. Without a moment's hesitation, she offered her own barn and her son's help. Her son, as we learned, was also a wireless operator by profession.

Thus we installed our wireless set in its third location. On the next day, having checked to see that there were no German radio stations nearby, we again established contact with headquarters. I left town, feeling a little more cheerful.

As the front line drew closer to Bobruysk, we were ordered by our command, in late November, to move our wireless set to Brest and to recruit a group of loyal comrades to service it.

This was no easy task. We needed people and money, and, in addition to that, it was very hard to get a permit to leave Bobruysk in a westerly direction. Our hopes centered around a German-language schoolmistress. Her knowledge of German was very good. We learned through our contacts that the Nazis often asked her to translate important papers. We also learned that she was planning to go to Germany, not because she had any particular liking for the Nazis but because she was afraid of what the future might hold. This we considered very important.

I entered into negotiations with her. Treading warily, I explained to her what was needed, whom we wanted to send with her to Brest, and what was going to be done there. She agreed to go on our terms and also to get permits for us. Three would go to Brest—the schoolmistress, the wireless operator masquerading as her niece, and also the operator's sister, who would go along as a domestic servant. We wanted to create the impression that a well-to-do family was fleeing from the Bolsheviks.

Next we had to find a good dress for the wireless operator and provide her with a couple of good trunks for her own belongings and for the wireless and batteries. In addition, we had to furnish the necessary food supplies. We did not have the means to do this. However, Samsonik gave us some money and we scraped together the rest from wherever we could. Finally, everything was ready.

We arranged that they would leave on July 16, 1943. I was not able to get to Bobruysk that day, but I soon learned that the wireless set had reached Brest safely and had begun to operate again.

Chapter 8

"The flag!
The Polish flag!"

More than half a million Poles were executed or died from torture and maltreatment because of their resistance or suspected resistance activities. They stubbornly fought back from the beginning of the war.

Tadeusz Komorowski, better known as General Bor, became the leader of the well-trained home army, which took continuing toll of the Germans and their matériel. This is his account of the ill-starred Warsaw uprising of August, 1944:

The men took up their positions at windows, in attics, and on chimneys. The entrances to the blocks were then closed and barricaded from within. A sentry in the courtyard forbade all inmates any access to the street, for fear that the final preparations might be revealed to the enemy. Thirty minutes before zero hour, all preparations were completed. The soldiers brought out their arms and put on white-and-red armbands, the first open sign of a Polish army on Polish soil since the occupation. For five years they had all awaited this moment. Now the last seconds seemed an eternity. At five o'clock they would cease to be an underground resistance movement and would become once more regular army, fighting in the open.

At exactly five o'clock thousands of windows flashed as they were flung open. From all sides a hail of bullets struck passing Germans, riddling their buildings and their marching formations. In the twinkling of an eye, the remaining civilians disappeared from the streets. From the entrances of houses, our men streamed out and rushed to the attack. In fifteen minutes an entire city of a million inhabitants was engulfed in the fight. Every kind of traffic ceased. As a big communications center where roads from north, south, east, and west converged in the immediate rear of the German front, Warsaw ceased to exist. The battle for the city was on.

It so happened that just before the action started my staff and I found ourselves involved in a fight which might well have proved fatal for us. I went to my headquarters in the Kammler factory just before four. It was situated in a part of the city which was completely unknown to me. The buildings faced two narrow, parallel roads, Dzielna and Pawia streets. Both were dead ends closed by a wall surrounding the ghetto. On the other side of this wall was a large area of charred ruins. Our headquarters adjoined another factory on the ghetto side, which belonged to the tobacco monopoly. It was occupied by a German garrison and, like all such buildings, was guarded by two pillboxes. Each of the two streets was covered by one of these pillboxes, because this factory looked out both ways. Altogether it was an unhealthy neighborhood.

At five o'clock the whole surrounding sector was to be occupied by the Kedyw Battalion, one of the crack units of the home army. It had been tried out in many street fights and partisan actions, and there was no doubt that it would ably accomplish its task. Its commander had been there before us, had taken his bearings and formed a detailed plan. His unit was to smoke out the Germans from our immediate vicinity. But events did not go quite according to plan.

I walked toward the Kammler factory and approached to within fifteen yards of one of the pillboxes. Through the slit I could see the barrel of a machine gun trained on the street; the pillbox was occupied by alert German soldiers. I reached the building which was to be GHQ [General Headquarters] and, with the utmost caution, was allowed to enter. Inside the factory, the guard platoon had assembled with its commander, Lieutenant Kammler, owner of the factory, who reported to me at the gate. His men were all workers from the factory. On the day of the rising the whole organization was transformed into a fighting unit. The men had an excellent appearance; I eyed them with approval. When I asked Lieutenant Kammler how things were in the vicinity of the factory, he said, "Not too good. During the night the Germans increased their garrison in the tobacco factory to fifty men. They have two machine guns."

"How many men are here with you?" I asked.

"Thirty-three actually on the spot," he replied.

"And what arms?"

"Fifteen rifles, maybe forty grenades, and a few filipinki."

Filipinki were grenades of our own production. They had been used with great success in sabotage and in street clashes with the Germans, and they had great explosive power.

I told Kammler to remain quietly with his platoon and not to reveal his presence until the expected Kedyw Battalion had arrived and occupied the tobacco factory at five o'clock, as planned. I then went up to the second floor, where the general staff, the government delegate, and the chairman of the Council of National Unity had already assembled. Engineers in one of the neighboring factory sheds had begun to install radio equipment.

Suddenly, from the empty street overlooked by our windows came the sound of an approaching lorry. I went to the window and saw a heavy lorry carrying a few German railway police. It passed the first factory entrance and turned into the second, which probably had now been opened. A thought immediately flashed through my head: our sentry at the gate would have a rifle in his hands. A clash was inevitable.

At the same instant, two rifle shots rang out in quick succession. The lorry suddenly reappeared in reverse and simultaneously, through the other gate, emerged Lieutenant Kammler, revolver in hand, with two other soldiers. Kammler killed the driver on the spot, as well as two other Germans standing in the lorry. The nearby German pillbox immediately opened fire and machine-gun bullets sprayed the street. Kammler, with his two companions, leaped for the gate. From the tobacco factory we could hear signals and warning shouts.

Together with the chief of staff I hurried down to see what the actual situation was. It appeared that in the same building there was a German store of railway uniforms which they had been removing for the last few days, and the lorry had come to pick up another load. At the sight of an armed Pole, the German next to the driver seized his weapon. He was too late, however; the Polish sentry beat him to it.

At any moment we could expect Germans from the nearby garrison to arrive on the scene. Brief orders were shouted and our platoon was swiftly posted at windows and gates. When I returned upstairs, I could see German soldiers in full equipment occupying the house opposite. Machine guns from the two pillboxes sprayed both streets constantly. One burst crackled through our room, spattering a line of holes across walls and ceiling. Glass flew and dust and plaster filled the air. The Germans in the windows of the house opposite were within a grenade's throw of us; high factory windows were no protection.

I proposed that the government delegate, other civilian officials, and a few of the women with us should go to the back of the building, but the women refused. I was relieved to see that, with the exception of the secretary of the government delegate, no one was showing any sign of nervousness.

All unarmed persons were put to work barricading the gates below. In little more than a minute, both gates had been reinforced with barrels, handcarts, tables, planks, and furniture, of which there were mercifully plenty about. Everything movable was pushed against the windows of the ground floor to provide as much cover as possible. The buildings formed a fairly large group, provided with several exits and a number of places where an intruder could easily enter unobserved. Our thirty soldiers were completely lost in all these buildings.

I looked at my watch. It was half-past four. The incident had started fifteen minutes before and we had to defend ourselves unaided for half an hour at least, before help would reach us. The soldiers watching the Germans through a small crack in the gate reported that they were obviously preparing for an attack under cover of the machine gun. It was firing insistently at our window at fifteen yards' range.

"For God's sake," said the chief of staff, "we can't let them force their way into the building. Once in, we'll never get them out again with the arms we've got." Then, turning to the men, he said quickly, "Which of you is the best grenade-thrower?"

Two came forward at once. Grzegorz told them to get two filipinki each and come with him to the second floor. There they met with another difficulty. The big heavy window was closed. They had to get it open to throw a bomb, and to show themselves in the window would have caused an immediate reaction on the enemy's part. However, they managed to smash the window with a length of iron piping. At once the whole German fire was directed on it. They succeeded, all the same, in throwing a filipinka in the direction of the machine gun. An explosion followed and the machine gun was silenced.

After a while we saw two dead soldiers being pulled away from the gun by the legs. This discouraged them for a time from attacking us, but they retaliated with hand grenades. One grenade severely wounded two of our soldiers. A little later I was informed that the wireless station had been damaged.

Meanwhile, the German police, whose barracks were in Leszno Street, three hundred to four hundred yards away, hurried in to help their comrades. In our narrow street another heavy German lorry appeared, filled with police armed with tommy guns and grenades. Obviously, however, they did not realize the exact location of the fight. The Germans already on the scene gave warning signs and shouted to them to stop, but the men in the lorry did not grasp what was happening and drove on under our window.

This was just what our men had been waiting for. From a window, another filipinka landed plumb in the middle of the lorry. It swerved suddenly, hit the wall opposite, and burst into flames. In a few seconds, thirty-five enemy dead and the wreck of the lorry were all that remained in the road.

Then Lieutenant Kammler reported a new danger. I followed him to the other side of the factory, overlooking the ghetto. From a window he pointed out a large circle of police closing in on our factory across the ruins of the ghetto.

Kammler was worried. With the small force and arms at our disposal, this new attack was beyond our control. Instinctively, I looked at my watch again. It was already five o'clock. All over the city the fight had begun. The expected Kedyw Battalion should now be starting their attack on our district, but I could see no possibility of their reaching us. Both streets were by now so well covered by machine guns that even a mouse would have had difficulty in slipping past.

Minutes passed. We were still covered by fire on all sides. Our shots were rare, but well aimed. Now the sound of firing in the city reached us and the line of advancing German police was stopped by an attack on their rear.

At six we had another alarm. Our spotter on the roof started shouting desperately for help. Six soldiers at once dashed upstairs. It appeared that the Germans had attempted to reach us through the roof and our sentry in the chimney had been badly wounded in the head. The Germans had managed to reach the attic, and it was only there that they started a fierce exchange of fire with the men who had rushed to help.

It took fifteen minutes to wipe out the Germans, but we had our losses too. The wounded spotter was replaced by two others, with orders to report to us every few minutes. It was now clear that the insurrection had already engulfed the center of the city and our district, but we could still see no sign of relief, and its chances of reaching us looked slender. The Germans, too, had their worries. They were perturbed by the noise of fighting behind them, and their attempts to force our factory ceased.

It was just after seven when, to my astonishment, two soldiers from the Kedyw Battalion reported to me. I asked them how they had managed to get through to us when every route was under enemy fire. They replied cheerfully that they belonged to an advance patrol and that the rest were following them. They had got through from Okopowa Street by blasting their way through the walls of attics, which enabled them to travel partly on the roofs and partly through the attics. Their tough journey had started several hours earlier—in fact, as soon as they had been warned by the sound of the first shots from the factory.

Half an hour later, the main part of the battalion began to come in. Soon the situation had changed to our advantage. The Germans were on the defensive, and we went over to vigorous attack.

About eight o'clock I heard more shouting from the attic. This time it did not signify alarm, but joy. One of the soldiers came down and asked me in great excitement to follow him at once to the chimney stack. There we were greeted by the spotter on duty. "The flag! The Polish flag!" he shouted, pointing. "Our flag—right in the middle of the city!" From the roof a wide view of the capital enabled us to see the blaze of the fires. From the tower of the highest building in Warsaw, the sixteen-story Prudential Building which dominated the whole center of the city, flew a large flag. I concentrated my gaze. No; it was not a Nazi flag. Now I could see the white and red. After five years, the Polish colors were once more floating defiantly over the city. Looking more closely, I saw that similar flags were already flying from the cupola of the Post Office Savings Bank, from the tower of the town hall, and from other buildings.

This was the first sign, the first report on the course of the fighting that I received. I tried to make out where the fires were located. Over to the west something was burning close to the Western Station. The clouds of smoke were black and dense and might be from burning petrol. Probably we had fired a German fuel dump. Several buildings in the center were on fire, one of which must be the Central Station or perhaps the wooden huts the Germans had put up in its vicinity.

The glare over the city, the smoke rising from burning houses, and perhaps even the flag on the Prudential Building—all these should be visible to the forward Soviet troops on the Warsaw bridgehead. We could clearly hear their continuous artillery fire. The German heavy guns were replying to the Russians from this side of the Vistula now—from the west, beyond Powazki. I went down to speed the sending of two messages to London, which, however, did not go off until August 2, owing to the damage to our transmitter.

1

WARSAW.
August 1st, 1944.

To the Prime Minister and the Commander-in-Chief:

The date for the beginning of a struggle to capture Warsaw was jointly fixed by us for August 1st at 17.00 hours.

The struggle has begun.

Home Delegate and Vice-Premier of the Polish Government.
Commander-in-Chief, Home Army.

2

WARSAW.
August 1st, 1944.

We began the fight for Warsaw on August 1st at 17.00 hours; arrange immediately for ammunition and arms to be dropped at the lights (specified) and also in the squares giving on to the city. . . .

As the fight to capture Warsaw has begun, we ask for Soviet help to be supplied by an immediate attack from outside.

Home Delegate and Vice-Premier of the Polish Government.
Commander-in-Chief, Home Army.

My first message to the soldiers fighting in the capital read:

Soldiers of the capital!

I have to-day issued the order which you desire, for open warfare against Poland's age-old enemy, the German invader. After nearly five years of ceaseless and determined struggle carried on in secret, you stand to-day openly with arms in hand, to restore freedom to our country and to mete out fitting punishment to the German criminals for the terror and crimes committed by them on Polish soil.

BOR.
Commander-in-Chief, Home Army.

The wireless station was unfortunately still out of commission. Technicians had been hard at work on repairs all night, and the messages had to wait. As yet the world knew nothing of the beginning of the Warsaw rising.

In the night a heavy rain damped down the intensity of the fires which burned fiercely in the city and suburbs. At 3:00 A.M., while it was still dark, our men broke into the tobacco factory. Part of the German garrison was killed and the rest taken prisoner. The pillboxes presented the greatest difficulty, but they were finally destroyed by filipinki at 5:00 A.M.

The wireless expert reported that spare parts were essential for the repair of the damaged sets. They pointed out that one of

our underground stores of signals equipment was a few streets
away, about five hundred yards off. The necessary parts could be
got there, but to reach the store was a difficult and dangerous
undertaking.

Two men were sent over. By morning neither had returned.
Later I learned that both had been killed on the way. At dawn,
another volunteer offered to make the effort. The fact that no one
outside Warsaw knew what was going on made people at GHQ
feel uneasy. Half an hour later, the soldier returned in triumph,
bringing the necessary parts. Before noon on August 2, we
finally managed to contact London with the first messages.

*The uprising was doomed to failure, to a great extent because
the anticipated Russian support never came. Quite the opposite:
the armies under Marshal Rokossovsky pulled back from the east
banks of the Vistula. The Poles capitulated on October 2, leaving
fifteen thousand killed, wounded, or missing.*

Chapter 9

"The Jews
had been warned . . . "

Denmark's independence was lost on the same day that Norway was invaded. Unlike Norway, which resisted bitterly, Denmark did not attempt to retard the progress of the overwhelmingly powerful conqueror. Instead, Danes bided their time and made life increasingly difficult for the invader—from passive acts of "freezing" all Germans with disdain to active and outright sabotage.

Carlo Christensen, a foreign service officer, was one of those engaged in a tremendously dangerous and humanitarian task: that of spiriting Jews out of the country. Christensen, now Cultural Counselor of the Danish Embassy in Washington, where he has served since 1945, told of some of his own exploits in a book published in Denmark after the war.

It was one of the last days in September, 1943—not long after that unforgettable August 29 when the Danish government ceased to function, along with Parliament, and King Christian X was made a prisoner in his own castle. It was a day when we all realized that our defenseless country, which had been occupied since April 9, 1940, was in the hands of a gang of brutal criminals. The air was poisoned with threats and uneasiness, and more and more of the Danish people burned with desire to make an earnest effort to become a part of the Danish underground movement, which had proved to be a serious threat to the occupation forces.

I was sitting at my desk at the visa office in the Ministry of Foreign Affairs at the Christiansborg Castle in Copenhagen. The telephone rang, and I heard a voice which I recognized at once, although no name was mentioned. It was that of a Danish police officer. Something in his voice put me on the alert and gave me a strange feeling of uneasiness, which was intensified when he asked me to meet him as soon as possible, as he had a matter of great importance to discuss with me.

I went to him immediately at the police visa office for Danes. As always, the busy office was seething and humming; groups of nervous and excited people were crowding in front of the desk. They wanted to get out of the country and had come to the visa office to apply for visas to Sweden—the neutral and promised land beyond the Sound, only fifteen miles away from Copenhagen.

It was evident that the majority of these people were Jews. In view of the criminal, brutal, and horrifying actions that took place in German concentration camps, it was not surprising that the Danish Jews looked to the future with fear, a fear that grew from day to day.

"I have important and very serious news," the police officer told me in his private office, "news that I have no right to keep to myself, and I therefore ask you to pass it on to the Ministry of Foreign Affairs." He went on, "In a few days the Nazis will start to persecute the Danish Jews and deport them to German concentration camps."

I knew that such a categorical statement by the police officer left no room for doubt. He had good connections at the German visa office in Copenhagen—an office he visited every day on official business.

I did not ask any questions and decided to submit the information to the Ministry without delay. It was received with some skepticism, as the German administration in Copenhagen had recently given the Danish authorities firm assurances against any surprises of this kind. But since the same news came to the Ministry from other sources, and since the president of the Jewish community had also been so informed by a prominent member of the Danish parliament, every precaution was taken to be prepared for what turned out to be inevitable.

I informed my superior in the Danish resistance movement, and information now came from many directions, whereupon the rescue of the Jews was organized within a couple of days.

The first task was to find some place for them where they would be secure until we could get them to Sweden. We hid them in attics, in cellars, in churches, in hospitals, and even at an institution for the mentally ill.

It was not easy to calm these unhappy people as they waited in feverish anxiety for the hour when they would reach safety in Sweden. Terror and fear brought many close to a breakdown, and many, unfortunately, had to wait several weeks before we could take them over.

One of the Jews, a tailor, had been lodged with his wife in a small room in an attic. One day he said to me, "Do you see that open window? It will never be closed. If the Gestapo comes to get us, we will jump out and get it over with. They will never get us alive. They will never get us to be murdered in a concentration camp."

I had in my younger days lived for some years in a little town on the west coast of Jutland, where I had two close friends. One of them was the chief engineer and the other the captain on the Motor Vessel (MV) *Mathilte,* plying between Jutland and the town of Copenhagen, where the ship moored right in the heart of the city at Nyhavn, close to the King Square. There the German high command had its headquarters in a hotel.

I went down to the ship one morning after it had just arrived, and told my two friends what was going to happen, suggesting that we use *Mathilte* in the rescue work. At first both were somewhat hesitant about the undertaking—not only because they were concerned about themselves, but mainly because they were responsible for their crew of eight and because they knew that the owner of the ship would not grant permission for the ship to be used for this purpose.

The captain assembled the crew in his cabin and told them the story. Their response came without hesitation. They all agreed to help.

On her first crossing the small craft carried twenty passengers. The refugees boarded at intervals in broad daylight—one at a time, or a woman and a man together. It took about three hours to get everybody on board. They were, of course, secretly checked. I was there the whole time myself.

Once I noticed that one of the refugees appeared nervous and indecisive, as though he were afraid to go on board. I went over to him, took his arm, and remarked jovially, "Well, hello, Hans Peter, how nice to meet you. Listen, let's go on board and have a beer with the mate—he's an old friend of mine."

As soon as the passengers were aboard they were shown aft to a room under the officers' mess. It was not at all comfortable and had no conveniences of any kind, but it was large enough to hold twenty to twenty-five people. The entrance was covered with a hatch, which fitted so exactly that it was practically invisible.

While the refugees were boarding, the ship was being loaded with sacks and barrels of sugar, beer, and other goods, and trucks were coming and going. There was plenty of activity and noise, and outsiders would never have guessed that anything unusual was going on.

About five o'clock in the afternoon everything was ready for departure. Before the ship could leave the harbor, it had to get clearance from the Germans. German navy police officers came on to inspect the ship's papers and the cargo, to ascertain that everything was in order. Often the crew had to move some of the goods so that the officers could be sure that no one was hidden on board. They didn't find the secret hiding place.

I breathed more easily when the Germans disappeared, and soon afterward the *Mathilte* sailed out of Nyhavn and chugged up the Sound.

She kept her usual course until she was well past the island of Hven, located in the middle of the Sound about ten miles south of Elsinore.

As there were no ships around, the captain ordered all the lights to be put out, and at the same time the vessel left her course and headed for Sweden. When she got close to the coast and in Swedish territorial waters, the crew put on her lights again and she was soon approached by one of the Swedish coast guard vessels.

When the Swedish ship came alongside, *Mathilte* was hailed by an officer: "Have you got refugees on board?" And the answer was, "Yes, we have."

The Swede came back: "Have you got Danish beer?"
They got both.

On that first trip, just before the refugees boarded the Swedish ship, one of them made a moving speech thanking the men who had helped them across to the Swedish sister nation, which was about to grant them asylum. He prayed for the early liberation of Denmark and said that all the refugees would look forward to the day when they could return to their own country again. On that day, he said, they would come back to a Denmark that could continue its thousand-year-old history as a free country.

The men promised that they would bring many more of their Jewish countrymen to safety—and so they did.

For many weeks, the ship carried twenty to twenty-five refugees to Sweden on every trip. Everything went well, and about 350 Danish Jews were taken to safety. This was only a small portion of the seven thousand who went to Sweden by some means or other, but however the others got there, they were always assisted by people who had the same determination to help their persecuted countrymen as the officers and crew of the *Mathilte* did.

I said that everything went well, and that meant that every one of the refugees whom we took aboard got to Sweden safely. But the operation was not without tension and strain on the nerves.

On a trip in the beginning of November we had on board the police officer who had informed me that the persecution would start in early October, along with other personnel from the Danish visa office. All of them had been very active in the rescue of the Jews as well as other political refugees.

The police officer had been informed by the contact he had in the German visa office that the Germans had found out about their "illegal" activities, and an order for their arrest had been issued.

With his wife and two children and three other persons— two of them ladies working in the visa office—he went underground, as it was called, and contacted me. Even though the ship was already filled with twenty-five Jews, I agreed to take them to Sweden immediately.

We were fairly sure that my connection with the rescue work was not known to the Germans, and that the *Mathilte* was not suspected of any illegal activities. Nevertheless, we took special care in getting the seven persons on board. At intervals of several minutes, they got on one by one and finally, I came along, holding the hands of the two children, appearing to be sightseers.

The chief engineer was standing at the gangway with his pipe in his mouth, apparently relaxed with not a worry in the world.

I hollered to him, "Hello—how nice to see you. Are you off again for Jutland?"

"Yes," he said, "come on board and have a drink." The children disappeared down into the overcrowded room where we now had thirty-two people.

Shortly before the German police came to clear the ship, I was sitting in the captain's cabin with the Danish police officer. He handed me the keys to his office and asked me to be sure that the head of the Danish police force was given them and that he was informed about the closing of the office and the departure of his staff and family. I left the ship more nervous than I had ever been. In a house across from the ship, I watched until the German inspection was over and the ship steamed out of the narrow canal toward open water.

I then went back to my office and informed my superior what had happened. For the first time I told him what he must already have suspected—that I was a member of the underground.

Mathilte, meanwhile, sailed up the Sound, following the course plotted by the Germans. As soon as the ship had passed the island of Hven, it was to steam off course as usual and head for the Swedish contact vessel. The captain gave his usual order to put the lights out.

A few minutes later two German motor launches suddenly came alongside the ship. Many searchlights bathed the deck in a dazzling glare. There was nothing to do but to stop the ship and await developments.

The Germans came on board and demanded to know why the ship sailed without lights. Perhaps because they had refugees on board? As the captain tried to give an explanation, the chief engineer appeared and said, "Captain, I think we have found the trouble."

Suddenly, all the lights went on again. But the Germans were not convinced. They demanded a search of the ship from mast to keel, from bowsprit to tiller, and immediately proceeded to do so. They did not find the hiding place. The refugees realized when the ship came to a full stop that something had happened, and when they heard the German voices and the many footsteps on the floor above, they expected the worst.

The searchers made out their report while the refugees waited in breathless silence. Finally they disembarked and the danger passed.

Mathilte did not dare to sail into Swedish waters at this point, but instead followed the Sound to the north, passed by Kronborg Castle at Elsinore, and continued north some thirty miles to the Swedish peninsula, Kullen. There the refugees were taken ashore by a Swedish boat.

Soon the ship followed its normal course to Jutland, and on its return trip to Copenhagen five American fliers shot down into Jutland made the voyage to Sweden, and from there to their base somewhere in England.

As the months passed, the vessel took many American and British fliers and parachute agents, sent over from Great Britain with instructions for the Danish resistance movement, out of the danger zone to Sweden.

The Germans were furious because the police officer and his staff had escaped. In their special broadcast, which almost nobody listened to, they tried to throw a cloak of unreliability over the police officer. They insinuated that he was bought by the "criminal Jews" who were behind the resistance. They also described the two young ladies as his dubious girl friends. But radio propaganda of that kind defeated its own end.

The captain was called to the Gestapo headquarters in Copenhagen, and was asked again and again if he had taken the police officer to Sweden. He told them that he was a good and loyal Dane who would not do anything wrong. He was released.

Then a very young lady, the daughter of an editor of one of the leading newspapers in Denmark, and married to a Jew who was already in Sweden, came to my office and asked for my assistance. We decided that we would take a chance and let her and her eighteen-month-old baby on board after the

German inspection. She could stay with her child in the mates' cabin, since there was no other space.

Just as the ship was leaving the pier, we saw the lady and her child at a porthole, smiling and happily waving good-bye to us on shore. I was horrified. Fortunately, nothing happened. The Germans had left, and people on the street who were waving to the beautiful child most likely thought that they were passengers on the ship.

The rescue of our Jewish countrymen was not the work of a single man, and it was not solely the work of the officers and crew. It was not the work alone of the many Danish fishermen who took a large number of the refugees to Sweden, nor was it the work exclusively of the members of the resistance movement. It was in a sense the work of a whole nation—impossible without the cooperation of people from every level of the population and of the Swedish who opened their doors to the refugees.

Before the persecution actually took place in Denmark, and even up until the time that the transport ship with the five hundred captive Jews was anchored in the Sound for a few days, the hope was cherished that the Germans would accept a Swedish offer of asylum for the Danish Jews.

But it was not accepted. The government never received any reply to its offer, which was submitted to the Nazis by the Swedish minister to Berlin. The Danish Jews captured were taken to Theresienstadt concentration camp in Czechoslovakia.

The reason for the transport ship's delay in the Sound outside Copenhagen was the simple fact that the Germans had hoped to get most of the Jews on board. They simply could not believe it possible that seven thousand of them had disappeared right under their noses.

But the Jews had been warned. On September 28, 1943, the Danish prime minister, Hans Hedtoft, went to the president of the Jewish community and told him that the German action against the Jews was going to take place in a few days. The following morning, which was the day of the Jewish New Year festival, the congregation was informed that the time had come.

On October 1, the persecution of the Jews became a horrible fact. At 9:45 P.M. that night, all telephones in Copenhagen were cut off and the hunt for the Jews began. Those who had not left were dragged out of their houses. The Nazis drove them along the streets tied to each other like animals. They were taken to the harbor in Copenhagen and led aboard the transport ship to await the departure for what would be the end of their lives.

The great majority of the Jews who were arrested by the Germans were old and, in many cases, poor. Some were taken while they were still praying, but all of them could have been saved if they had only followed the instructions they were given that morning at the synagogue from the resistance movement. Despair, and the belief that their lives had come to an end, motivated them to stay on in their homes to be captured by the criminals.

Most of the Jews outside Copenhagen—and there were quite a few in Jutland—were saved. Those who were not were rounded up and placed on a train of cattle cars. The train stopped at the different towns and picked them up. Several committed suicide rather than be taken to the concentration camp. People who had given shelter to the Jews were arrested and members of the resistance were killed by the Germans during the rescue actions.

After the German failure—and it was a failure—the Germans apparently wanted to make a good impression on the Danes. The Danish newspapers were commanded to print the message that since the criminal element of the Danish population had now been removed from Denmark, the Danish military personnel who had been interned for some time would be released.

All of Denmark protested against this sanctimonious manifesto. The commander in chief of the Danish army protested. All branches of Danish scientific life, of the arts, trade, and industry, protested. And the Danish church protested more strongly perhaps than anyone.

By the end of the year, there were still Jews in Denmark—those married to Christians and those partly Jewish. As the conditions in Denmark grew worse from day to day, many of these people felt that they were no longer safe and decided to go to Sweden.

On every trip in 1944 the *Mathilte* carried some of these people, together with political refugees, saboteurs who had to get out of the country at least for a while, and members of the resistance movement who had to reach neutral Sweden for liaison purposes. The Danish brigade was also growing in that country.

The Nazis had seized the Danish police force in September, 1944. Many were taken to concentration camps; others went to Sweden, although some stayed on in Denmark as members of the resistance.

Because of the growing sabotage against factories working for the Germans and against railroads when German troop transports took place, the Germans became more and more irritated. Inspection of fishing boats and ships became more thorough and took place more frequently.

The *Mathilte* was moored at Nyhavn, and the captain and I were discussing the situation. The captain thought it would be better to stop while the going was good, or it would end in disaster. I made him promise, however, to take passengers on the next trip, as I had many refugees whom I had to get to Sweden.

The ship was scheduled to depart on the morning of the next day. This was unusual, but the Germans would no longer permit the ships to sail when it was dark.

The night before, we began to embark the refugees. We continued cautiously and at long intervals until three o'clock in the morning. The passengers were instructed to bring warm clothes and food, as the trip could be a long one before we were able to get over into Swedish waters.

About 10:00 A.M. the ship was ready to sail.

But the German police inspectors would not clear her, because the Sound had been filled with mines during the night. We hoped for better news during the day. But evening came, and the sailing permission had still not been given. The refugees confined in the small compartment were very cold, for there were no heating facilities. The long waiting period made them restless. We managed to get hot meals and some tobacco to them, and we waited and waited.

We waited for seven days. The British had filled all the waters between Denmark and Sweden with mines. We could not, of course, get permission to sail. I visited the refugees every night. I brought illegal papers for them to read and informed them about what was going on. We fed them as well as we could, and they were permitted to walk on the deck, one or two at a time, when it was dark.

At last the sea-lane was swept for mines. Then the captain was informed that the *Mathilte* was to sail to the customhouse in the Copenhagen harbor for a very thorough and exhaustive search. And the ship had to be there within two hours.

We felt very uneasy about this. We had no way of knowing the extent of this search, and we did not know the reason for it. Other ships had been examined like that and police dogs had been used, which meant the danger of their discovering the refugees would be multiplied.

I told the refugees about the situation, and that I had to put them ashore at once in broad daylight. It was unavoidable that this would be noticed by people, perhaps even by Germans, and we therefore had to camouflage the true state of affairs.

As the refugees went ashore, the captain and the chief engineer shouted after them, "So you thought you could get a free trip to Jutland? Nothing doing, and don't ever try that again."

It worked. Nothing happened. People were standing at the pier laughing at the incident; no one caught on to the true facts.

I had told the refugees where I would meet them in small groups. During the morning I had them all put up at temporary lodgings again. Ten of them—all Jews—were sheltered at a mental institution, others in the epidemic ward of a hospital, and the rest in a church.

Within a few days we had all except those at the mental hospital taken into Sweden by other routes. Those ten went over on the next trip to Jutland, in spite of the fact that the captain had said he would not take any more refugees to Sweden because the Germans had looked everywhere on the ship for refugees during the search at the customhouse. They had still not found the secret room.

The chief engineer agreed, however, to take the last ten refugees without the knowledge of the captain. We invited the captain to a splendid dinner that night and I praised him for everything he had done for Denmark, for the refugees, and for humanity.

He made what he called the only speech he had ever delivered and gave credit to the crew without whom it could not have been done. It was a wonderful evening.

When we came back to the ship late at night, the ten passengers had been taken aboard. The next morning the *Mathilte* sailed out of Copenhagen on her last illegal trip.

The captain waved to me, happy and smiling. He did not know. At the next call in Copenhagen I went down to the ship. I was apprehensive. What would he say? Surely I had failed him.

He was rather pleased about the situation, he said, and he told me what had happened. As *Mathilte* came north of Elsinore the chief engineer arrived on the bridge and said, "We have to make the last trip to Sweden. We have the last ten Danish Jews on board."

"All right," said the captain. "Let's get them ashore."

Part 3
Day to Day Existence

Part 3

User to User Experiences

Chapter 10

"The Nazis
did not permit strikes . . . "

Hitler exploited the people's continuing need for food to gain the physical services of millions of workers in the countries that he had conquered.

Jean de Vos was a Belgian aeronautical engineer. To make sure that he would "volunteer," his ration card and those of his wife and children were confiscated until he agreed to work at the Daimler-Benz aircraft plant near Berlin.

De Vos' story, as told to writer Richard Baxter, affords an insight into life within Germany during the early days of the war. He arrived at the factory, jammed with thirty thousand workers:

I was taken to a long dormitory where some two hundred men were sleeping in bunks ranged in tiers; the floor was bare and the long room was without furniture. It might have been a work-house ward.

I was shown a vacant bunk, provided with two thin blankets and a pillow, and told to get some sleep, as I would be taken to the factory in a conveyance the next morning at 6:00 A.M. with the day shift.

Most of the men in the dormitory were Dutchmen, though there were one or two Belgians and a few French. They were not a happy crowd, and before I went to sleep I was given much to think over. A fellow countryman who occupied the bunk over mine started a conversation.

"I suppose you think you are in clover now?" he asked. "This is just hell. I volunteered to work to save my wife and kids from starvation, but they spell work with a capital W here."

"What is the food like?" I asked.

113

"Just fit for pigs," was his answer. "But what can you do? They shot twenty Dutchmen last week because they refused to work on the food given them. Colored water they call soup, and black bread every day—and not enough bread to keep a man alive, either."

Men and women were expected to work seven days or nights each week, and to receive seven days' leave after three months' work—or rather they were promised seven days' leave. That they did not get it, unless they knew how to arrange matters, made no difference. They just had to work when ordered or suffer the consequences.

The Nazis did not permit strikes or arguments.

They had a way of dealing with discontented workpeople which was calculated to crush any desire to grumble or display resentment.

Generally, conditions at the Daimler-Benz factory were not bad when compared to other factories in Germany. Within their powers the directors did their best to make life for their employees tolerable, and the food provided in the canteens was the best obtainable under wartime and blockade conditions.

Unskilled workmen, recruited by the thousands every week in Germany, were specially trained in schools attached to the factory. During their training they received pay which, although comparatively small, was sufficient to meet their normal expenses. For those who were brought away from their homes at a distance, accommodation was provided either in Berlin or in specially built hostels in the forest.

We in the forest derived a tremendous benefit from the fact that the woods abounded with deer, hares, rabbits, and wildfowl. It was impossible for the deer to escape, owing to the high wire fencing, and consequently they provided a valuable addition to the general diet.

Outside the forest was a large farm owned by the directors of the works, and there the land was cultivated to supply all the vegetables needed in the canteen, so that generally we were well provided for.

I must not let it be thought that the workers in the factory there lived in luxury so far as food is concerned. Admittedly, after my period of starvation in Brussels while I was unemployed, the food provided was luxurious to me, but actually it was not sufficient in quantity nor varied enough to keep working men and women in full health.

There was a tremendous shortage of fats and sweets, such as sugar. The vital vitamins were lacking, so that every other day vitamin pills were given to the workers to make up for the lack of vitamins in their food.

In the factory we were allowed two meals a day in the canteen. These consisted of vegetable soup and bread on three days each week, meat one day a week, and occasionally a fish meal or meat soup; mostly the meat was horse flesh two days a week, and a meal of sausage and vegetables on the other day of the week. Such meals were allowed without having to surrender coupons.

In addition, however, one could always buy meat and give up coupons. Although the prices charged were high, they were far below those prevailing in the cafés and restaurants of Berlin.

The deer and game in the forests were not served to the workers free. Those dishes could be brought in so long as supplies lasted. Mostly the fortunate ones were those who held the higher posts in the works—the departmental managers, draftsmen, designers, and higher inspectors, whose purses not only permitted them to buy the delicacies but also to bribe the canteen manager.

It did not take me long to discover the secret of how to obtain more than my share of the limited food supplies and the little extras that went to make up for some of the hardships we had to endure. Bribery was everywhere rampant in Germany. So long as one was prepared to pay the price and knew how to pass a bribe to the right person, one could get along fairly comfortably. It was a very costly business, and liable to be dangerous. There were, however, few officials in the Fatherland who could not be tempted by the offer of a bribe; my experience was that, having bribed one, a second promptly showed his hand and was not slow to suggest threateningly that he was prepared to inform the authorities of the fact that number one had been bribed unless hush money was paid to him also.

Working at the bench next to me was a good-natured German with whom I struck up a friendship. Carl Hartmann was his name, and he had been employed by the Daimler-Benz people in their works for several years. He was well over military age and had one son serving in the army, and he himself had been a corporal in an engineer regiment during the last war.

I told him of my uncomfortable lodgings, and he suggested that perhaps I would like to lodge in his home.

"You could have the bedroom that my son used to have," he said.

"Heil Hitler," I replied, laughing, "but that sounds good to me."

Hartmann gave me a rather strange look.

"Did you really mean that?" he asked. "I thought you served with the International Brigade in Spain." Then he dropped his voice to a whisper, glancing round him quickly before he added, "I thought you were an anti-Fascist."

"So I am," I admitted. "I was merely joking when I said that."

"Good," he said, "but never let anyone know. Be careful whom you talk to here. The place is full of agents of the Gestapo who report on everything they see and hear."

It was not long before I was introduced to the black market, and discovered that so long as one was prepared to pay the price and could be relied on to keep a secret, it was possible to buy almost any kind of commodity.

Foreigners could obtain more supplies than the Germans and with greater ease. The fact is that few shopkeepers would trust a German. There were too many informers anxious to curry favor with the Gestapo for the black market trader to take the risk.

But the very rich and the higher officials of the Party, not to mention the Gestapo officials, were always well supplied with every kind of commodity, no matter how great the shortage. They had to come first, and unless they did, there was trouble for the shopkeeper.

Bribery and corruption were rife throughout Germany. If one had money, there was scarcely a thing which was impossible to accomplish. I firmly believe it would have been possible in many cases to bribe one's way out of a concentration camp. The cost, however, would have been so great that none could have met it, for it would not only have been the initial bribe but the subsequent demands made by "officials" who actually had no part in the business. Germans talked to each other, and each seemed bent on enriching himself—hence the organized blackmail which existed.

In Berlin, afterward, I found there was a growing tendency on the part of men and women who had money to keep it in their homes or hidden in places which they regarded as safe, rather than leave cash in the banks.

My introduction to the black market came through a word dropped by Carl Hartmann.

"Foreigners can buy where Germans cannot," he said one evening; and since there was a distinct shortage of some kinds of food in the Hartmann home, I decided to see if I could manage to buy.

Quite casually I entered the shop of a trader in foodstuffs. As the store appeared to be entirely without goods of any sort, although it was compelled by law to remain open, I decided to test the shopkeeper.

In faltering German I asked for sausage and margarine, at the same time jingling the money in my pocket and giving the man a look which, unless he were a complete fool, he could not fail to understand.

"You are a foreigner?" he asked.

"Of course," I replied. "A Belgian, but I have volunteered to make planes for Germany, and I am working at the Daimler-Benz factory."

"That is good," he replied, "but I have no food to sell, unfortunately, even though you have ration cards."

"Come," I urged, "surely you can find me something. I need food before I go to work tomorrow morning, else I cannot do my job well. Besides, I am ready to pay what you ask, and tell no one."

He was a bit diffident at first, but since there was no one else in the shop and the blinds were drawn, he thawed. A greedy, grasping fellow, that shopkeeper was. He could not resist the chance of robbing a foreigner and adding to his profits.

We had quite a long discussion about the evils of controlled prices which were hampering traders and making every difficulty, about the dirty tricks played on traders by the Gestapo informers, and about the way some of the Gestapo demanded as their right far more food than their rationed share.

"And they get it, too," he moaned. "Unless I let them have it, and often not even charge them for it, my shop would be closed tomorrow. It was better in the old days," he whispered, "but no one dares say so to a German."

We got on famously, and I left the shop with a huge sausage tucked away beneath my coat, not to mention some margarine and half a dozen tolerably decent cigars, which I had bought to give to Carl.

The purchases cost me a small fortune, but I had broken the ice and was assured that whenever I needed foodstuffs, I had only to let him know. If any supplies were available, they would be mine, but of course I would have to be cautious and tell no one.

For weeks after that I was able to buy little presents of food for the Hartmann household, and once I even managed to buy a whole goose which I somehow smuggled home.

My purchases in the black market certainly did much to make life more pleasant, but the cost was high. Yet all purchases in the black market were not paid for in cash. Traders developed a new racket which operated among themselves.

The new system was based on the fact that clothes were almost unobtainable. The ordinary civilian in Berlin wore patched and worn suits which, even a few months before, he would not have worn in public. Boots, too, could only be obtained by special authorization and then by giving up an old pair which had been established as beyond repair. The new boots which the Germans were told to wear were made of a sort of American cloth upper, with wooden soles. They cost anything up to two pounds a pair.

A new kind of shoe was being tried out as I left Germany. It was made of plaited straw uppers, with a thin, metal-covered sole, quite pliable for walking but by no means comfortable. They cost much less than the boots.

In most trade newspapers, curious advertisements began to appear. Dealers in foodstuffs were advertising their clothing needs. Of course they didn't openly state that they wanted to buy. The Germans were too cunning for that. Instead they advertised that a dealer in foodstuffs was anxious to discover a tailor who could make up a suit from material supplied at the earliest date.

This is how the business operated. A tailor, in return for supplies of rationed food, would make up one or more suits of clothing from the cloth which had been obtained by the foodstuffs dealer. How the man got hold of the cloth in the first place was never inquired into, but it was usually the proceeds of a robbery. That didn't matter. The foodstuffs dealer needed suits, the tailor needed food; so the matter was arranged in secret, and the food shortage in the shops increased.

It was a bitterly cold night that November when I witnessed the first of the big raids over the capital. My landlord friend and I had been working the day shift, and we returned to the city by underground train only a few minutes before the sirens sounded their warning.

The moon was shining brilliantly, lighting up the streets as though it were full daylight.

We were walking slowly toward Carl's house when the wailing commenced. At the first notes of the siren, there was a stampede from the streets. The pavements, which a moment before had been crowded, were instantly deserted. Marshals were shouting and excitedly shepherding the frightened people into the basements of houses.

There were no public shelters in the streets as there were in London, to protect the pedestrian who might be caught out in the raid. Every house and block of flats had shelters in the basements—shelters which were actually poor affairs, the ceilings merely being supported by timbers and sometimes steel balks. They provided no real protection, save from splinters and possibly from the blast of a bomb exploding in the streets. Although the Germans made every possible effort to conceal the true casualties in raids, and declared that most of the small number which occurred were due to people not taking shelter, I know that thousands were killed in the shelters or buried beneath tons of debris from which they could not possibly have been rescued.

Even the Berlin tube railway provided no protection against bombs; it was too shallow for that. Yet every night thousands of frightened Berliners shut themselves down in the tube stations and used the tunnels after the train services had stopped.

The Berlin authorities provided bunks in the tube for the regular users, in the same way that the London authorities did, but with this difference: While Londoners could claim to be tolerably safe from bombs in their tubes, no such claim could be made by the Berliners.

The people were panic-stricken and trembling in the tube on that night. All the time they moaned, and their cries sometimes even drowned the noise of the thousand and one guns firing overhead. One woman became so hysterical that she started to scream, adding to the fright of the children.

The heat became insufferable, for there was no air or real ventilation. It made me feel ill. Personally, I would have much preferred to take a chance in the open, sheltering in the doorway from bomb splinters, than spend hours in a Berlin shelter; and I told the marshal so. But it was useless.

"You will obey orders," he said firmly.

"And die of suffocation," I retorted.

There was no lull in the firing; all the while the noise was like thunder. At particularly heavy explosions the people shuddered and one or two screamed.

"Bombs!" they yelled.

They were quite unable to distinguish between the sound of guns firing and the dull heavy thud of bombs. As my experience in the Spanish Civil War enabled me to tell the difference, I tried to help maintain the morale of the women.

"Rubbish," I exclaimed. "No bombs have fallen yet."

"Silence!" the marshal shouted. "Your opinion has not been asked."

The marshal was as terrified as the others in that cellar. I noticed that he had taken the best place in the shelter for himself—a fairly wide space, quite close to the door, where there was a sort of brick buttress jutting out, one of the main supports of the building. That fellow was going to look after his own skin.

The guns were roaring when above their noise came the dull unmistakable *thunk* of a bomb, and the appalling crash of the explosion. The floor of the cellar trembled and the door, which had been closed, flew open. Men, women, and children yelled in complete panic. The marshal was visibly trembling, his mouth wide open and his eyes staring. He made not the slightest attempt to calm the panic-stricken people, for he was also seized with panic.

In the hubbub, I managed to worm my way toward the door and escape unnoticed up the stairs.

I reached the street and peered out through the space where the door had been before that bomb fell. Directly opposite, a large store was burning furiously, the flames leaping high above the building. Farther along was a whole heap of rubble and stones—all that was left of a cinema which had been used as a store for military equipment and clothing. Broken glass was everywhere. It was really a terrifying sight. In the sky, great beams of light of many colors were weaving strange patterns, though actually there was no real need for searchlights, so light was the moon.

Shells were bursting by the thousands high in the heavens, and above the noise of gunfire I could hear the constant drone of the raiding planes. Then came the whistle of the falling bombs and the shattering crash as they exploded.

The street was absolutely deserted. The fire opposite was left to burn. People who might have been injured or buried in the debris of the shattered cinema, and a few houses which had also been smashed, were left to their fate.

The Berlin ARP [Air-Raid Precautions] services did not rise to the rescue, and the fire brigade was perhaps too busily engaged in taking cover to trouble about so small a matter as a big fire in a store that might be serving as a beacon to the raiders. Clearly the ARP had been caught napping, or else was so badly organized that it could not cope with a real raid.

The planes came over in wave after wave to wreck and destroy.

It was almost dawn before the guns ceased firing, although for hours before, there had been no sound of planes or screaming of bombs.

When the people were finally permitted to leave the shelters, it was daylight. The fire opposite was still burning, and at last the fire brigade had turned up to attend to it. Police and soldiers were digging among the debris of shattered buildings, and other workers were erecting great plank boardings to hide the buildings which had suffered.

Berliners were not permitted to see the scars which the raiders left. It was an offense even to linger and stand talking near a damaged building.

For a whole week Berlin's tube railway was out of action following the raid, and the journey to and from work had to be made by bus. It was a slow and tiring business and unquestionably affected production seriously.

The managers of the different departments in the factory were constantly complaining and finding fault. We were charged with deliberate slacking and threatened with punishment, but nothing violent happened. Everyone's nerves were on edge. It only needed a few more raids, sustained night after night, to have seriously upset production and industry in and around Berlin.

The raid provided Berlin with an appalling shock. No one ever believed it possible for RAF planes to come in such force and do such damage in a single night. The people had been doped with constant and liberal quantities of Nazi propaganda, assuring them that they were absolutely safe and that the RAF was a spent force which would not dare to penetrate far into Germany. Like a lot of sheep they had accepted what they had been told. Now Berlin was stunned, unable to believe what was there before their eyes.

With the advance of winter, the sufferings of the German people were increased a hundredfold. There was the impossibility of obtaining a sufficiency of warm clothing; people who had not been able to lay in a store of clothes and boots during the spring and summer months, when the pinch of the British blockade was not so keen, had to shiver.

Worse still, unless they could make secret purchases of food in the blackout, they had to go hungry. Despite the fact that they had ration cards, there was no guarantee that the shopkeepers would have sufficient supplies to meet even the minimum quantities of food that each person was entitled to. The Nazi leaders and the Gestapo had to be served first.

Then there was the problem of fuel for warming the homes. Coal was strictly rationed, as were the briquettes made from treated coal, and in Berlin itself wood was simply unobtainable. In the big modern block of flats provided with central heating, the apparatus was kept out of order. There was no fuel for the furnaces. Oil for heating stoves could not be bought, and electric or gas heaters were out of the question, owing to the rigid system of rationing.

It was a terrible winter for everyone. Frankly, I welcomed leaving home for the factory, for there it was possible to keep warm. At home one just stayed in and shivered.

Nor was it possible to go to a restaurant to eat food. Every meal consumed called for ration cards, and as the number of cards dwindled, the future prospects grew worse.

During the late summer, when events were beginning to take a bad course for the Nazis in Russia, there was a general speeding up in the factory. Somehow production had to be increased and at the same time men had to be released for service with the forces.

Almost daily, fresh batches of workers from one or another of the occupied countries arrived to take over the jobs vacated by Germans who had been called up. More and more women and girls were put to work filling the vacancies, but still production lagged.

Machines were constantly out of action due to a need for repairs; they were worked until they stopped because of the breaking of a vital part.

The engineers were too busy dealing with other essential repairs to come near a machine which was still working, or else they were waiting for the delivery of spare parts. It was always the same. No spares to be had, and no men to fit even the few spares available.

The consequence was not only that production fell off, but that the number of serious accidents increased. Day after day workers, both men and women, were injured from operating defective and worn-out machines. There were, as I have said, thirty thousand workers in the big factory, and accidents were happening every day, with often as many as fifty people being hurt in a single day.

The injured were given what first aid was possible in the works and then carried to the hospital, where an overworked staff of doctors and nurses sought to attend to them.

When I first went to the factory, there were twenty doctors who worked in shifts. Toward the autumn of 1941, that number had been reduced to three doctors and three students. The others had been called up for service.

The same state of affairs prevailed in other factories. Throughout Germany there was a terrible shortage of skilled medical men, a shortage which had been increased by banning Jewish doctors, most of whom had either fled the country, were confined to ghettos, or worse still, were in concentration camps.

Owing to the lack of skilled doctors, men and women in Germany were dying from minor ailments. What would have happened if a serious epidemic or illness had broken out then, with a population already suffering the effects of semistarvation and long hours of hard work and strain, one does not dare to speculate.

As day succeeded day, the demands for increased production were continued. At first the workers were urged in the national interests to put more energy into their tasks. Then, when men and women failed to accomplish the impossible, no matter how willing they might be in attempting it, they were threatened with penalties and severe punishments.

The machines constantly breaking down added to the worries and difficulties of the working people and of the management also. The management were at their wits' end to find efficient engineers to patch up the broken machines and secure the needed spare parts.

But never was an idle moment permitted. In September, work at the factory became absolute slavery. An eight-hour day was a thing of the past. Men and women were compelled to work for ten to twelve hours and even more. I know that I was literally worn out when I had finished a day's work and actually welcomed the opportunity of going to the cheerless hostel to seek my bed.

De Vos ultimately escaped to Spain, then to England, and ended the war fighting with the Free Belgian forces.

Chapter 11

"The soap powder
is all soda . . . "

The unhappy and unfortunate Polish people, whose soil was the Nazi's first battleground, suffered proportionately the most severe attrition of any of their European victims. In excess of half of a million Poles were executed or died from torture, neglect, or wholesale genocide.

At least seven million more, one-fifth of the 1939 population, "vanished" during the long, bloody conflict. They perished—unidentified—from the bombing of cities, from gas or "extermination" chambers, or from being unable to withstand the privations of six years of strife.

How one woman managed the day-to-day practicalities of living is told in a book written by Maria Brzeska in 1944. Using her knowledge of French to join in the resistance, she taught that language to a group of children within a secret school:

In Warsaw, Lvov, and Kraków, in the small Polish towns and scattered villages, it is the woman who, like her sister in Britain, has to bear the burden of running the home, of earning to keep the home going, of looking after and educating the children. And of her problems, those of feeding and clothing her family are the most important and the most difficult.

The German rationing system provides bread, potatoes, jam, soap, and soap powder. Fats are regarded as quite unnecessary for the Poles. All through the war they have not been allowed fats once. Meat, sugar, and flour are issued two or three times a year, before the great holidays, at the rate of 10 decagrams [3½ ounces] per person.

The wartime bread in Poland is as black as earth, as sticky as clay. When you cut it, it sticks to the knife; when you eat it, it clings to the teeth, and it weighs down the stomach for hours afterward. It consists of all sorts of substitutes: lupine seeds, chestnuts, sawdust—the percentage of flour is the lowest of all. The Germans issue flour for bread rations when it is beginning to go bad in the military stores. The wet, solid lumps have to be broken up and dried, then milled again.

During the early days of the war, it was difficult to bake anything resembling bread from this material. The shelves of the bakeries were stocked with flat, heavy cakes which were done outside, but sticky and damp inside.

This black and indigestible bread is nonetheless the chief item of food now in many homes. Yet there is always a shortage of it, and the ration is roughly 15 decagrams [5¼ ounces] per day for the adults and 10 decagrams [3½ ounces] per day for the children.

Potatoes are issued more generously; the ration fluctuates, depending on the harvest. The potatoes kept during the winter go bad, however; after they are sorted, usually only about half are fit for eating.

So far as the rest of the rationed treasures are concerned: The jam, rarely issued, is made of beetroot wash sweetened with saccharine. The soap powder is all soda. The dark gray cakes of soap, which are either sticky and soft or hard and rough, feel like sand and at best can only be used for washing the hands.

Every autumn brings a battle which calls for great ingenuity and resource, for one's ability to live through the winter depends on the extent to which the larder can be stocked in the autumn.

An old item of clothing can be exchanged for several kilos of butter, but lard is more difficult. Home-rendered fat must suffice for the winter. Colza oil is comparatively the easiest of oils to get.

A little flour and groats must be obtained either by exchange or as part of one's earnings. Fine yellow millet grains, coarse-husked barley, and barley meal have become the main dishes on Polish dining tables.

From time to time salt goes right off the market. In any case, white salt is always a rarity and the dark block salt, much more salty and hardly at all refined, disappears from the stores for weeks at a time.

After a couple of years, herbal tea seems to get better and better. Another drink is made from a decoction of wild strawberry leaves, to which a drop of rum essence is added. Even the Germans have forgotten the taste of real tea and coffee, which vanished from the market in the second year of the war. The shortage of sugar, however, is a serious blow. "Saccharine crystals," sold by lads surreptitiously on the streets, are costly and difficult to obtain.

If you have a large income you can get everything in the black market, especially in Warsaw. But only those exceptionally privileged can pay 200 zlotys [$8.80, as one wartime zloty roughly equals $.11] for a kilo [2¼ pounds] of butter; 140 zlotys for a kilo of sugar; 35 zlotys for a kilo of old cow. An egg costs 7 zlotys, a liter [about 1 quart] of milk costs 12 zlotys. But everyone must get hold of money for bread, flour, and groats. And for those articles the prices are high too—about 20 zlotys for a kilo.

Nonetheless, the people in general are not starving. Those who are better off help the poorer; the village comes to the aid of the town. Of course, there are days of despair in the countryside before the harvest is ready, and there is hunger typhus in the towns. Even though pillaged by the invader, Poland is a predominantly agricultural country and manages to feed her people. Every little scrap of garden and even the town squares are turned into rye and potato plots.

Apart from the shortage of food, there are many other things one has to do without—the most troublesome and perhaps the most dangerous shortage being soap. During the earlier years of the war almost every woman made her own soap for laundry purposes, while some families even made the manufacture of soap their main source of income. Unfortunately, tallow followed all the other fats off the market so the price of homemade soap leaped up and it became inaccessibly dear to everyone.

Gum, needles, thread, and string (except paper string) cannot be obtained at all; paper is rationed in very miserable quantity even to German offices.

One of the blackest features of life under the German occupation is the shortage of fuel. Warsaw has spent winter after winter in unheated homes; the price of coal, when it is available, is out of all proportion to the average earnings. A ton of coal costs 2,000 zlotys [about $200]. During the early years people had to resort to electric heaters, but in the third year of the war the Germans rationed electricity and gas. These supplies were then turned on for only two or three hours a day, and after a few months certain districts had to do without light altogether.

Often it is more difficult to clothe than to feed your family. In this fifth year of the war, the infants, who some years ago could manage with any old thing, such as articles made out of their mothers' dresses, are now grown children who have got to have boots, clothes, and coats.

And of course fashions have changed. Much ingenuity has been required not only to clothe but to adorn oneself.

Clothes have been worn out, remade, and darned in every possible way. Everything has been in wear for at least four years and, in the majority of cases, the people have not had any possibility of renewing their wardrobes during the war. From March to October the women go bare-legged, wearing wooden-soled shoes in the summer and chiefly rubber footwear in the winter—though wooden soles are also common then. Hats are not worn from early spring to late autumn, and in winter heads are covered with warm kerchiefs, or caps made from scraps of material or crocheted from wool used over and over again.

The Germans have issued no clothing coupons whatever to the Polish people, and no boot or shoe coupons either. Without clothes rations, the Poles are forced to buy illegally. But prices rise from day to day. A year ago a pair of women's shoes cost 800 zlotys, and woolen cloth for a man's suit cost 300 zlotys per meter. Stockings could be bought for 300 zlotys, and a meter of poor-quality cambric cost 128 zlotys.

The clothing situation is still worse in the countryside; in the villages the peasants usually have one workday suit and one for Sundays. All summer the children run naked.

In the large towns, despite all that has happened and all their difficulties, the women have not given up caring for their personal appearance. For that matter, it is very important to look after oneself, for a well-dressed man or woman is less troubled by the police. Neat clothing and a confident air increase one's safety.

The streets of fighting Warsaw—of Warsaw, the underground capital—are almost unrecognizable.

To begin with, the streets are dirty, gray, and poverty-stricken. The damage done in the bombardment has become more evident and more unpleasant, now that the ruins have been cleared away. The great blocks of houses which had threatened to tumble down were pulled down. Warsaw has been swept clean of ruins and now the heart of the city is like a desert. At every step, squares, gaps, and streets with unexpected débouchés recall the days of the siege.

In many cases the houses have been pulled down only as far as the first floor, and now lone one-story houses stretch for miles on end, like those of a provincial town. The better-preserved blocks have shops with small, miserable windows, but the others are all covered with German propaganda posters.

Two factors give the streets an impression of universal indigence: the empty shop windows and, even more, the outward appearance of the people. There is absolutely nothing in the shops. Food shops sometimes make a show of mustard and vinegar, but even those articles are difficult to get, and the windows are adorned with boxes surmounted by the inscription "*Leere Schachtein*" [empty boxes]. Yet to leave the window empty or to close the shop would be "sabotage," so the shopkeepers sit patiently freezing behind their counters, waiting for closing time.

The gray, unchanged window dressings, the dirty walls of the buildings, and above all else the poor wretched appearance of the passersby give the Warsaw streets a certain monotony and a touch of sadness. In these circumstances the more fashionable streets of Marszalkowska and Nowy Swiat have approximated the standards of the workers' districts of Wolska Ochota.

Restrictions on the use of oil fuel have led to a great diminution of traffic. Taxis have disappeared completely. Only military cars are seen in any number.

The drozhkis with their drivers have returned to favor, and the drivers have not lost their sense of humor. Because of the absence of telephones, the old messengers in their red caps have come back. One would relish the old-time charms of nineteenth-century Warsaw if it were not for the nightmare of reality, which permits no sentiment.

Of course, the trams remain the chief means of transportation. Overloaded and wheezy, they grind along, their always-defective brakes screaming as they come to a halt. The trams move along slowly with people clinging all over them, half-hanging off the steps, climbing on one another, knocking out the windows. Only in the front part of the car, clearly marked "for Germans only," two or three people sit comfortably spread out; beyond the rope separating the two parts, the Polish section heaves and seethes. People travel packed together and never buy a ticket. This evasion is deliberate and long-standing. The two conductors and the numerous inspectors are unable to control this situation, and the German-owned power station sees its income falling off seriously every day.

Yet the most characteristic feature of the wartime street in Poland is the street trade. The forbidden, hunted street trade, the paradise of smugglers—despair of the German police and salvation of the people. Bawling hucksters, impudent, with tongues never at a loss. The rascals of lads, omnipresent, the plague of the Germans—the incomparable children of the streets.

If you have any money, you can buy anything you like in the Warsaw streets. Until 1942 it was still possible to provide yourself with a second outfit of clothes, "as good as new," in the Kercelak market. But later the Germans drove in lorries to this free market and, with machine guns at the ready, pillaged the goods from all the stall owners. The smugglers themselves were carried off to forced labor.

Nevertheless, for five years now the Third Reich has been waging war against the Polish black marketeers, and it has lost all along the line.

As I was walking along Chmielna Street in Warsaw about noon one day I was the witness of a roundup of hucksters selling "finest white bread." Cars drove up, and in a moment the street was empty. A convoy of six lorries carried off the two hucksters with their baskets of bread. Hardly had the lorries turned the corner when the whole street was noisy with cries of "White rolls, sausages, Kraków sausage made from the finest pork."

The enterprising and indestructible street traders play a useful part. They make it possible for the people somehow or other to survive, if only by barter, and with their effective sabotage, they undermine the German system of food rationing. The scolding hucksters are capable of rising to heroic deeds, such as the time they fought to release truckloads of children who were being carried off to Germany. The small urchins selling cigarettes and matches are also skilled at selling secret, illegal papers and periodicals; in broad daylight they will go about shouting, "Extraordinary supplement—Mr. Churchill's speech," in Polish, of course. And it is they, lively as quicksilver, who give the mournful, dirty streets their tempo, spontaneity, and even their humor.

In the endeavor to give permanence to that which at any moment may be destroyed, an enormous number of marriages are taking place in Poland. Here the family is experiencing a definite revival, and life which everywhere else is terrorized finds shelter within the four walls of home.

The Germans haven't left us much of our homes, so far as the material aspect is concerned. The housing problem is another of the difficulties of life under the occupation. All the public buildings have been requisitioned as offices and departments; schools and educational institutions have been taken over as barracks or hospitals. The Germans like to set up their offices on a large and bureaucratic scale, and they require much room.

All these evictions and removals associated with the requisitioning of accommodations for office and military uses could have been a nuisance rather than a plague, if they had been carried out in satisfactory circumstances and with the good will of the occupying authorities. But the Germans have done all they can to intensify the miseries of their occupation by adding that of homelessness.

It always depends on the humor of the official from the *Wohnungsamt* [housing department] whether the time allowed for removal is two weeks, or (as is most often the case) three

days, or even "at once." And it also depends on his humor
whether you may take your things away, or whether you must
go out with a suitcase—"a document case," as everyone puts it
jokingly.

I have friends in Kraków who have been evicted five times.
It often happens that people are evicted from their new homes
two weeks after they have entered into occupation. The people
go begging to the housing department—not for accommodation,
for there is no talk of that—but to find out where they can live
to insure that they are not evicted again in a short time.

Ignoring the possibility of losing the roof over one's head,
one always has to reckon with a less unpleasant form of the
housing crisis—the requisition of part of one's dwelling space.
Much depends on the way the space is disposed of.

You may have a four-room flat. Then they may quarter in
your home a German family with many children, a wireless
blaring away day and night, and a mastiff (the German's favorite
dog) trained as a guard. The queues for the kitchen and bathroom make it necessary to rise at 5:00 A.M. in order to get to
work on time.

The continual "dwelling traffic" which the Germans have
created is aimed simply at reducing the people to a state of
lassitude and anxiety, of loathing even their family corner. Yet
compared with the dangers, the terror, and the threats of deportation, imprisonment, and death, this housing persecution is
really less terrible. So the people console one another by saying,
"Why get worked up about the problem of housing when tomorrow I mayn't need a house?"

This kind of reasoning kills all desire to possess a decent
house. On the contrary, the worst kind of accommodation is
sought. An out-of-the-way street is selected; all comforts—a bath,
even electric lights—are avoided like a plague. Every comparatively comfortable home at once attracts the Germans, so the
people never attempt to make their homes convenient or beautiful. No one repairs or renovates anything. The carpets, the curtains, the pictures are kept well hidden. The worse a home can
look, the more certain one feels in it.

I once found an acquaintance of mine standing on a ladder
pulling down the ceiling of her bathroom.

"I must give the impression that the roof might fall in at any moment," she explained, in an excess of devil-may-care humor.

One officer who was billeted with me was distinguished by very sentimental family feelings. On his desk stood a cabinet photograph of his wife, who was in Berlin, together with his two children in their Sunday best. He sent his family food and silks pillaged from Jewish shops, and he wrote and received letters a mile long. His twelve-year-old son was a very promising young spit, for in one letter he asked, "How many Poles have you killed, father? I expect at least a hundred."

The major proudly read this letter to me and declared that the boy was being splendidly brought up in the *Hitlerjugend* [Nazi youth organization].

However, these devoted family feelings did not prevent the model husband from bringing a different girl home almost every night. When I grew impatient with these girls' demands for baths, clean linen, and food, and threatened to report the matter to the Wohnungsamt, the enterprising major turned a Jewish family out of the next flat and there set up lodgings on his own account, requisitioning part of my furniture for the purpose.

When I told him one evening that I had no clean bed linen, he turned out all the contents of my cupboards on the floor to make sure I was telling the truth. Then he went out for a few minutes (it was eleven at night) and brought back several sets of linen, a down quilt, and a pillow. A stenographer-typist and the young lieutenant who had brought her with him had only one remark when they saw their hero returning with the spoils: *"Ah, der Meister!"* ["Ah, the master!"]

The Germans in the government are treated with hatred and contempt by the people whom they oppress. They themselves see the moral abyss which lies between them and the Poles, and they are always declaring that they are among enemies. They attempt to break down the morale of their Polish cotenants by all kinds of torments and insults. A German colonel living in the home of a professor's widow forced her to carry his suitcases to the station. Another officer threw thirty grochen [less than five cents] to his hostess, crying, "It's time you got your ladylike ambitions out of your head."

The opinions which were formerly held, that Germans behaved more or less decently in accordance with their origin or occupation, have long since disappeared. It had been said that the military men were better than the Gestapo, the Austrians or Bavarians than the Prussians. All these fairy tales have been dispelled in the reality of life in Poland.

An acquaintance of mine had to give accommodation to a member of the Gestapo, a regular drinker, who felt particular hatred for the concert grand Bechstein which stood in their drawing room. He banged his heels on the pedals, broke the keys, snapped the strings. After a few weeks he was transferred, and he left the piano in a miserable state.

The next tenant was a charming doctor from Munich. He was indignant at the conduct of the vandalizing colonel, and asked permission to have the instrument repaired. He played Chopin on it beautifully, and his hostess had to resist a strong temptation to listen. Two weeks later he also left, loading the piano on a lorry to go with him, and so satisfactorily elucidated the difference between a cultured and uncultured German.

The very difficult material conditions compel everybody to work always to the utmost limit of their strength. The German offices, many of which employ Poles in subordinate capacities, start work at 7:30 a.m. and close at 6:00 p.m.; but wages and salaries fluctuate within prewar limits and are insufficient to meet the minimum of everyday requirements. So other sources of income have to be sought during times which should be spent in rest. The continual overwork, and the exhaustion of physical strength owing to the inadequacy of the food, make it still more difficult to overcome the omnipresent depression.

Yet it is easier to bear everything, even the worst material privation, than to grow accustomed to the burden of continual fear of the worst thing of all—something unknown, yet always expected. Every quiet night slept through at home is an achievement. Every day got through without mishap is a small but important gain.

Fear invariably accompanies life in Poland; nothing is free from fear. But even with this gnawing anxiety, the most daring and courageous enterprises are undertaken and carried through.

Despite the constant fear, the people remain calm and dignified and maintain their inflexible bearing toward the Germans. But it is not natural or easy; it calls for a continual, conscious effort, an unbroken tension of will.

At times when roundups are proceeding, every venture into the street may be the last that one will make. When they go off early in the morning to work, every member of the family says good-bye to the others; in the evening they greet one another with a feeling of relief. Every delay in someone's arrival causes alarm, often despair. And so, in everyday life, as in conspiratorial work, punctuality is the first and most scrupulously observed regulation.

During roundups it is a difficult and dangerous task to get to one's place of work. Thousands of precautions are observed; the more populous streets and squares are avoided, and often the route taken is much longer. But all this is not of great importance—human life has completely lost its value, and almost everything depends on chance and luck.

But it is not always possible to observe, or, having observed, to avoid the brigand dressed in civilian clothes coming round the corner; one never knows when the fatal *"Kommen Sie mit"* ["Come with me"] will be heard. New roundup officials, new victims emerge from houses and side streets. From single shadows they gather into little groups and are directed to the green lorries cunningly hidden in the narrow street ravines.

Those crowded into the lorry still have a moment in which the heart beats with at least a sigh of hope; they can still hope for the lighter of two sentences. As they turn the corner, they will see in a moment whether they are being carried off to the Labor Bureau in Lubelska Street, or to the Montelupi prison. The tiny card dropped discreetly on the road leaves a hint to their families, which will wait in vain for their return.

This chain of events—street, prison, camp, grave—is the road taken after the "political roundup." Such a roundup may last a day or, with intervals, for several months. It comes like a thunderbolt and overtakes one without cause, in an unexpected place and time.

After such a political roundup, which is a repressive measure born of the desire to break the will of the nation and to destroy its very core, no one but Germans and *Volksdeutsche* [members of the German ethnic group] are set free; old people, women, and children are taken.

Sometimes a friendly gateway brings salvation on a broad, busy road; sometimes it is possible to flee in the confusion. But on a small, quiet street there is no escape. The ends of the street are guarded by SS men, and rifles with fixed bayonets protrude from every gateway. One hears the cries of the hapless victims, the roar of "Halt!" and the departure of the laden lorries.

Roundups for work are carried out in the same fashion, but they have another function. These manhunts have their own definite seasons, determined by the course of agricultural work. The first wave is in the early spring; there is another in the summer before harvesttime, and another in the autumn for the potato lifting. Those rounded up on the streets have their identities and their papers examined, and the certificates of the Labor Bureaus are generally honored; whereas during the political roundups even the most important papers certifying that the person is engaged in valuable labor are laughed at.

Those carried off to work become the slaves of the Germans. How many will survive the exploitation, hunger, humiliation, and bombing? How many will return? There are over a million of them. The Germans are destroying the Polish nation by making a dual selection: The young, healthy, and physically strong are sent to forced labor; the intellectual world is dying in the camps.

The women are waiting faithfully for their absent husbands, sure that they will come back just as they went. And as long as there is a woman in the family, even in the poorest home, the children's eyes can watch with confidence for the door to open each evening. How anxious these children get for the safety of their mothers, how earnestly they try to show their attachment!

In my own circle, I had two young boys who had lost their father in Mauthausen concentration camp. The older, ten years old, was the devoted protector of his hard-working mother. In the days of despair after the tragic news of his father's death, he looked after his brother so completely that his mother did not have to worry about him at all. He taught his brother to read and write, and besides attending a secret high school, he earned money by making toys from plywood.

Often, after a day's work, I went home with their mother. The boys were always standing by the door, waiting every day. They stood holding each other's hands, waiting for the bell to ring as if afraid their mother might not return at all.

Imprisoned, deported, oppressed like their husbands, the women are today the core of the family and protectors of the aged and the children. They work beyond their strength at two or even three methods of earning money; yet they have no help in their home, and when they return they have to wash, cook, clean, and carry coal (if there is any to carry).

Even those women who belonged to the class of "idle rich" in prewar days have now forgotten that such things as hairdressers and dressmakers ever existed. On the dark, frosty mornings they go clattering off to work in their wooden-soled shoes. They return home laden with baskets of potatoes and other food, obtained by miracles of ingenuity. They freeze with cold outside the shop windows, they type with frozen fingers, they scheme all kinds of trade and barter, and every day they manage to find something for the children to eat.

These women teach the children who cannot attend school. They all live with one idea, that of surviving and living to see better days.

Among the many profound changes of this war has been one very important and significant change. The masses of peasants have finally been brought into citizenship. Numbers of peasants and workers have joined the ranks of the underground with a fervent desire to fight not only for a free Poland, but for a Poland of free people. The vigorous development of the peasant press at a time when every printed page may have to be paid for with a human life is the finest proof of this spiritual and intellectual uplift of the village.

Peasants bringing goods to town have helped in another nationwide problem. In large numbers they take gifts to the Prisoners' Relief Organization, the basis for the greatest part of the food parcels sent to civilian prisoners and prisoners of war.

The professional classes and intellectuals of Warsaw, Kraków, and other towns will all their lives bless the mysterious food parcels which arrive with the anonymous note: "Help from the village." Only after three years did I discover that their work is organized by the Peasant's party, which does all it can to keep alive a class of society which the Germans are mercilessly crushing. Those twenty kilos of flour, groats, or peas, the scrap of fat, mean much more than salvation from hunger. They are a part of the work to build a new confidence, a new and genuine cooperation between town and country in Poland.

Chapter 12

"I am smiling for my life . . . "

*Many of Germany's Jewish people felt fortunate to be "slave la-
borers" instead of prisoners in concentration camps. One of these
was Catherine Klein (Kate Cohn, actually), wife of a Jewish
doctor in Berlin. About a month before war broke out, her husband made his way to England but she could not go with him. In
1943, while working as a slave laborer, she managed to obtain a
forged passport in the name of "Francesca Borelli." To create the
impression that Catherine Klein was dead, she left her authentic
identification papers and a suicide note by the river Spree. Then
"Signora Borelli" boarded a train for Switzerland.*

"Where is the luggage to go?" inquires the customs official.

"First to Zurich," I tell him.

"Ticket and passport, please."

My escort [the Italian travel agent who was paid to get her
passport] eagerly produces both from his pocket and hands them
to the official, pretending to be quite calm. But I can see that his
hand is shaking.

Two pairs of eyes are firmly glued to the official at his desk,
following his every movement. With the stiff self-importance
typical of his class he opens a huge book, then closely scrutinizes
the first page of my passport. I hold my breath.

The Italian, in his anxiety, keeps a perpetual sugary smile
on his face.

The official spells out in a loud voice, "F-R-A-N-C-E-S-C-A
B-O-R-E-L-L-I," entering my name into his book.

"Where are you living? I mean, are you residing in Berlin?"

I begin to stammer. In my excitement I have completely forgotten where I am supposed to be living. Where was it? Was it Kaiserin Luise Platz, or Königin Luise Platz, or perhaps Augusta Viktoria Platz?

I look to the Italian for assistance. He is gasping for breath. Evidently he has not the faintest idea.

"Don't you understand German? I am asking you, where in Berlin are you living?"

An awkward silence follows.

After what seems ages, the voice of the Italian suddenly breaks in: "Madame lives—lives at—Seven Viktoria Luise Platz."

This seems to satisfy the official's curiosity. He merely notes it down.

"Open your luggage."

My fingers are quite numb while I fumble in my handbag for the keys.

The Italian firmly takes the bag from me, extracting the bunch of keys with miraculous swiftness and unlocking my suitcases for me.

Every article is carefully examined.

I may now close my suitcases.

They each get a pink label fixed across the locks: "Passed by the Customs," and are taken to the luggage van by the porters.

Longingly I follow them with my eyes until they disappear. How I envy them! They have passed their final test and are now on the road to liberty. Whereas I—shall I ever see them again?

Thinking of my passport, I have serious doubts. Only this morning did I realize the passport was finally in order. Uncle Ruggero [who altered and forged passports] had done his best.

Glancing at the document on which my life depended, I have to admit that two superfluous die-stamps have actually disappeared from the photograph. But on closer examination I find that the paper where they had been has lost its color completely and has also become considerably thinner. The overlay on a spot just on the back of my photograph shows the paper so badly damaged that only childish trust or criminal negligence could keep an official from realizing that the passport has been tampered with.

To divert attention from the damaged area, Uncle Ruggero

had hit on one of the oldest forgery tricks. He had sprinkled a blob of water on the opposite page, thus blotting the writing. Quickly closing the passport, he had transferred the ink to the damaged page, and it had certainly made it look a mess, which might fool an unsuspecting official.

The Italian was quite beside himself in his exultation over this masterstroke, and I had to remind him repeatedly of the fact that it was not only the Gestapo who were guarding the frontiers. They were reinforced by picked SS troops, well versed in every branch of trickery. Nothing would escape their attention. "You must realize what this means: Gestapo and SS. Do you believe in miracles? I don't."

Then it was time for the Italian and me to go to the station. And now I am all set for the part of an Italian lady just about to be off on a pleasure trip.

Languidly I walk along the platform. While producing my ticket for inspection, I make a lot of fuss—rearranging my handbag, looking at myself in my mirror, bringing the powder puff into action. The Italian urges me to come along.

I take no notice and calmly walk across to the bookstall, looking at the titles which are barely visible in the blacked-out station hall. Finally I decided on a magazine, the front page of which shows a German U-boat crew that has achieved a record number of sinkings, proudly displaying their brand new decoration and singing the popular little song: "*Denn wir fahren gegen Engeland.*" ["Because We Sail on England."]

I think to myself, Don't you show off. Now it is *my* turn to go to England.

The train is rather full. Mostly men in uniform.

I find myself a corner seat in a first-class compartment. Putting my small suitcase on the luggage rack, I spread a traveling rug on my seat. The Italian warms to the part of helpful escort and gives a splendid performance. Somehow I manage to whisper to him that I would prefer to be left alone in the compartment. So he takes up his post outside the open window of the train and, partly in Italian and partly in German, he gives me some last-minute instructions—not so much intended for my own benefit as for the ears of my fellow passengers and anyone else who might care to listen.

I can see the stationmaster's right arm raised slowly, pompously, with Prussian exactitude. I hear the engines beginning to fume, and for the last time I look at the city I once loved so much; all I can see of it is the sooty gray station wall.

Good-bye, Berlin. Never will I see you again. The train is beginning to move. The last thing I notice is a nervous twitch on the Italian's face.

I sink into my soft seat and close my eyes, trying to relax. There is nothing further to be done. Fate will have to run its course. All I can do now is sit and try to remain inconspicuous.

It is bitingly cold in the unheated compartment. I bury myself in my rug. By the light of the bluish blackout lamp, the faces of my traveling companions look rather ghastly. I keep looking at my watch. Oh, only twenty minutes have passed and the journey to Basel, on the German border, takes thirteen hours. Silent and reserved, we all sit in our respective corners, mostly with our eyes shut.

I go to sleep, apparently for quite a while, for when I wake up there are two new faces in my compartment.

". . . and I just went and tackled that schoolmaster. 'Sir,' I said—and when I say 'sir' everyone knows what to expect—'Sir,' I said, 'do you think that I put my children into the world that they should be taught when Homer wrote the *Iliad?* Sir, you cannot stop the march of time,' I said. 'We Germans have to concentrate on more important subjects these days. The whole world is waiting to be ruled by us and our children. Sir, you had better impress on these young minds the only theory worth knowing, the only theory we acknowledge today—the racial theory,' I said to him."

This avalanche of words comes from a little fat man now sitting opposite me who, decorated with countless swastika badges, continues to provide samples of his general outlook on life and is applauded vigorously by two officers.

The train stops at a station. Looking out, I discover in the first gray light of dawn that we have reached Frankfurt am Main.

While I was asleep we must have passed through that part of the country where I spent my childhood, I think to myself. The place of my birth lay on the way. And I managed to miss it. How I would have liked to say one last farewell to that particular spot of the earth, even in the dark of night. Although I have no friends left there any more, I would have liked to say good-bye to the trees, the houses, the streets of the sleepy little town where I spent the peaceful, happy years of childhood and adolscence.

In another six hours' journey we will reach the frontier; I am frightened of these six hours.

Again the faces of my companions change. This time I have two quiet, reserved civilians in my compartment. They take no notice of me.

Each turn of the wheels brings us nearer the frontier. I am getting restless, my arms and legs begin to feel heavy like lead, breathing becomes difficult, I cannot sit still any longer. So I go into the corridor where the temperature is below zero. But the extreme cold eases my aching head.

There is no one about except an elderly gentleman smoking a cigarette. I seem to represent the answer to his silent prayer; he wants to have a morning chat. And before I can take any precautionary measures he has asked me where I come from, where I am going.

"Oh, you're going to Switzerland, too? Are you as nervous about it as I am?" he asks me. What did he say?

"Yes, I am terrified of the frontier," he confesses. "It is such an uncanny feeling. Here we are in the midst of war and suddenly you come to a country where it might quite easily happen that you find yourself sitting next to an American or an Englishman without even knowing it. My wife at home is trembling for my safety; she knows what I am like. I cannot keep my mouth shut. For two pins I would get up and tell these foreigners exactly what I think of them. But I must remember that I only got my exit permit as manager of a dancing troupe, trying to arrange for an extensive tour through Switzerland, to bring back foreign currency. So I suppose I will have to keep my mouth shut, in the national interest."

The train stops at Mannheim.

It is getting much emptier now.

Returning to my compartment, I find it occupied by the Duke of Windsor.

In speechless surprise I stare at him.

The gentleman laughs, "Now, young lady, don't you start

telling me that I look like the Duke of Windsor—I just could not bear it. In peacetime it used to be a magnificent joke; but now I would not mind wearing a placard round my neck: 'No, I am not what you think I am. I happen to be a good German.' "

"That wouldn't be a bad idea at all," says a bony hooknosed civilian who has also just come into the train. "The state should force everyone to display a badge clearly indicating the nationality of the wearer. If you make a study of racial history as I have, you will soon find how easy it is to be fooled by members of inferior races. Just look at the Jews, for instance. Some of these Jew-women have managed to acclimatize themselves so well, through being permitted to live among us Aryans, that even nature has come to their help. It amounts to mimicry. Only the other day in Prague I had a most distressing experience. I must add that it was in the evening; I ran into a girl near the Wentzelplatz and spoke to her. I can tell you she was blue-eyed, blonde, tall, slim, straight little nose, small well-made mouth. I looked closer and suddenly discovered a yellow Jew star. That was a lesson to me. I won't be taken in again so easily."

I feel how he fixes his glance on me while talking, how he takes stock of the red of my hair, the blue of my eyes.

"Soon there will be no Jews left anywhere," our delightful fellow traveler continues to air his views. "The Jewish question will solve itself automatically. We have seen to that. But what we Germans should take into serious consideration is the introduction of badges for all non-Germans. If you once make it clear to yourself how many Poles, Russians, French, Dutch, Czechs, Danes, Americans, English, and other conquered nationals will be working for us here after the war, you will realize that it will require some means of differentiation between the masters of this country and the vanquished."

Feverish scarlet spots appear on his cheeks and I can see how he already imagines himself strutting along the pavement, swinging his whip over the bent, crushed figures of the foreign work-slaves, who have to walk in the road. All the time his eyes do not leave my face for a moment. Although I am listening intently, I have so far not shown by a single gesture whether I agree or disagree.

"My superiors knew what they were doing when they put me into my present post," he continues. "I am so thoroughly versed in these matters that nothing escapes me now, nothing at all."

Again I feel his searching glance and I need all of my self-control to present a picture of equanimity which I am far from feeling.

I should like to go to the washroom and take a sedative. Cautiously I remove the passport from beneath me—I hope my weight has pressed it to open at the desired page—and put it in my handbag. But I dare not get up; my knees are trembling too much.

All the while the express is racing toward the frontier.

The fear, bordering on certainty, that this devil knows exactly who I am, that he is sent here by the Gestapo to catch me, and that he is now playing a cat-and-mouse game with me— that fear drives me nearly crazy.

The way that creature is talking. The way he keeps staring at me all the time. The way each one of his words seems to be meant for me, and me alone. There is no doubt in my mind, he is a Gestapo official.

And again I feel his eyes on me. I feel how he enjoys watching my fear, the pleasure he finds in keeping me guessing. I suppose he will only snatch me at the last moment, just when I am reaching out for freedom.

No! The cry comes from within me. No, you won't get me. Not alive, anyway! And as if haunted by a thousand ghosts, I rush in sheer terror from the compartment into the corridor. I could scream aloud in torment. The torment of miserable helplessness, being a victim once more, waiting in a kind of hypnotized stupor until it pleases the enemy to fell the final blow.

Outside, the dancing-troupe agent has apparently been waiting for me. He refuses to let me pass.

"Well, young lady," he says, and his voice comes to me as if out of a mist, "now we'll soon be over the worst. My mother, who used to be a devilishly clever woman, dead these twenty-five years—no, let me see, it must be twenty-seven years this March—my mother used to say . . ."

Murmuring an excuse, I hurry swiftly past him and lock myself into the washroom.

Catching hold of the basin, I try to steady myself. My legs are shaking so much that I am hardly able to stand upright. Tears are rolling down my face.

So near the goal, within the very reach of life itself, and now it will have to be death after all!

The train is steaming toward the frontier.

I shall have to act quickly if I am to escape the Gestapo. In a few minutes' time we will reach Weil, the last German station before Basel. That is where German customs and passport officials will board the train; it will be too late for me then.

I open the window.

A gust of icy-cold fresh air blows in. The country is covered with snow, and the bare branches of the trees are weighed down by it.

Now the sun is breaking through the clouds. What a picture of perfect peace. It looks like an enchanted garden.

I breathe in deeply.

Gradually hysteria and fear leave me, and sanity seems to return.

I look at the embankment. To have to end up among the rubble down there! What a ghastly thought.

No, I don't want to die! Not now, when I have got this far. I want to start life again, join my husband, return to normalcy.

Catching sight of myself in the mirror, I discover that I look absolutely wild, with strands of hair falling over my face.

While repairing the damage with combs and hairpins, I begin to wonder if I have not been imagining things. Surely if this man were really a Gestapo official, he would not have talked so much. And just as only three minutes ago I was fully convinced that this man was my deadly enemy, I am now quite certain that he is nothing but a pretentious ass.

My head feels clear and calm now, but my limbs are still trembling.

From the confusion of my fears and obsessions there suddenly comes the thought of my good old standby, the only one that the Italian was able to provide—my sedative. Yes, I shall take two of the Luminal tablets.

On and on races the express; soon we will reach the frontier. Upon trying the water taps, I find that there is no water. The pipes are frozen. How am I to swallow my tablets? With endless trouble and by sheer determination I manage to get them down at last, even without water.

The mere fact that I have swallowed them makes me feel calmer at once. But then the drug really begins to take effect. Soon I have regained complete self-control.

I rearrange my hair, renew my makeup, use lipstick and lots of perfume, and, without blinking an eyelid, Francesca Borelli, the Italian glamour girl, sweeps back to her compartment.

My fellow passengers seem to have been discussing me, for they stop talking the moment I reenter the compartment. Their gossip must have been of a harmless nature, as the friendly smiling faces are eager to testify. Even the pseudo Gestapo-man has interrupted his recital of revolutionary schemes and measures and is concentrating on a few interesting-looking sandwiches, which he consumes with a repellent mixture of relish and noise.

The train comes to a standstill.

Outside our window a station poster appears: "Weil."

That means that the decisive battle is at hand. Outside, a railway guard calls out for the benefit of those who might still be unaware of the fact: "Last station before the frontier."

For months I have been afraid of this very moment, day and night. In my waking and sleeping hours I have imagined how I will feel, wondering how I can possibly stand the strain, expecting to find myself trembling with excitement, neither being able to see, to hear, or to take in what is being said. And now I find that I am in complete control of all my faculties. I feel not a vestige of fear; I am best compared to a robot who neither thinks nor feels any emotions.

Rising from my seat, I let the window down, and with absorbed interest I watch the greater part of the train being disconnected. Our express consists of only two carriages now. I watch three frontier officials in uniform leave the station building, coming slowly across the lines and climbing into the train, locking all doors behind them. The engine starts to move again.

I feel as if I were watching a play being enacted. The tension takes hold of me and I share in the general excitement, but the idea that I am personally involved in this, that in a few seconds' time the final curtain may fall on my own life—that idea does not even occur to me.

Yet it is inevitable that I should remember a few of the many tales circulating in Berlin, especially more recently, of frustrated attempts to escape. Will the tale of my own unsuccessful attempt soon be spreading among those left behind?

Being now thoroughly under the influence of the peace-giving drug, I am not even worried by excited voices coming from the next compartment. The passport control officials are in there now.

Something seems to be wrong.

I discover that my three fellow travelers are much more nervous than I am. The Gestapo-man is furiously biting his nails while the "Duke of Windsor" suddenly has the urgent wish to go to the restroom. Hardly has he opened the door when it is pushed back from the outside by a sergeant major, who shouts at him, "Stay where you are."

Next door the babble of voices rises to a concert pitch. Although we are all listening intently, we unfortunately cannot hear one word clearly. Then suddenly all is still.

In the corridor outside our compartment window the white face of the ballet manager, followed by a huge soldier, passes. Our eyes are still following this ill-matched couple when our door slides open.

"Heil Hitler, passport control."

Even the Luminal tablets fail me now. No dose would be large enough to counteract the sudden spasm of fear running through my body. My instinct for self-preservation revolts at the idea of giving myself up without a final struggle. My lips are beginning to quiver, my teeth are chattering, and I am trembling all over.

"Heil Hitler," replies the fellow on the seat opposite mine. His face has become hard and repulsive again, now that he is no longer munching sandwiches or biting his nails. He just smiles at the official without attempting to produce his identity papers.

"What happened just now with that ballet chap next door?" I heard him whisper. "The man seemed harmless enough to me."

"You never heard such impudence," one of the officials answers, still breathing with fury.

"Impudence indeed," chimes in the other official. "I have had plenty to deal with on this train, but that was the crowning glory. You will get your report in Basel."

I stare at my compartment-mate. So my first instinct was right. He belongs to the Gestapo. Apparently his job is to watch us for a few. hundred miles before we even reach the frontier. Or is he only investigating particularly suspicious cases, such as mine, for instance?

Now the official holds my passport in his hands. As intended, he opens it on the photograph page and, hardly glancing at it, turns a few pages until he comes to my transit visa to Switzerland. Undoubtedly of greatest interest from his point of view is the German exit and reentrance visa, which he examines minutely. In my trembling fear, I feel that he is taking hours over it. But, at last, even this comes to an end. Apparently satisfied, he turns a few pages back, now looking at each one separately.

I am only fearful of the damaged back of my photograph. Miraculously, he seems not to notice it at all. Meanwhile, I feel the searching glances of the other official and his colleague opposite me, watching my every move. I smile in splendid unconcern. I am smiling for my life. I cannot stand the oppressive silence any longer. Someone must speak.

"Will I have to change at Basel?" I ask.

No reply.

The inquisitor has come back to the photograph, examining it much more closely now than before, comparing it with my face over and over again.

Suddenly he starts.

Lifting the book quite close up to his eyes, he exclaims, "What's this? Something exceedingly queer." Each one of his words strikes me like a whip.

Nevertheless, I keep smiling. There is no change in my expression, none at all.

He waves to the other official to follow him and they both leave the compartment, posting themselves in the corridor with their backs to me, consulting.

My face behaves splendidly. It is still smiling all by itself.

The honorable gentleman opposite me watches my every move.

I can hear quite distinctly one of the men saying to the other, "There is something fishy here." And clearly I hear the other one reply, "Try to tear off the photograph. Let us see if the stamp runs on underneath it."

All the while the train is hurrying toward the frontier.

My thinking apparatus has stopped functioning. I am possessed of fear—naked, wild fear. I feel as if I were being slowly strangled to death.

A voice comes from outside: "We had better investigate the whole thing at Basel."

The game is lost.

The rope around my throat is tightening. There is no way out for me now. I am not even free to choose my own death. Jumping out of the window is out of the question, and the only other possible way is barred by the officials.

Again comes the voice: "I believe the die-stamp must have slipped here."

"Yes," replies the other. "Underneath it seems to be quite all right."

And they continue their whispering.

In a minute they will be back in the compartment, they will take me between them, and we shall start on a road from which there is no return.

Farewell, liberty; farewell, life.

How long does it take—days, hours, minutes? Suddenly I hold my passport in my hands again.

"Do you understand German, madame?" one of the officials asks me.

"I was born in Berlin," I tell him.

"On your return there, you will have to go to your consulate at once and ask for a new passport. You will have nothing but trouble with this one. Never have I seen anything like it. The die-stamps are in the wrong place, and the mess behind the photograph! We wouldn't permit a German to travel about with a passport in a condition like that. Heil Hitler!"

And they are gone. The nightmare is over.

My lips are positively aching from the petrified smile I have kept on my face during the ordeal. And yet, I must not drop the mask yet. The unwavering stare of the gentleman opposite me warns me that I am still in the power of the Third Reich.

Here is the official back again, too.

"Have you any newspapers, magazines, books? You are not allowed to take anything across the frontier." I hand him the magazine I bought at the bookstall last night. It is confiscated for the benefit of the Red Cross.

"How much money have you with you?"

I hold out handbag and wallet.

"I want to know how much money you have?"

"Sixty-five marks."

He neither checks up nor comments on it. And he is gone.

I gradually awake to the certainty that this is no dream. These are no phantoms of my ever active imagination. I have passed the final test, I have graduated with honors. It is all over now. I have won. Liberty is mine now!

The train is slowing down, and we are passing houses, streets; we draw into a station.

Basel, Badisher Bahnhof, still part of Germany.

We all have to leave the train.

There are not many people left who climb out of the two carriages.

The three frontier officials, with the ballet manager in their midst, disappear quickly into one of the station buildings. A door slams behind them. I stare after them for quite a while. And then a huge wave of gratefulness engulfs me, flowing through my veins, making my pulses beat faster. How easily I might have become the fifth of that party! Thanks to a kindly fate, I have been saved from defeat by what now seems a miracle to me. And for the first time in years, a simple little prayer of thanksgiving rises to my lips, such as I was taught when a child.

As from another world, a friendly voice sounds in my ears in unmistakable Swiss dialect. It comes from a Swiss porter offering his services to me.

"No, thank you, I can manage my two little suitcases by myself. It's only to the next platform."

"To the next platform! That's what you think. That's how it used to be in peacetime. All that is changed now. You have to walk on foot into Switzerland. Quite a long way through no-man's-land. There will be a few formalities to go through; you had better let me help you."

I agree to everything. Only quickly away from German soil. No time is to be lost.

"Have you changed your ten marks into Swiss francs yet?" The porter remains quite unperturbed. "You get a much better rate of exchange here."

I am burning to get away but show no signs of impatience. Playing my part to the end, I change my ten marks and deposit a sum of money for the return journey. This is the last time that the Nazis grab money from me, I reflect with joy in my heart.

My porter and I start off on our way. It is a walk between two worlds, but for me it means much more: the road from death into new life.

Slowly, slowly, we wander through a long covered tunnel. There is no one about. Our steps resound in a sepulchral silence.

Suddenly the corridor widens into a glass-roofed hall and much to my horror we are again confronted by German uniforms, five of them. German luggage and foreign currency control.

All five descend on me like a storm, snatching my cases and handbag, searching every corner.

Is there no end to these Nazis at all? I sigh to myself, as I pass on with my good old porter.

"How much longer until we get into Switzerland?" I ask him a few moments later.

"Switzerland? We have been walking through Switzerland these last three minutes," he replies.

Mrs. Klein (Cohn) rejoined her husband in London, where they live today.

Chapter 13

"Women prayed for the safety of the enemy . . ."

Yugoslavia had paid dearly for denying safe transit to Hitler's armies en route to Greece to amend Mussolini's fiasco there. When the German army marched into Yugoslavia on April 6, 1941, it held a five-division advantage in troops that were well trained to use their modern weapons. The plucky little Balkan country with its pitiful cavalry divisions was subdued in slightly more than a week's time—taught, as the Nazis put it, "a terrible lesson." Thousands died in Belgrade during a Palm Sunday vengeance bombing.

Surrender to the Germans did not mean toleration of a Nazi occupation, and guerrilla fighters in all parts of Yugoslavia rose against their oppressors. All too soon, however, conflicting sociopolitical aims seemed more important than a common patriotism. Unalterable differences split the partisan ranks. During a struggle for power that lasted long after the Germans had been expelled from the country, both the invaders and the Yugoslavs were victimized by the guerrilla groups.

Lena Yovitchitch, the daughter of a Yugoslav diplomat and a Scottish mother, stayed in Yugoslavia despite the urging of British friends to escape to England. After her brother Milan joined the army—later to be captured by the Germans—she left her Belgrade home and spent most of the occupation in the small Serbian village home of a girlhood friend, Mila, whose brother, Stoyan, was a prosperous local farmer.

These are some of her experiences at the village with the Nazis and with the marauding Chetnik guerrillas:

When the resistance began fighting internally, the Germans

153

asked for nothing better. It was a quicker way to quell rebellion and to annihilate the Serbs than the Germans could have devised, causing no loss to themselves.

Mikhailovitch [leader of the Chetniks] and his forces were principally engaged in operations against the enemy in Serbia, which was cut off from the rest of the country during the German occupation. As Tito and his partisans [a leftist guerrilla group which opposed the Chetniks] were confining their activities to regions beyond Serbia, they did not concern our daily lives. On the other hand, small detachments of Mikhailovitch's men, who roamed the woods and hills within a stone's throw of the town where I lived, were an ominous reality.

During 1943–44 German troops stationed in the town of X. steadily decreased until only a negligible number remained. In consequence, the bands of Chetniks entrenched in the neighboring hills and woods became bolder and bolder. They frequently made reconnoitering expeditions, penetrating to the center of town. They were easily recognizable by their long hair and flowing beards. (It was a tradition of the Chetniks to let their beards grow during warfare; it was also a sign of mourning among the peasants, who did not shave for forty days after a bereavement.) Sometimes they disguised themselves as priests—orthodox clergy wore beards and long hair—thereby fooling the Germans, but not the Serbs.

News of the presence of Chetniks in town would quickly spread and cause alarm. If it came to a clash of arms and German soldiers were killed or wounded, German revenge would fall upon the town's inhabitants. Haunted by fear of reprisals, women prayed for the safety of the enemy, in an inverted prayer to safeguard their menfolk.

One day in the middle of summer in 1943, the sleepy little town of X. was startled by the sound of rifle shots. A skirmish had suddenly sprung up between a small company of Germans and a band of Chetniks. The faces of citizens going about their daily tasks became blanched with fear, and in an instant there was a mad rush through the streets as women fled to their homes and men took the shortest cut to the hills for refuge. They knew that if so much as one German lost his life, a hundred Serbs would be arrested and shot. But the encounter that morning was quickly over, and the Chetniks made good their escape. There were no casualties on either side, with the exception of a German who was wounded.

A curfew was immediately imposed and the streets were cleared; everybody was ordered to remain indoors with blinds drawn. The front rooms of Mila's house had iron shutters, a more effectual protection than blinds, and these were hastily closed and bolted. Not a sound came from outside as we waited.

After a while the heavy tread of soldiers was heard and surreptitiously I looked through a peephole in the shutters. On either side of the pavement men of the Wehrmacht were advancing with slow and measured step; their faces were ashen, their jaws were set, and every muscle was taut as they furtively looked right and left, afraid lest Chetniks were in hiding, ready to shoot if they got a chance. So the Germans crept along like tigers, preparing to hurl themselves in whichever direction danger threatened.

An hour or two passed and nothing happened; the curfew was lifted and normal conditions were resumed. Mila hastened to the farm to warn her brother not to return home until she sent word that he might safely do so; the possibility of reprisals accounted for the fact that there was hardly a man to be seen in X. But in a few days the affair died down; the wounded German "fortunately" survived and the incident bore no consequence.

In 1943 the Chetniks once more adopted tactics of sabotage in order to impede German activities: obstructing railway lines, cutting down telegraph poles, thwarting and hampering the enemy as much as possible. This was commendable; however, in the opinion of many Serbs living in the country, it was questionable whether hindrances inflicted upon the German war machine were sufficiently important to compensate for the price paid in reprisals and the enormous sacrifice in human lives.

At this time a certain Mr. Harrison, sponsored by the BBC, gave regular broadcasts from London in the Serbian language, inciting the people of Yugoslavia to intensify acts of sabotage by every means in their power. This advice was ill received by listeners in X., in whom it aroused bitter resentment. They considered it proof that Britain understood little about the internal situation in the country and cared less about the persecution of the people.

Telegraph poles in the district of X. suffered severe damage at the hands of the Chetniks. The destruction was always accomplished under cover of darkness, and the Germans would no sooner make the necessary repairs than the work had to be done all over again, for the Chetniks allowed the enemy no respite. There were no reserve supplies of telegraph poles; consequently the original ones were shortened after every assault, until the wires hung dangerously low overhead. The dwarfed effect was rather comic. More active measures were needed to cope with the situation, and the Germans finally decided to spare themselves further trouble by making the Serbs responsible.

Every night shifts of men between the ages of twenty and fifty were assigned to keep watch, their lives pledged as security for the telegraph poles. Stoyan took his turn at mounting guard. When he started out for an all-night vigil, we who remained at home to sleep in comfortable beds were beset by anxiety for his safety. We did not know what might happen during the time he was on duty.

Whether in rain or snow or bitter winds, men tramped the high roads to safeguard the poles. And nights were long in the winter.

Stoyan carried a flask of *rakija* [Yugoslavia's native brandy] in his pocket, not so much for himself as for those who were not in the fortunate position of having a barrel of rakija in the cellar. He was generous and kindhearted, qualities which singled him out as a good sort. Everyone respected him. He had few genuine friends, however, perhaps because he did not encourage intimacy.

The watchers made bonfires at which they warmed themselves from time to time, telling jokes and stories to keep up their spirits. But when dawn came at last, they were exhausted and had to go home to snatch a few hours' sleep before beginning the next day's work.

Night duty, in addition to the constant anxiety, was a strain on Stoyan's health. An attack of grippe developed into an inflammation of the ear and for several weeks he was confined to bed. During this time a number of telegraph poles were cut down by the Chetniks. No one seemed to know when and how the raid occurred, but the harm was done and fear of reprisals gave rise to acute alarm. Terrible consequences were prophesied.

Snow lay thick on the ground; it was extremely cold. One evening while Stoyan was ill, we were sitting round the supper table when the dogs began to bark furiously. Someone was heard thumping at the garden gate, which was locked after dark. Mila rose to discover the cause of the commotion, but before she reached the door a servant burst into the room, exclaiming breathlessly:

"Germans are at the gate wanting to be let in!"

At that moment we saw two soldiers in the courtyard. They approached the house, keeping the dogs at bay with their rifle butts. Impatient at being kept waiting, the men scaled the high wall, breaking their falls by jumping into a mound of snow.

Mila received them in the hall and inquired their business. By way of reply, they produced a warrant for Stoyan's arrest in connection with the affair of the telegraph poles. Unperturbed, she invited them to deliver it in person, mentioning that her brother was ill.

In order to reach the bedroom, it was necessary for them to pass through the dining room where the family was assembled. On the threshold the soldiers paused for a second, clicked their heels, and saluted. Observing that we were at supper, they murmured "Mahlzeit" ["Good appetite"] before following Mila into the next room where Stoyan lay in bed.

As the door opened, Stoyan sat up and, removing the bandages swathing his head, took the proffered warrant. He scanned it and said, "I am ill, but as you have orders to arrest me, here I am."

Putting his words into action, he threw back the bedclothes and was about to rise. But the soldiers restrained him. They were perhaps impressed that he made no attempt to use his illness as a pretext for evading arrest. Rejecting the aggressive methods usually adopted by Germans in authority, the men spoke kindly.

"Bleiben Sie nur rühig," one of them said, "die Sache eilt nicht." ["Just stay quiet, there is no rush."] And without another word, they left the room.

In the hall they lingered, conversing with Mila, expressing surprise and pleasure at her knowledge of German. To be able to speak their language was to meet the enemy halfway, they thought. One of the soldiers had suffered from inflammation of the ear and sympathized with Stoyan, volunteering advice on methods for relieving the pain. He was a German, but he was not without fellow feelings.

"Gute Nacht!" he said, as he turned on his heel. "Vielleicht sehen wir uns noch einmal dienstlich." ["Good night! Perhaps we may see each other again in an official capacity."]

Mila did not reciprocate the sentiment—she had no desire to see either of them again, whether on business or otherwise.

Citizens held responsible for the destruction of the telegraph poles were arrested and imprisoned, but upon an urgent appeal to the commandant they were released on bail. The German authorities meanwhile counseled together and it was finally decided that, owing to certain extenuating circumstances, the incident would be overlooked on payment of a ransom of a million dinars.

This sum taxed the resources of the inhabitants of X. to the utmost. It was, however, a matter of life or death, and everyone considered it a sacred duty to make a contribution toward the fund. Stoyan and other citizens who were in a position to give liberally headed the list of subscribers, and between the big sums and the little sums, the total was collected and handed to the commandant. German rancor was appeased and the condemned men were saved.

By the middle of 1944, Allied victories had reached a conclusive stage, and it was evident that the Germans were playing a losing game. They began to withdraw their troops from Serbia and other parts of Yugoslavia in order to fill the gaps in their ranks on the battlefields of Central Europe.

In the autumn of 1944, German troops left X. for good, and the guerrillas from the neighboring woods established themselves in the town and took over command.

Toward the end of the war the Chetniks became disorganized and scattered, losing contact with their leader. Certain of them took matters into their own hands, acting without consulting headquarters and in some cases leaving records that were not always to their credit. When they were in authority in X., constant demands for contributions of money were made on the inhabitants, who were threatened with dire reprisals in case of noncompliance.

The Chetniks were anxious to fill their coffers while the opportunity served. Money alone did not satisfy them; they were in need of shirts, pants, socks, towels, and miscellaneous goods, which were collected in organized drives from house to house. The civil population had already been fleeced by the Germans; but when asked to give to the Chetniks, they gave whatever they had and gave gladly, for these were their own people.

Guerrillas were seldom seen in broad daylight; they employed emissaries to carry out their orders—unobtrusive figures charged with delivering messages, who furtively tapped on the window or knocked at the door. An "official message" consisted of a scrap of paper upon which was scribbled a sum of money with instructions when, where, and to whom it was to be made payable. Transactions of this kind took place at lonely outposts, as a rule, and the greatest secrecy was observed.

On several occasions Stoyan was summoned to make arbitrary payments which he found increasingly difficult to meet. His reserve funds were exhausted, and he was finally obliged to draw upon the savings accounts in the bank, which were intended for his children. It was a bitter concession, and one that was hard to take.

Life passed from one state of uncertainty to another. The departure of the Germans brought little improvement to our situation. In fact, we were worse off in some ways than before. Liberty and safety were still beyond the horizon. Resentment at new forms of tyranny were keenly felt by all, but it was dangerous to say a word that might be overheard or misinterpreted. Several men in X. lost their lives for openly condemning the course adopted by the guerrillas.

Among those killed whom I knew personally were two businessmen, a schoolteacher, and a gentle, well-educated man— a lover of animals, who had been in charge of the kennels in the royal palace at Belgrade before the war. In the dead of night these innocent victims were ordered to rise from bed; masked figures armed to the teeth hustled them into a waiting vehicle, and they were driven away to an unknown place. Nothing more was heard of them until after the war ended, when it was learned that they had been murdered in cold blood and buried in a pit scantily covered with earth.

Not until the spring of 1945 did Lena Yovitchitch leave the village and her friends to return to Belgrade. By birth a British subject, she applied for and received a passport for England. On November 2, 1945, relatives greeted her arrival on British soil and "with a heart filled to the brim with thanksgiving I recognized my brother Milan." Miss Yovitchitch continues to make her home in Edinburgh, Scotland.

Chapter 14

"Laughter is nearly extinct . . . "

Hitler's only opportunity to fly the swastika over English soil was his five-year tenure of the Channel Islands that lay no more than ten to thirty miles off the French coast. For centuries a part of Great Britain, Guernsey, Jersey, Sark, and Alderney were inhabited by forty-two thousand people.

All Nazi gestures of friendship were met with cold disdain. There was no underground with attendant sabotage, only contempt and annoying little obstructions. Fiction concerning these islands in World War II may have given an amusing word picture of the conqueror's sojourn. However, privation, abuse, and tragedy followed in these parcels of land as they had elsewhere after the Nazis came. And some of the men who were sent to prison and to labor camps in Germany did not return.

Two residents of Jersey, Reginald Maugham and Horace Wyatt, recalled after the war what the occupation meant to the Channel Islanders. The first account is Maugham's. His description of the arrival of the invaders in the town of St. Hélier is peculiarly reminiscent of German tourists in peacetime.

All day long you might have seen German officers and men burdened by packages and parcels, hurrying to their billets. These men, I learned, entered business premises intent on exhausting the goods for sale and were provided with money especially for the purpose. Jewelry, gold and silverware, watches and clocks, men's and women's clothing, underclothing, furs, haberdashery, footwear, toilet articles and perfumery, fancy goods—nothing was missed. Even uncut bolts of cloth from the

tailors' shops, household linen, blankets, sheets, curtains and curtain material, carpets and linoleum—all were feverishly bought
up. When these classes of goods were finally depleted, the in-
satiable buyers turned their attention to gas heaters, electrical
apparatus, ironmongery—anything, in a word, that could be purchased, packed up, and sent away.

It was not long before shop windows, completely or almost
completely bare, were boarded over—partly to safeguard their
expensive and irreplaceable plate glass, but chiefly because there
was nothing left to display in them. Soon the larger and more
commodious premises—Burton's, Woolworth's, and the Fifty Shil-
ling Tailors—were taken over and transformed into a soldiers' canteen, a wine and spirit depot for seized and requisitioned wines
and spirits, a propaganda center for the diffusion of Nazi litera-
ture, and the like. But large stocks of alcoholic liquor were
centralized at other places. Champagne, brandy, and other luxu-
ries of the kind, unprocurable by the civilian population, were
earmarked for the use of the German officers.

Very soon after the arrival of the German troops, dances
were arranged by them in the two principal dance halls of St.
Hélier. No German festivity, of course, can possibly be a success
unless accompanied by large quantities of German beer. Beer,
therefore, was imported in great quantities to insure such a
spirit as the Teutonic mind regards as festive.

The dances were attended by all ranks—officers, noncommissioned officers, and men. But after several of these gatherings
had failed to attract a single female member of what might be
called the *haute société* of the island, great disgust was expressed
by the officers, whose "conquests" had perforce to be limited to
domestic servants, the young damsels from behind the various
lesser counters of the business world, and—others.

Toward the end of 1940, probably to mark the disappointment of the officers at their failure to attract the ladies of the
island to their balls and dances, indulgence in this form of
amusement was suddenly prohibited.

A year or so later, a number of German theatrical and
variety companies were brought over, as well as German films
for the local cinemas—where, however, manifestations of applause or displeasure were sternly forbidden. At the same time,

hordes of French prostitutes were imported and lodged in hotels and empty private houses, which were thus readily transformed into convenient brothels for the use of German officers and others.

About this time complete control of all ports and harbors was vested in a German port authority. This control also applied to every description of vessel, including fishing boats. No boat could proceed to fish without a license. As a consequence, enthusiasm for fishing—not for many years very exuberant in Jersey—received a further setback. Moreover, as the Germans insisted on appropriating the greater part of each catch, the amount of fish left for the public was negligible.

The autumn of 1940 brought a shiver of apprehension to owners of the twelve thousand-odd motor vehicles which, up to the arrival of the Germans, had circulated freely upon the roads of the island. Teutonic cupidity doubtlessly being stirred up by the spectacle of all these smart and—for the most part—well-kept cars and lorries, a notice was inserted in the press ordering registration with full particulars of all motorcars, motorcycles, and other gasoline-propelled vehicles. A few days later, an order from the field commandant directed that private cars were to be presented at specified centers for valuation and purchase for the use of the German army. Vehicles were examined and tested by persons appointed for the purpose, in the presence of a German officer. In many cases, the cars were retained by the Germans; in others, owners were directed to drive them home again and to keep them in their possession until further notice. Cars in the latter category were said to be reserved, and a document to that effect was affixed to their windshields. In the settlement of prices there appeared to be no sort of consistent rule; for, while owners of the smaller and less expensive types frequently received reasonable and often fairly high prices, great indignation was expressed at the valuation of higher-class vehicles.

In due time all the cars which had been reserved were called up and taken; the owners received, in place of cash, a curious document in the nature of a bond, issued by the Island States. This interesting piece of paper informed the recipient that it entitled him to receive the amount stated therein six

months after the conclusion of the war! I framed as a curio the
bond addressed to me, entitling me to rather less than one-third
of the value of a car which I had handed over with rage and
bitterness. For about two years it adorned the walls of my study
until one morning when, to my profound surprise, I received
an intimation that, on presenting the bond at the Treasury, the
sum due to me stated thereon would be paid. And it was.

I suppose I was lucky on the whole, for there were some
who, three years later, had received for their vehicles neither
bonds nor cash.

Late in the summer of 1940 a regulation was adopted by
the Island States decreeing that household furniture and effects,
abandoned in their houses by persons who had hastily quit the
island, should be stored in the custody of a designated official
and in no case sold or otherwise disposed of until forty days after
the return of the respective owners. It was time. By the early
autumn, innumerable cases of burglarious entry in such premises
were reported almost daily. Day after day, wholesale thefts
engaged the attention of the harassed police. In a few cases
arrests were made and the stolen property recovered, but, in
the great majority, it was never seen again.

In the weeks that followed, some progress was made in
giving effect to the Island States' directions, but, before more
than a small fraction of the work could be completed, an order
from the German commandant stopped all further progress. This
order prohibited the removal of furniture of any description
from abandoned houses, such furniture being required at short
notice for the use of the army of occupation.

A few weeks later, administrators for persons who had left
for England were ordered to present within five days duplicate
inventories of all stored furniture belonging to such persons.
Soon afterward, all single mattresses left by the evacuees were
ordered to be handed over forthwith; for days after that,
lorries piled high with this class of bedding, in all states of
preservation, might have been seen proceeding in the direction
of the indicated depot. It is perfectly safe to say that these,
together with the whole of the furniture commandeered, were
forever lost to the unfortunate owners. While it is highly im-
probable that any claim would ever be made for the return of

the mattresses after their use by German soldiers, the fate of the furniture—much of which was of considerable value—is less shrouded in mystery, for much of it was openly shipped to Germany.

It was credibly stated that during the later phases of the war, great quantities of household effects, together with similar articles looted from French occupied towns and villages, were loaded into trains at neighboring ports, destined for German centers which had suffered from our bombing. These trains bore white painted notices stating that the contents of the wagons were spontaneously presented by the sympathetic people of France and the English Channel Islands to unfortunate German families, to atone in some degree for the barbarous and inhuman destruction wrought upon innocent and defenseless German civilians by murderous Allied aircraft.

The larger and more important houses taken over as quarters for German officers, even if furniture and appointments were not exported, were despoiled. Thus senior officers residing in one house, who took a fancy to pictures, carpets, or other objects of value seen in premises occupied by men of junior rank, would unhesitatingly order such objects to be sent to them for their use. In this way the original owners, returning to Jersey at the end of the war, might spend months, perhaps years, in tracing, recognizing, and reclaiming their property—discovered sometimes miles away in the involuntary possession of persons possibly unknown to them.

Empty houses were treated in a shocking manner. In many, dividing walls between rooms were roughly broken through; staircases were torn down for firewood; toilets were choked up and, where this happened, cellars and basements were used as lavatories until the premises became untenable, at which time they were evacuated and other dwellings occupied with similar results. In one private home at St. Brelade's, the drawing room afforded accommodation for a number of pigs. In many cases, houses tenanted by German troops were left in such a sorry condition that they were only fit to be pulled down and re-erected.

A military zone, which included all coasts and coastal roads, was declared in May, 1941. Persons residing or having business therein were compelled to provide themselves with special passes. Curfew in these areas, moreover, was fixed one hour earlier than elsewhere. The general idea underlying this order was to keep the public away from works connected with island fortification, which was now proceeding apace. At the same time, the sea beaches as well as the land behind them were heavily mined. Dogs seen trespassing in the forbidden zone were ordered to be shot.

Later in the year, for billeting purposes, the inhabitants of Jersey were ordered to deliver schedules to a specified authority, showing the number of bedrooms and other rooms in their houses, the number of persons habitually sleeping there, and full particulars regarding lighting, cooking, water supply, and drainage. At a later date, German officers and soldiers were compulsorily billeted in a number of private houses. In many instances, I was informed, these men were inoffensive and gave little trouble; but in others, especially if the family included girls and young women, the conduct of the Germans was sometimes odious. Any attempt to restrain them by force was the immediate signal for the drawing of a revolver or a bayonet; this was almost certain to be followed by some trumped-up charge which consigned the unhappy parent, husband, or brother to a more or less lengthy term of imprisonment during which, of course, the house and its remaining inmates were left without protection.

The spring of 1941 witnessed the first of a number of epidemics of burglary which broke out during the German occupation of Jersey. In addition to thefts from evacuated houses, tradesmen's shops were the scenes of these nocturnal visits with great regularity and frequency. The time selected was usually the eve of the issue of rationed foodstuffs, tobacco, and cigarettes. In many cases, these goods were swept away in such quantities as to arouse suspicion that there was already a black market growing steadily for their disposal.

By this time, the German authorities had begun the importation of a number of police officials, who were billeted in the various hotels. They were not apparently connected with the notorious Gestapo at first, but appeared to fulfill the functions of spies upon the civil population, at times making themselves, by their harsh and brutal churlishness, one more terror added to life. They would violently force their way into a place where wireless (at that time officially permitted) was being listened to, and, characterizing the communiqué being broadcast as "lies, lies," would brusquely order it to be turned off. These men would impudently intrude into private conversations, demanding the meaning of some overheard remark made or expression used.

On one occasion at a well-known hotel, one of these blackguards observed that an old lady was wearing a brooch in the form of the familiar badge of the Royal Air Force, which had been given to her by her son. He scowlingly ordered her to remove it, which she naturally refused to do. The German then ordered her husband, a retired Indian judge, to be summoned.

On the latter's arrival, the demand was still more offensively repeated, and the police officer expressed his intention to tear the brooch off the lady's dress if his order were not obeyed. The indignant husband, unfortunately losing his temper, threatened that if this were done, he would knock the policeman down. Whereupon the German, drawing his revolver, called in a subordinate and, violently taking possession of the brooch, arrested the furious judge who was immediately removed on a charge of resisting police authority. He was sentenced to a lengthy term of imprisonment on the Continent. Distraught with grief, his wife took to her bed and died. This incident, and its pathetic sequel, aroused great and widespread indignation.

But spying on the civil population continued and, as time went on, became almost commonplace. It took a variety of forms.

After the final confiscation of wireless receiving sets, every effort was made by the German authorities not only to discover persons who had had the courage to retain them, but also those who communicated wireless intelligence to their friends and neighbors. These latter were often pleasantly accosted in the street by well-dressed persons speaking perfect English. They would be asked in cheery tones if they had had any news that day from one or another of the fighting fronts, or whether or not it was a fact that such and such a city had been taken by the Allies, or again, after lamenting the increasing scarcity of some commodity, whether or not it was still obtainable in England. If a definitely informative reply were elicited, the individual approached would be asked how he came by his knowledge and in all probability would soon find himself undergoing a grueling examination, with disastrous results, before the officials of the Gestapo.

Spies—frequently females—would stand in the milk queues with their jugs and listen to gossip. Conversations in the streets and in omnibuses, in particular, were also liable to be overheard by the ubiquitous German spies. You could not safely refer in any way to the war or to war intelligence outside the security of your home, and not even there if you were unwise enough to employ servants of continental nationality.

There were some misguided individuals who would foolishly carry with them written transcripts of the various wireless communiqués. Upon discovery, or upon denunciation by persons with a grudge (which occasionally happened), such people were dealt with most severely.

Throughout the years of the German occupation of the Channel Islands, the occupying authorities, in Jersey at any rate, received large numbers of anonymous letters from local people denouncing fellow islanders and others for possessing hidden wireless receiving sets. These missives, conceived in a spirit of contemptible spite, frequently resulted in serious consequences to persons accused, whose homes were promptly and thoroughly rummaged from basement to attic. There can be little doubt that spies were tempted by the rewards for denunciations which the German authorities are said to have offered; it was not unknown, it must be regrettably admitted, for one member of a family to denounce another.

Horace Wyatt reports:

We are now in the depths of our second winter of discontent. The weather is unusually severe with alternate rain and heavy snow, and the discomforts of our position are steadily piling up. All gas heaters in the sitting rooms, bedrooms, and passages have been disconnected. Also, all gas-fed apparatus.

Thus gas can only be used for cooking, and the hours at which a supply is available even for this purpose are strictly limited. One result is that those who depend on gas for lighting are left in darkness earlier in the evening. Candles are at a premium and only a few people have any left.

The solid fuel monthly ration for the average house is two two-hundredweights of wood and one of coal or coke, which means restricting fires to one room and then lighting up only when the cold is intense. Hot baths are an almost unheard-of luxury and hot-water bottles cannot be bought. Of course, people are feeling the cold more acutely than normal, while subsisting on a diet almost innocent of fats, meats, and sugars. Very few have any superfluous fat left on them, and for lack of heating our houses are getting clammy and damp.

Nearly everyone has lost a lot of weight. Personally, I have gone down four stone [fifty-six pounds]. But till now many, if not most, of us do not feel any the worse for it. There are certainly some who have positively benefited by the compulsory slimming process. Thus the impossibility of our overeating and having too much to drink has, in fact, done us some good.

The meat ration—including bones, skin, gristle, and offal— was reduced to eight, then to four ounces a week. The male tobacco ration—and tobacco is definitely useful for staying hunger—fluctuates around twenty cigarettes, or the equivalent in pipe tobacco, per week; women get none at all. Other rations also vary from time to time, but the standard is about five pounds of bread, two ounces of sugar, and—until recently—one ounce of tea a week. Now the tea ration has stopped completely and the price of tea in the black market is soaring. Some people are brewing substitutes of grated parsnips and beets, or blackberry leaves. Potatoes are not yet rationed, but there are signs that they will be before long.

Over and above our regular rations we get a sort of "surprise packet" every other week, as the result of our representatives in France. The extras vary in kind and quality. A few examples from recent months are: a cake of (so-called) soap, four ounces of macaroni, two ounces of cooking fat, one pound of jam, one hundred saccharine tablets, three ounces of barley semolina, four ounces of coffee substitute, and a very small tin of tuna fish.

We hardly ever get two extras in one week and sometimes we get none at all. Irregularly, and not as a ration, some Camembert cheeses arrive, but they are often uneatable after such long delay.

It is almost impossible to buy anything in the way of clothing, except for an occasional vest or pair of socks, and the island is beginning to manufacture clog-soled boots and shoes.

Petty restrictions and annoyances are steadily piling up which, I suppose, is only to be expected, taking into account the German love of organization and detail. For instance, we are all "registered" and nobody is allowed to sleep away from home without giving notice. We have to carry our "identity cards" with us everywhere, and a list of the inhabitants of every house must be posted inside the front door. The possibility of aerial bombardment seems to be admitted by an order that all attics be cleared of inflammable material. The rule of the road has been altered from the British to the continental one.

The quality of the occupying troops is not what it was, and they seem to be wavering in their conviction that they have as good as won. But, for all that, their confidence not long ago was such that they fully expected to finish with Russia within two months of the declaration of war. It may be due to the fact that this expectation has been disappointed, like their earlier anticipation of the breakdown of Great Britain, that they seem to be getting more touchy and sensitive.

Recently some girls committed the heinous crime of writing the letter "V" on a wall or pavement. Until they handed themselves over to "justice" and were sent to prison for a considerable spell, platoons of local householders had to patrol the district throughout the night and the locality was temporarily deprived of its wireless sets. The Germans have, by the way, continued the "V" campaign by the *tu quoque* method and have been busily painting "V's" on their buildings and cars—though what the sign can signify in German, I am at a loss to understand.

Gasoline supplies are shorter than ever and the bus services are as curtailed as a Manx cat. One's friends—those of them who are left here—are becoming more and more inaccessible. One feels rather like an animal in a cage. The mere fact that you can't get out makes you want to, and there is always the underlying fear that some day your keeper will forget to bring you your dinner. But the lack of food, to my mind, is far less distressing than the lack of variety of companionship and the terrible inadequacy of communication with anyone outside the islands. Everybody has said, to everyone he knows, everything he thinks about every subject there is to discuss, so often that everybody is rapidly getting sick of everybody else; tempers grow shorter and laughter is nearly extinct.

This to my mind is one of the worst features of the situation; this and the feeling imposed upon us that everything is circumscribed, hampered, supervised, and overheard.

All the days are exactly alike except that Thursdays and Sundays are rather worse than others. On Thursdays the shops close at 12:30 instead of 4:00, and the very limited bus services of other days are further reduced. On Sundays there are no shops and no buses at all. Otherwise all the days are the same. Entrapped on this island, you cannot even break out of bounds and suffer the consequences.

Chapter 15

"Doctors are men just like any others . . . "

In November, 1942, the Sixth Army of the German Wehrmacht stood on the Don, between the Don and the Volga, and in Stalingrad itself. At the end of November the long-expected offensive of the Red army was launched.

Two hundred fifty thousand were encircled when the Russians broke through the flanks of the German positions. Forty-five thousand wounded and sick were flown out to German hospitals by transport planes before the surrender. One hundred thousand fell during the battle, froze, starved to death, or died of diseases; over ninety thousand were taken prisoner. The majority of those captured were wounded, or suffered from frostbite, exhaustion, malnutrition, and sickness. Of these ninety thousand, the weakest stayed behind in Stalingrad.

Dr. Hans Dibold, one who remained, describes their fate. His story begins on January 28, 1942.

Combat groups, decimated units, baggage trains, men of the auxiliary services, sick cases, and wounded, hobbling soldiers with frozen feet wrapped in rags streamed into the city. Not all of them had an order to proceed to an appointed spot as we had. Our last order had read, "The group is to be led into the GPU [Russian political police] building."

That had been five days before. Now we were waiting. What would become of us? The fighting soldier has no idea what the morrow will bring, and in captivity everything is doubly uncertain. Only during the last few days had we felt that we were approaching a different phase. From the open steppes we had entered the ruins of Stalingrad. We were closely hemmed in.

The winter sun peered through the battered dome of the GPU building. There was a cellar below the room under the dome which was accessible by a narrow entrance beyond the edge of the rubbish heap. Dr. Markstein of Danzig was standing there with the interpreter Haszy. I went up to them. We waited for the Russians.

The last German soldiers who were still able to walk had left the building. There had been no capitulation. That there was to be no return of fire was all that we had been told. Our place as doctors was with the sick and wounded. We had hung a small Red Cross flag at the entrance to the cellar. It would be a pointer for anybody to the kind of life we alone had to preserve from now on.

Some days later Karl Markstein, former divisional doctor, was permitted by the Russian captors to visit some of the German medical units remaining in the area. Encountering a colleague, Dr. Fritz Stein of Prague, he asked that both stations—Stein's and his—be transferred to a formerly German-held hospital, which was actually a house adjoining the GPU building. Hans Dibold's narrative continues there:

Two days had passed when a Russian surgeon general accompanied by a German-speaking adjutant turned up and demanded several doctors from the prisoners of war for a hospital in which, he gave us to understand, there were over a thousand wounded with only three doctors to attend them. We reported at once, took a chilly farewell of the others, and went to the main entrance. We were accompanied by Sergeant Major Bätz from Coburg, the medical orderlies Kummer and Franzl from the Wienerwald, and the interpreter Haszy.

We stepped outside. A Russian truck was waiting. The truck stopped. We climbed out and followed the Russians. They swiftly mounted the slope. Halfway up the ravine we came to a small plateau. On the far left of this stood a little bare tree; a stake was driven into the ground beside it, carrying a crooked wooden board with the inscription in red letters: "Prisoner-of-War Hospital 1."

The Russian surgeon general who had conducted us here strode across the plateau to the entrance of a tunnel which opened onto the path at the far right-hand corner. The great opening was framed with timber, and broad wooden steps led some ten yards downward; then at right angles to them a long, dark gallery began, leading off into the hillside to the right. Far inside, to the left, a small, murkily crimson light smoldered. The Russians went in front, lighting the way with electric torches.

We learned that we had arrived at the large hospital to which we now belonged: the one with over a thousand wounded and only three doctors. The doctor in charge, the field surgeon general Schmieden, had been the divisional doctor of an infantry division. Beside him stood Dr. Leitner and Dr. Mayr, who both came from upper Austria. They were joined by a protestant army chaplain named Priesner, and a Major W. At the entrance the interpreter Schlösser and the two medical orderlies Kronenberger and Rosner, both from Vienna, were waiting.

The doctors shook hands with us. Sleeping places were allocated to us. Accompanied by a medical orderly, we stepped back into the gallery and followed it to the left, into the interior. The red light of the tin lamp gleamed somberly on the wall. The flame burned low. The black, tarred walls gleamed stickily. The gallery was scarcely wider than the length of a man's body.

After no more than a few steps we had to take care not to tread on dressings wrapped around frostbitten feet, for the sick were lying right across the gallery, one beside the other, on the bare earth. In the smoke and the dismally crimson glow of light we surmised, rather than saw, that the gallery branched out; everywhere, forms were lying packed close together, wrapped in sooty clothing. From time to time a furious cry of pain arose, either close at hand or far in the depths of the gallery: someone had touched another man's frozen feet or wounded arm.

The medical orderly led us into a spacious side chamber. It was divided by pillars down the middle; with its dark walls, it resembled a morgue. Here the orderlies, water carriers, and kitchen hands lived. We saw that the majority were busy; some were lying down, and of others we heard only their voices.

Our man Kummer fitted up a double-tiered bunk of boards and set it in the far right-hand corner. Dr. Markstein chose the upper berth on the side open to the room, Dr. Stein took the middle place, and I reserved the one by the wall. Kummer, Franzl, and Bätz occupied the lower tier.

As a surgeon, Dr. Stein was assigned to the operating theater. Dr. Markstein and I were put in charge of two galleries each. Dr. Leitner and Dr. Mayr, the two doctors already on the spot, looked after the sick and wounded in the other galleries.

Each of us was given a medical orderly as an assistant. I was allotted Franzl. In a chamber fitted as a dispensary we were each handed a cardboard box without a lid. It contained a small quantity of dressings and medical supplies and a piece of candle. Now we could go to work.

In accordance with the Russian custom, those who worked were given more to eat than those who were not working or who were incapable of work. And, just as in the annex to the GPU, so here in the Timoshenko bunker: Dr. Markstein had to speak up on behalf of the newcomers to obtain for them their fair share of the food. The view still prevailed that only brutal egotism was of any use. It had not been considered that if the community went under, it would drag down individuals with it. Consequently, even our medical work was concentrated on individual cases, and not on improving conditions generally.

Dr. Schmieden was a very fine, fatherly man and a gentleman, and he was undoubtedly a good doctor. But without the requisite authority and without power to issue orders, he no longer carried the necessary weight to overcome the opposition of the commandant, who withdrew all the men fit for work and sent them to Beketovka. The commandant hardly seemed open to any approach. But quite possibly the Russians themselves were not in a position to assure food, light, and warmth to serious cases. To move the sick would certainly have condemned them to death in the conditions of the steppe winter. In all probability it was this consideration that reduced Dr. Schmieden to inactivity.

But the Russians soon came to regard this inactivity as evidence of our ill will, and even of a deliberate intention to let the prisoners die in order to deprive the Soviet state of labor and so do it injury.

For a long time we had no suspicions whatsoever that the

Russians were thinking along these lines. We only realized that they quite seriously believed we were deliberately and consciously letting our comrades die when they openly accused us of it. They did not understand that the incredible conditions were the consequences of incredible hardships, of a complete breakdown. They suspected ill will and inefficiency. Only when we finally learned how to make ourselves understood did our medical work have any success.

From that moment, we knew we could count on the Russians' help. They, on the other hand, knew they could count on our unconditional cooperation. But we still had to travel a long road before this understanding was achieved.

Our immediate task was to compile a list of the patients as they lay in rows along the galleries. Then we had to visit our sick and wounded cases routinely twice a day, and whenever necessary to attend to their dressings, give them medicine, and convey the operation cases to the theater. The lists had to be revised every day; the names of the dead had to be struck out and the removals noted.

So I set out to write down the names of my patients. Franzl carried the light and the box with the dressings and medicines. We walked along, stooping, for the patients lay flat on the ground and could hardly raise themselves up; their voices were hoarse and faint.

My ears were ringing with the continual cry of "Doctor, Doctor!" I was called by the men I had already visited and those I still had to visit. The light traveled with us. For both sides, apart from a sip of boiled water, the brief moment in which our eyes met those of our patients were the only comfort we had then.

So we labored, passed from one case to another, gave comfort, administered powders to ease pain and to induce sleep, bandaged frozen feet, checked our lists, and preached patience.

Our patients grew worse and worse each day. Fungi began to flourish on the louse-bitten, sweaty, filthy skin, which formed blisters and peeled off. In places where there was no muscle between the skin and the bone—none of the patients had any fat—ulcers developed. Tetanus set in the wounds. The spasms did not last long. Too weak even to have spasms, the cases soon closed their eyes in peace. Then the dressings and medicines began to run short. Though our patients were in great pain, we could more and more rarely afford to change dressings. And we issued all we had left of our analgesia and sleeping powders. Wherever we could manage it, frostbitten toes were amputated.

It was difficult to get the patients through the overcrowded galleries to the operating theater without inflicting further torments on those lying on the floor. The bearers' strength began to flag.

In the operating theater Dr. Leitner and Dr. Stein worked turn about with two orderlies by the light of smoking lamps. Before long they both had to summon up their last nervous and physical reserves in order to remain at their posts.

When our morning labors were ended, we went to our sleeping quarters to eat. We drank our tea or the watery soup, ate our piece of bread; only rarely did we have herring to add to it. If there was still free time, we tried to lie down for a minute or two. Usually the furious itching goaded us to our feet again, and we deloused ourselves by the gloomy light of the tin lamp. We would soon set off again to make a round of the galleries. Every time we went, we were tormented by the anguish of being unable to help. We heard men call "Doctor," but we knew no answer.

On one occasion it became too much for me. I tried to postpone my tour of the galleries but then my eyes fell on my medical orderly, Franzl. He was younger and weaker than I, and he had been ill since the first battle of the winter; he lacked the medical man's sense of his duty, which should have kept me going. But the short, sickly youth was on his feet before me, and picked up the light and the medical box; he was ready without saying a word. I felt ashamed, got a grip on myself, and followed him.

We went with bowed backs to our comrades. The farther we penetrated into the interior of the bunker, the more space there was between one patient and the next. Where the western gallery branched off, a chilly dampness mingled loathsomely with the vitiated air. Water was streaming from the black walls. A traverse gallery led off to the right, which was darker, dryer, and more stuffy than the others. Here the sick were lying together in groups.

They were not really in my charge, but Dr. Mayr's. But on some days Dr. Mayr would not have yet visited them. So it was I to whom they called and implored. I must attend to their dressings, I must give them medicine, I must not pass them by. But I didn't have enough medicine, nor dressings, nor did I have the time or strength to look after them as well as my own patients. All I could do was to give one or two of them powders, say a kindly word, or appeal to their common sense.

Just beyond the point where the traverse gallery branched off, an old engineer from Vienna was lying. His features conveyed something of the worldly-wise sadness that sometimes ennobles the expression of the Viennese, who outwardly seem to be a gay people. As I passed him I thought of the city in which my dear ones were living, and all the brightness of a past day of pleasant charm. I went on wearily. The distant glow dimmed. At the end of the gallery the flame flickered low, and breathing became difficult. Only a few more men lay in the innermost corner.

By the evening our work and our strength were both at an end. We sank down in our bunks and waited for the lice. Our greatcoats served as sheets, our coats as coverlets, and our linen bags as pillows. My mosquito net hung on the wall. In it I dried the sticky bread before eating it.

At the beginning of winter, during the encirclement, my wife had sent me a dozen candles. A young lieutenant of artillery, Dr. Eymannsberger, had brought them with him when he flew in just before Christmas. A few days later he was killed, trying to take his howitzer forward to engage an attacking Russian tank in direct fire.

I gave half the candles to a group of my medical corpsmen as a Christmas present. On Christmas Eve they lit up their foxhole with them, in the Rossoshka valley. In Gumrak the entire group was wiped out by a bomb dropped from a plane.

I kept the rest of the candles. They gave me light at Christmas and at the turn of the New Year. Now I had only one or two left, so I was sparing in my use of them. Sometimes I lit this small light from home, and we fell to talking. Dr. Stein said, "If you want to come through the imprisonment, we must reckon on it lasting five years."

I agreed with him. And so in fact it did—for me.

Thus the days and nights passed. From time to time we went up into the open air for five minutes in the wintry cold. Once I met the commandant, who halted and recited a Russian poem about spring to me in a singsong tone. When he had ended, he threw an ecstatic glance at the naked little tree on the edge of the small plateau, then turned to me and said:

"Go and work, go and work!"

But I remained standing there for a moment longer. From the traverse road on the ravine side I caught a glimpse of the Volga. It was icebound.

Mortality among the sick and wounded increased. We were still without conclusive proof that typhus had broken out, but we noted more and more frequent cases of high fever, delirium, and pains in the head. During the evening talks with Dr. Schmieden, typhus and the plague of lice were almost the only topics of conversation.

I said to him, "By the time we come upon an absolute certainty among the many highly suspicious cases, twenty or thirty others will have caught it. That means the whole bunker will get it in a matter of weeks."

Like many regular military doctors, Dr. Schmieden was afraid of diagnosing an infectious disease a single day too soon. Instead, he asked, "But what will the Russians do if it really is typhus?"

One evening the interpreter Haszy reported sick. He was feverish and his mind was wandering. I diagnosed the characteristic typhus eruption, swollen spleen, and red eyes. A medical orderly went to Dr. Schmieden and declared that the patients were persecuting him. He, too, was running a fever. Men fell seriously ill whose conditions shortly before had passed as fit. Now Dr. Schmieden admitted that typhus was the only possible cause.

The Russians had not reckoned with a typhus epidemic on the scale to which it developed. This was proved by the fact that they did not more thoroughly isolate the doomed German army, and that they began to organize the fight against the epidemic rather belatedly.

But the new war waged far and wide across the Soviet western provinces. The disease laid waste town and country, displaced masses of people, and broke down all the natural boundaries which are the strongest defense against epidemics. As soon as the fronts came to a standstill at the onset of winter, typhus broke out. The native population frequently had only light attacks, but the soldiers had them more severely and were affected in much greater quantity.

The Germans commented, "We never had lice or typhus till we came to Russia. Such things do not exist in Germany."

The Russians said, "You brought typhus with you. We never had typhus cases before the war."

No wonder that it was difficult to organize a common struggle against the epidemic when the two sides were of such contrary opinions as to its origin.

The Russians eventually evacuated all typhus cases from the Timoshenko bunker, and Hans Dibold and his colleagues, who were also stricken with disease and fever, moved from the bunker galleries to Hospital 2B. It was here that a glimmer of under-standing and cooperation between the Russians and the German doctors began.

As soon as I was free of the fever, I fitted up a small sick bay in the inner bunker. In it we put the most serious typhus cases. One evening Dr. Deichel walked into the cellar more hurriedly than usual and announced:

"By tomorrow morning a history must be drawn up of every case. [The Armenian commandant] Blinkov's orders—otherwise we'll be shot, and so forth."

The case histories proved to be of great service to us. They provided us with documentary proof which helped us when putting the case for the patients. It was more or less at that time that our cooperation with the Soviet doctors began.

So far as we doctors were concerned, the whole question was one of winning the Russians' trust. Could we establish our work on a basis of facts and truth? We had two incorruptible collaborators: the Soviet doctors and the GPU, from whom we could expect justice if we succeeded in proving that we were right.

We heard the words, "You're treating the patients badly,"

time and time again. They were said quite seriously by people who themselves were not medically trained. Later on the time would come when we would be able to refute this charge.

Meanwhile, new threats arose. At the end of May, while typhus was still rampant, scurvy and malaria broke out. Dysentery and other intestinal complaints carried off victims every day. In addition to all this, we were faced with the menacing and fearful specter of death by starvation. Finally tuberculosis began to develop.

Soon after the German doctors and their patients made another move to Hospital 4, at Easter time, 1943, the anti-doctor offensive reached a climax. An open accusation of medical neglect and abuses prompted Hans Dibold's suggestion for a doctors' conference to study the high mortality rate and how to combat it.

It had been summer for a long time. Every day the sky was blue above the sand and the ruins, the barbed wire and the green of the steppe. The westerly wind blew fresh air and cooled our hot, thin bodies. The orderlies brought into the open air every man who could be moved.

The day appointed for the doctors' conference arrived. It was fixed for three in the afternoon. We had a room in Block 3 freshly done up for the occasion. The Russian staff had been invited and had agreed to come.

On the morning of that very day a Russian commission turned up. It consisted of a surgeon major who had charge of all the prisoner-of-war hospitals in the Stalingrad district, a professor of the Stalingrad outpatient hospital, and an officer. The commission scrutinized the sick wards and the hospital equipment very closely. We mentioned the forthcoming conference and all three promised to be present.

When the commission arrived, they settled down in front of us at the tables which had been intended for the speakers' use. Each speaker addressed himself to the commission and though it may have been difficult for the Russians to understand the speeches in German, they listened attentively.

The head physician opened the meeting. He welcomed the commission and went on to say that the conference had been called with the approval of the political commissar, in order to consider ways of reducing the high mortality rate among the cases in our hospital. He called on Dr. _____, who was to be the main speaker that day. And Dr. _____ spoke.

"There is no such thing as a hospital where nobody dies. Before we ask ourselves why a large number of cases are not cured, but instead die, we must ask the question: Why and how did these men fall ill? Only when that has been answered can we go on to ask if the treatment is responsible for their deaths.

"The men in this hospital have fallen ill because they have been infected with typhus, dysentery, and other intestinal diseases, and because they have suffered serious shock and hardship owing to the war and their imprisonment. They starved and froze, they could not endure the climate. They received food which was inadequate and to which they were not accustomed, and they did not get enough vitamins. They had to be housed in dark cellars and holes in the ground, they had no change of underwear and no clothes, and it was impossible for them to keep themselves clean.

"Many of them had been wounded and the wounds did not heal. Many of them had frostbite which could not be treated, and there were many other deleterious factors at work. That is why the men of this hospital fell ill. That is why most must be considered serious cases, and that is why the majority of these serious cases die.

"All these causes can be summed up in one word: War!

"What can the doctors do to combat this? They can try with the simple means available to recognize the nature of the complaint in good time. They can isolate the infectious cases. They can tend the sick and treat them, to raise their physical powers of resistance.

"But if we have to put our serious cases in cellars, on wooden floors, on bunks, on bare iron bedsteads, and on old blankets—if we have to give patients with high fever millet soup, salt, fish, and black bread because we have nothing else and cannot let them starve—if we are deprived of the sulfonamides we need to save patients suffering from dysentery and pneumonia—if we cannot get hydrochloric acid to combat diarrhea—then we doctors have no responsibility for the high mortality rate. Of course we make mistakes like any other doctors and any other men. But we must refuse to be saddled with the guilt for the high mortality. We accuse no one. It is wartime, and transport conditions are very bad. There you have the true causes of the high mortality."

The doctor spoke earnestly, quietly, and firmly, but not in an unfriendly tone. The Russian professor listened to him closely. The surgeon major wiped the sweat from his brow once or twice, but betrayed no reaction. The officer did not stir. Once or twice the major sent an orderly to see that there was more quiet in the house.

Now our surgeon spoke. He explained that even small wounds and superficial ulcers would not heal because our patients' bodies no longer had the strength to get rid of morbid tissues, or to renew the healthy ones. Then the dermatologist described the skin troubles of our dystrophic cases and mentioned the causes. Our consultant surgeon spoke on tuberculosis.

I was the last to speak:

"The course of an illness depends on a number of factors, among them the manner in which a patient's body is constituted —his inherited constitution and also what Tandler called his condition, meaning his present state dependent on his living conditions. The condition of our patients is as bad as can be. The term 'mesotrophy' might be applied to their body cells, cells which are no longer being renewed. They are aging and dying off. It is not the least surprising that our patients frequently exhibit states which we formerly associated only with old people. But old men, and old—in other words, prematurely aged—organisms die in greater numbers than the young. That is well known. And that, unfortunately, also applies to our patients."

The professor nodded his agreement several times.

After a brief discussion, the medical superintendent closed the meeting.

We had expressed our views clearly to the Russians. The major, the professor, and the officer departed. They made no contribution to the conference.

But it soon turned out that at the conference we had won their complete trust. From that day they helped us as much as possible. They often visited us and they felt at home with us.

They had learned that we were doing our best, and in Stalingrad we never again heard the charge, "You are treating your patients badly."

Doctors are men just like any others and, in the misery of Stalingrad, they frequently became patients, too. But those who at that time were too fearful or selfish to help missed the greatest opportunity of their professional lives.

Whenever we diagnosed a disease which we had never come across before, but which we had learned about at home from excellent professors, we felt all the thrill of a successful explorer. We could be deprived of all we possessed, but anything we had once learned, nobody could take from us. We had many a burden, yet we felt rich at times, poor though we were.

When at sunset we gazed across the green steppe, or when before retiring for the night we stood at the door and watched the stars come up, or when through the empty window frame of our room we cast a glance at the Volga, into our hearts crept a feeling of strength and happiness we had not known before. This will no more leave us for all the rest of our lives than will the great seriousness and the quiet sorrow of the time. This is the way men feel who have experienced much and who know they have stood the test.

No sorrow is without joy!

Chapter 16

"Hell has broken loose . . . "

Late in the war, Operation Thunderclap appeared to be a leaf torn by the Allies from the Nazis' book of terror: the saturation bombing of cities. Thunderclap was endowed with the dignity of codification in response to demands—at least implicit—to support the accelerating westward Russian offensive.

A further wallop to the remaining morale of the Germans appeared fully justified strategically to the military tacticians in London, even if the targets did not necessarily encompass important rail yards, factories, and barracks.

Dresden became Thunderclap's first victim. This famed art center was packed with people by 1945: one and a half million all told, including refugees, migrant and captive workers, and even Allied prisoners of war. Its peacetime population had at least doubled. Dresden was a rail and highway junction between east and west, as well as an area containing or adjacent to some industry—although not in a class with Düsseldorf, Stuttgart, Cologne, Darmstadt, Schweinfurt, Frankfurt and other names synonymous with heavy manufacturing.

It became a matter of some debate, later, just why Dresden was visited by successive waves of bombers, first British, then American, that pre-Lenten Tuesday, February 13, 1945. In retrospect Winston Churchill himself, one of the originators of Thunderclap, was hard put to justify the overwhelming assault.

But it had happened. And some lived to recount the horror.

Among these was a Swiss resident, a wartime employee of the city who was to remain nameless. However, his graphic account was later translated by a surgeon in Dresden, Dr. A. V. Borosini.

I had paid a visit on my bicycle to friends who were living in one of the suburbs east of the Elbe (Lössnitz) and was caught outside the city when the alarm was sounded. The nearest shelter I knew about was a restaurant several hundred meters away, but because of the storm my progress was very slow.

The first waves were roaring over me before I could reach that house, and when I saw that these planes were dropping light signals I realized to my horror that this meant a "surface bombardment." A carpet was being marked out. I still saw the big twin-motor planes which formed the advance force, as I stormed into the inn and its cellar. The attack was on.

In spite of being quite a distance from Dresden, we could hear the planes roaring over the town. They made a truly hellish noise, mixed now with that of the first explosions. Every time one of the big bombers seemed to be headed straight toward us and we expected in the next moment to hear the crash of an explosion in our immediate neighborhood, we realized shortly afterward that the machine had flown away again. Obviously, we were out of the zone of attack.

It was about half-past nine in the evening when the first wave approached. None of us in the cellar had a dependable watch, but I am certain that not five minutes had elapsed when I decided that I could not bear it any longer down there and ventured into the open. My family was as far distant from the center of Dresden westward of the Elbe as I was eastward at the moment, and I was now certain that nothing would happen to them. But I felt that I must reach them as soon as possible.

When I got outside I felt my way toward my bicycle, mounted, and rode several hundred meters farther until I had an unobstructed view over the whole town. The night had been dark when I went into that inn; all had been quiet, and the howling of the storm within the birch trees and pines had only accentuated the tranquillity. Now it sounded as if hell had erupted, because amid the ear-piercing roar of the low-flying bombers came an increasing number of explosions. It was a noise beyond the grasp of the senses, and all I remember is that I thought: Hell has broken loose!

And then I saw the rising of a flaming sea which, within a few minutes, inundated the entire city in one huge glowing wave.

From Loebtau to Blasewitz [sections of Dresden's Old Town, famed for its beautiful monuments and buildings], the entire area was in flames.

Huge red and yellow tongues of fire were roaring toward the sky. Streaming, trembling, madly onrushing clouds—dark brown, grayish yellow, red and white masses of smoke, which the storm whipped past the burning town only to have them replaced by new ones—intermingled with brilliant white, red, and yellow explosions out of which the big bombers seemed to rise like flocks of giant birds on their flight from hell. But they did not flee.

Like roaring creatures of fury and crazy beasts of destruction, no longer like engines, they leaped back into the sky only to make room for new waves which came behind them. The most agonizing nightmare could not approach the ghastly, paralyzing scene or whip up the mind to frenzy like this fascinating and horrible spectacle of Dresden's eclipse that took place before my eyes.

No pen is capable of describing the effect of such a holocaust upon a human being. Without ever having been through a big air raid before, I knew at once that here something quite different was happening, something which had not happened to any other German town. Here were no particular targets, no selected quarters. This time the raid was aimed at the destruction, the blotting out, of an entire city.

Imagine if a terrain such as the entire Manhattan district of New York should go up in flames within a few minutes, and someone should attempt to describe the picture and what he felt while looking at the blaze. I only know that I did not understand what my eyes were seeing. I stood in the darkness, paralyzed, numbed, with my eardrums aching from the hellish uproar of a night of death; but, in spite of the feverish activity within my brain, which undoubtedly existed, I did not grasp the meaning of what had happened. It was simply beyond comprehension, beyond the wildest imagination. It seemed actually unreal.

I shall never know how I found my way home that night. I vaguely remember that I went for hours through woods; that I ran, rode my bicycle, fell over roots, screamed, called, found my bicycle again, and went back and forth, seemingly without any sense of direction. When the first attack was over and I realized

that I had to get home under all circumstances, I already knew
that Dresden could not be saved. These waves and waves of fire-
spitting planes which had raced over the town had set everything
afire, everything in the word's most literal meaning. Dresden
was finished.

When the second attack came, there was no warning from
any sirens because the entire power system had broken down.
When the second holocaust, this mad dance of the elements,
began and still more fire and still more bombs rained down on
the already doomed city, I looked, silent and unmoved, down
from the hills of Lössnitz and thought, Now it will be completed.
This time there were at least five hundred four-motor planes at
work. Again the attack lasted only twenty minutes; again there
were about the same number of waves, which seemed to throw
themselves headlong into the flaming sea. Again, not a single
antiaircraft gun was firing, not a single night fighter had taken
off to attempt a counterattack. I knew that this meant the end,
but at that time I did not know how gruesome it had been for
those who had been overtaken by the catastrophe.

I rode twice through Dresden on my bicycle after the thir-
teenth of February, and what I saw was so ghastly that the pen
simply refuses to describe it. Since comparatively few explosive
bombs had fallen on the town, it was not too difficult to get
through. There were only a few bomb craters, but the nonex-
plosive bombs did not penetrate the paved or asphalted streets;
the fire had wrought the destruction.

Even the victims in the Grosser Garten were not torn to
pieces by explosive bombs, but were slain by a million incendiary
sticks which had been thrown down over that park.

Ten days after the attack, the mountains of bodies had not
been disposed of, in spite of the fact that big trucks had been
put into service to carry the dead as quickly as possible to the
mass graves. No one was taking the trouble to identify the
bodies. They were simply loaded into these trucks, often together
with debris and ashes.

I rode through this world of ruins, pushing my cycle over
beaten fragments, bricks, and debris, fighting my way through
the strange jungle and trying to get some orientation. Quarters
in which I had gotten to know every house, where I had found

my way on a dark night by means of familiar landmarks, I simply did not recognize in plain daylight.

The old part of Dresden—the town's center, the sections near the Postplatz, Pragerstrasse, the streets between the Central Station and the Porticus—had been so utterly destroyed that literally no house remained untouched. All this had been caused by fire.

Where some house fronts still stood, seemingly intact, it became obvious that they hid only empty, burned-out shells. The royal castle, the Catholic church, the world-famous Hotel Bellevue—all were in ruins. Half of the tower of the royal castle was gone. The celebrated tower of the Catholic church, that unforgettable work of Chiaveri which many art historians call the most elegant tower in the world, was still standing. In the no less famous Zwinger there remained some walls and a few facades, but they stood only as ruins above the debris.

Had it not been too dangerous to take pictures, I could have obtained some quite unbelievable photographs of the extent of the destruction. For instance, I saw the double T-girders of a building block erected in the nineties at the Albertplatz in Dresden-Neustadt, lying about coiled together like curlers. These iron girders were one meter high and wide, a size never again employed. I saw actual rows of streets in the center of the city filled with debris. It was obvious that there no one had escaped. In this section alone tens of thousands must have perished.

The vastness of the destruction within the Altstadt by the second wave of attack became clear to me from what I had heard from an SS man. Because the sirens no longer functioned, a few survivors of the first attack were trying to flee from the fire within the inner city when the second attack started.

This man had been among these people and had succeeded in reaching the Postplatz. When the first new waves came, he threw himself to the ground to be at least partially covered and grabbed the iron grating of the street drain beside the sidewalk with both hands. He needed all of his strength and will power to do so, because the fire suction which came from all the burning streets was so powerful that the people were drawn into the fire like dried leaves.

Whole districts the size of District 1 in Zurich—or the older part of Boston—were still inaccessible five to six days later. Even the lovely houses around the Grosser Garten had all been razed to the ground, and this wonderful park had become a grave for more than ten thousand individuals. Here, however, I did not depend on hearsay. I saw what had happened with my own eyes.

I rode one day to look up some Swiss friends and on my way had to pass through the Stübelallee in which the Gauleiter Mutschmann had had his fashionable residence. This thoroughfare consisted of two broad, four-lane streets; between them ran a promenade twelve feet wide, on either side of which there was a strip of lawn of a similar width. This huge thoroughfare was almost impassable, and the aspect of heaps of corpses everywhere was so ghastly that I did not wish to repeat the experience. On my return, therefore, I took the route through the Grosser Garten, never imagining that this was even worse.

Outwardly, one did not see much change there. The bridle paths, the promenades, and the little waterways of this famous baroque park seemed perfectly intact, with only here and there a fallen tree. It was all the more shocking to encounter with almost every step bodies scattered about, torn arms and legs, torsos without heads, and heads torn from their bodies which had rolled away like bowling balls. In some places the corpses were lying so thick that one had to push them aside in order to avoid stepping on arms and legs.

The Palais at the Grosser Garten, one of the most beautiful baroque buildings in existence, was of course destroyed. All restaurants and pavilions, the exposition halls, and the zoo had simply disappeared. Having once been present at a day attack near the Heller [a group of buildings in the middle of a big forest near Dresden] without getting hurt, I could understand what must have happened in the Grosser Garten.

The problem of getting transportation from Dresden to Otterwitsch, an insignificant, out-of-the-way little place, was appalling. We could not walk that distance, both because my wife was in her last months of pregnancy and because of our three small children. None of our friends who still had cars at their disposal could transport us, for lack of gasoline.

By what seemed a miracle, I succeeded in chartering a one-horse carriage to Radebeul at the cost of one kilogram (a little more than two pounds) of coffee. That does not seem much, but

I could have sold that coffee for at least two hundred marks (the equivalent of fifty dollars). We left our house at midday Saturday, but it was nightfall before we crossed the town; we did not arrive in Radebeul until Sunday morning, though the distance was only fifteen kilometers.

The whole railway system was in utter confusion and chaos. We were lucky enough to get tickets and seats on a train and arrived after a harrowing journey at Grossboten on the evening of February 25. This station, where our train stopped "for good," is about twenty-five miles from Leipzig. We found a train to Leipzig and from there were able to get a train to Bitterfeld, where we were to meet a train from Berlin, which was to take us to Konstanz.

The train from Berlin which was to take us to Konstanz was due at half-past seven in the evening. At 2:30 A.M. we saw it approach what was left of the station. During the hours of waiting we had fled twice with all our luggage into a nearby bunker because of repeated air raids on Bitterfeld. Now we stood with our children in the dark of night, chilled to our bones and trembling with fear, between the torn-up rails which represented the station. Thank God the moon was shining through the clouds, and we had no need to fear that one of the children might be lost in the dark. When we were actually inside the train, we breathed a sigh of relief, but that sigh was premature.

We had left our house at midday, February 24, but we did not reach Swiss soil until March 4. It took nine days for a journey which in prewar days did not require quite twenty hours.

The toll at Dresden will never be accurately known. Estimates vary all the way from 35,000 to 135,000. In all likelihood, many more perished in Dresden than later in Hiroshima.
Thunderclap could not be reflected upon by the Allies with pride.

Part 4
Prison Camps and Atrocities

Chapter 17

"I always found people who needed me . . . "

The many explosive ingredients which were finally to combine for World War II were in evidence long before September, 1939. Nazism, fascism, and communism were out of the test tubes and fulminating in both the '20s and the '30s. In the case of Germany's National Socialism, however, its chrysalis was primarily in Adolf Hitler's evil brain in the '20s or in the minds of his Brownshirt nucleus, waiting only for the next decade to spill over and infect an entire nation.

Two of many Europeans caught in this ideological vortex were Heinz and Margarete Buber-Neumann, active German Communists.

This is her story, in part:

From 1921 to 1932 I was a loyal member of the Communist party of Germany. In 1931 I was sent to Moscow as a delegate for my fellow employees in a big Berlin department store. When I returned to Germany I reported the splendid successes of socialist construction I had seen, and I presented a red satin flag embroidered in gold with the words "Workers of All Countries Unite" at a meeting of those who had sent me.

In 1935 my husband, Heinz Neumann, and I were ordered to Moscow by the Comintern. From 1928 to 1935 Heinz was one of the leaders of the German Communist party—until, in fact, he came into opposition to the deplorable policy of Stalin toward Germany.

When Heinz was charged with "political deviation" and removed from leadership of the German party, he was first of all sent to Spain as a political instructor. That was in 1932. Toward the end of 1933 he was ordered to Switzerland as a translator. In 1934 he was arrested by the Swiss police because his papers were not in order. The Nazis, who had in the meantime come to power in Germany, lodged a request for his extradition, and it was then that he was invited to Moscow. He was taken under police surveillance through France to a port and placed aboard a Soviet ship. I accompanied him.

From 1935 to 1937 we both worked in Moscow as translators. During these two years we were already political outcasts and really prisoners in all but name. Our every movement was watched and everything we did in public was noted. In April, 1937, he was finally arrested by the NKVD—the Soviet secret police, better known as the GPU.

In June, 1938, my turn came.

She spent three months in a detention prison awaiting the charges for her "crime," and then she waited again, until late that winter, before receiving her sentence.

A fortnight later I was called out for my fourth examination. It was a different room and examiner, a man who spoke only Russian. He handed me a document on which was written: "The examination has established the guilt of the prisoner, Margarete Genrichovna Buber-Neumann, who conducted counterrevolutionary agitation and organization against the Soviet State." At first I thought perhaps I had misunderstood what was written there, but he confirmed that there was no mistake. The examination had established my guilt.

I went up to the desk and the GPU officer handed me a typewritten sheet of paper.

"Can you read Russian?" he asked. I nodded.

"Good enough to read this?"

There was that ridiculous name again: "Margarete Genrichovna Buber-Neumann." And my social status: "Socially dangerous element." And the sentence: "Five years' reformatory labor in a camp." [This turned out to be the Siberian concentration camp, Karaganda.]

We came to a fixed railway carriage without wheels, in which prisoners were kept until the transports could be put together. Before we went in, Nadia Bereakina [another prisoner], who was more experienced than me, whispered, "You mustn't say you're a political; say you're a prostitute or a thief." I had no time to ask why, and we were hustled through the door into a long compartment separated down the middle by a wire netting which reached to the ceiling.

We stood helplessly about. There seemed no room for us anywhere. Only Nadia had managed to find a place to sit. Now I understood her whispered advice. For a prostitute, they were prepared to move up, but not for a political.

On one occasion [at Karaganda] I was working in a gang, sorting out frozen potatoes. We stood in the potato dump, a gloomy moldy place, and searched in the icy mess for potatoes which might still be eatable. Next to me a criminal was working. Probably she was as tired and disgusted with the work as I was, but her reactions were different; she kicked me in the ankle irritably. At first I thought it must have been an accident, but I couldn't see how.

"What's that for?" I asked in some astonishment. Her only reply was to kick me again, and this time there was no doubt about the intention.

I protested angrily, and immediately she struck me in the face. Boiling with indignation, I went for her and in a moment we were engaged in a fierce scuffle. The others pulled us apart. The "brigadier" of the gang was a political.

"Grete," he hissed in my ear, "be careful. Don't get into trouble with the criminals. It's dangerous." He knew, of course, that I could not have started the trouble, and he seized the offender and hustled her off. She then flung herself to the ground and indulged in a fit of hysteria, kicking and shrieking. They pulled her to her feet, still kicking, and dragged her up the cellar steps into the fresh air.

I stood there almost in tears from humiliation, now that my anger had drained out of me; but suddenly another woman came up to me, and before I realized her intentions she had hit me between the eyes, so that I literally saw stars. My blood rose again at this second unprovoked attack and I gave her a blow every bit as good as she had given me. In an instant the second fight was on.

My unknown enemy shrieked and cursed and threatened to kill me. We were soon separated and the other woman was hustled off in her turn. My brigadier was very upset.

"Why did that have to happen?" he said in despair. "That was Tania, the bosom friend of Djura, the first woman. She's one of the most dangerous furies in the camp. If she says she'll kill you, she will, if we're not careful."

I was depressed by the whole disgusting business, but he seemed to attach more importance to the scuffle than it warranted. However, the politicals decided that I was not to go out alone again; if I went to the latrines, I must always be accompanied by someone. I consented to this unwillingly and I carried it out strictly for a while, but it was a burden.

After about a week, when nothing had happened and the thing seemed to have been forgotten, I went out to the latrines alone. There was snow on the ground and there was only a narrow path to the latrines. While I was still a little distance away a woman came toward me, and I recognized Tania. I would not show my fear by turning around and going back, and as she came close I stepped to one side in the snow to let her pass. My legs were trembling and my whole body was alert for an attack. She stopped.

"Have you got a fag?" she asked.

"No," I said. She looked at me for a moment.

"Oh! It's you, is it? Well, never mind. Forget it. I've forgotten it."

In 1940, Mrs. Buber-Neumann was handed over to the German Gestapo during the period of the Russian-German friendship pact.

On Saturday, August 2, we started off for Ravensbrück. There were fifty women in the group and we went by prison coach from Stettiner railway station in Berlin. My anxiety and depression and fear of what was to come were so great that I hardly remember any of the women who shared the narrow compartment of the prison coach with me.

The train stopped at Fürstenberg in Mecklenburg.

Outside the station were two covered lorries, and we were rushed along to them and herded in as though the loss of a single minute would be fatal. The shouting and bullying were obviously part of a deliberate plan to frighten and intimidate us. Our "reeducation" had begun.

After a short drive, we came to a gate. The woman in charge handed a list to the guard, who counted us, and then the gate swung back and we were hustled through into the concentration camp Ravensbrück.

Everything at Ravensbrück was done with typical Prussian thoroughness. A prisoner was passed from hand to hand until every detail was complete and she had become a permanent inmate—registered, photographed, listed, and uniformed. After we had gone through all this, we were taken to the washroom which was fitted with showers. We had to undress and wash ourselves under the showers, and all our things were taken away.

The attendants were in white. They were also prisoners, and on their arms they wore a small triangular cloth whose color indicated their status: red for politicals; lilac for Bible students (or Jehovah's Witnesses); red and yellow in the shape of a star for political Jews; black and yellow for Jews who had been guilty of "racial offenses"; black triangles for asocials; and green for criminals.

After our clothing had been taken away, the long-feared procedure of looking for lice began. When it was all over we were left sitting around the room on benches, naked and shivering with cold, waiting for the next procedure. It was a medical examination, and a pitiful travesty it was.

After this "entrance examination," we were given prison clothes: a shift of coarse material, ridiculously long knickers, the striped dress we had already seen, a blue apron, and a white cloth to bind round our heads. In this rig we were marched barefoot to the accompaniment of much shouting to Block 16, which was the block for new arrivals.

When we had finally gone through the long and complicated process of registration, I received the triangular piece of red stuff with a number which stamped me as a political and a regular inmate. The Block Senior (prisoner-warden) then instructed us in the way to show proper respect to the SS officials. As soon as addressed, we had to spring to attention with our arms close to our sides and say smartly, "Protective Custody Prisoner X——. Y——. No——." My number was 4208.

Forty-two hundred women lived there in sixteen huts in 1940. At that time Ravensbrück had only one street of huts, but later there were three. In addition to the living huts, there were huts for clothing and utensils, two tailor workshops, two sick bays, and a large laundry. The camp square was surrounded by the kitchen huts, the offices of the SS commandant, the baths, an SS canteen, the aviary, and the prison block.

The Ravensbrück camp lay in a hollow. To the north beyond the camp wall was a rise of sandy land on which grew a few stunted pines. Toward the south the ground sank gradually and ended in a morass. Later this was incorporated into the camp, filled in, and built over with further huts.

The first block which had been built in this way gradually sank into the soft ground, and in order to lessen the weight, the second block was left without a proper roof and covered instead with tarpaulin sheets. Toward the end the overcrowding was very bad, and to add to the miseries of the prisoners, the drainage was constantly overflowing. In the summer months the huts in this low-lying part of the camp were permanently surrounded by a cloaca of filth which froze hard in the winter.

A small concentration camp for male prisoners, holding about one thousand men, abutted our ground. In the west, behind the buildings of the *Kommandantur* [local headquarters] outside the prison wall, lay Fürstenberg Lake. Prisoners who were sent outside the camp to work declared that it was surrounded on all sides by water and marshland.

During my years of incarceration I had ample opportunity for seeing my fellow human beings without their normal civilized mask. It is not so easy to watch oneself. When people ask me how I managed to survive seven years of concentration camps in Russia and Germany, I can only say that, apart from the fact that my physical condition was always good and my nerves well balanced, I never let myself slide into a state where I lost my self-respect. And above all, I survived because I always found people who needed me. Again and again I made friends. It is only under such conditions that the true meaning of friendship can be learned.

Apart from the real criminal and asocial elements, most of the women were ordinary human beings—housewives, mothers, and young girls who differed very little, if at all, from the housewives, mothers, and young girls outside the camps. In the first years there were very few conscious enemies of the regime in the camps—just the "old" politicals and the Bible students. Later their number was increased by women from the resistance movements in the occupied countries. These latter women found it easier to stand the camp life. They had fought for a cause and the fact that they were now in a concentration camp was proof of their danger to National Socialism. It strengthened their self-respect and helped them to hold their heads high.

But the majority of the prisoners were "innocent"; they were unable to understand why this terrible fate had befallen them at all. Each of these prisoners hung with all her being to the memory of what she had left behind: her husband, her children, her home. And here she was now, despairing and helpless in a concentration camp, with no knowledge of how long she would have to stay there. She was drilled like a soldier and made to react like an automaton. At no time of the day or night was she ever alone. Everything she did was done in the company of others. At every step, at every word, she came up against strangers—strangers who were suffering as she was. Among the hundreds in her hut there would be perhaps one or two to whom she felt attracted, but the majority she would find odious and intolerable in all their ways and habits.

She was made to work excessively hard; she was half-starved; she was made to stand still and freeze. And it even happened that she, an adult human being—whether an older woman, a mother, or a young girl—would be shouted at, bullied, and even beaten.

Every newcomer in a concentration camp goes through a terrible period in which she is shaken to the core, no matter how strong her physique or how calm her nerves. The suffering of the newcomers became worse and worse each year in Ravensbrück, and in consequence the death rate was highest among them. According to character, it would take weeks, months, or even years before a prisoner resigned herself to fate and adapted to existence in a camp.

During this period the character changes. Gradually the interest in the outside world and in the other prisoners declines. The reaction to horrifying events grows less intense and does not last so long. It is a process of hardening, until the news of death sentences, executions, floggings, and even atrocious tortures causes no more than a faint reaction of horror which is over in a few minutes. Then there is again laughter and talk, and the camp life goes on as if nothing had happened.

I observed the change in myself. I remember that when I was a newcomer, I was shocked and horrified when the women fainted at roll call and in particular when a gypsy woman suffered the same heart attack each time because she was unable to stand immobile so long. And yet in 1944, when I had to go to the sick bay for something or other, I calmly picked my way through the dying as they lay in the corridor choking out their lives.

Concentration camp was not like an ordinary prison. The one great blow, the loss of freedom, was only the first, and after that you were made to suffer deliberately and often. Blows were bad but there were worse things—constant provocations and constant humiliations. When the SS struck, you dared not strike back. When the SS bullied and insulted, you had to keep your mouth shut and never answer back. You had lost all human rights, without exception. You were a living thing with a number to distinguish you from the other unfortunates around you.

Unconsciously, you were tempted to revenge yourself on your fellow prisoners for the injuries you had suffered. I am not thinking here of those prisoners who occupied some post and were able to maltreat those in their charge. No, I mean the ordinary women prisoners.

This was at its worst amongst the asocials, most of whom had not the faintest vestige of human solidarity. With them it was a fight of all against all. But the same thing in a milder form could be said for the other prisoners, even among the conscious politicals. They were envious and jealous of each other. If one seemed to get a trifle more food, a slightly larger piece of bread or sausage, there were immediately hateful scenes of anger and resentment.

In the first years the politicals, asocials, and criminals were kept separate in German concentration camps, but later on, particularly when the camps became overcrowded, the practice ceased. Like the GPU in Russia, the SS discovered that nonsegregation made it easier for them to manage the prisoners, for it tended to increase the rivalries, jealousies, and differences that already existed.

Then in the winter of 1944–45, there was another large inflow of women.

As the Russian advance drove deeper and deeper into Europe, the concentration camp at Auschwitz was evacuated and the women were brought back farther into Germany. Several thousand of them arrived at Ravensbrück, half-starved and exhausted by the terrible journey. They were crying desperately for water and none was given to them. The kitchen prisoners asked permission to give them coffee substitute and this was allowed, but when the great tub of hot liquid was wheeled out to them, hundreds of women fought madly to get at it first. They kicked, punched, and clawed each other, and in the scrimmage much of the coffee was upset on the ground. It was only after camp police and SS overseers had clubbed right and left that some sort of order was restored and it became possible to distribute what remained of the coffee.

The Auschwitz prisoners were a very different type—or perhaps it is more correct to say that they had been made into a very different type by conditions in the extermination camp. Only the toughest had any chance of survival there, and the one aim of all the prisoners was to remain alive. They were brutal both in appearance and manners. In the first period after their arrival, it was possible to recognize a prisoner from Auschwitz at a glance.

They had not been in the camp long when a rumor went round that, in order to lessen the pressure, all old and unfit prisoners were to be sent to another camp in Mittweida for light work. The prisoners of one block after the other were paraded and an alleged doctor named Winkelmann, who was said by the Auschwitz prisoners to have chosen those to go to the gas chambers, walked up and down the ranks indicating by a jerk of the thumb who was to go to Mittweida. The old and unfit were taken away in lorries.

A little while later new Block Seniors were chosen from amongst the "old" politicals to go to the youth camp Uckermark, which lay a little distance away beyond the workshops, and where youthful offenders had once been held. When they arrived, they found the old and unfit prisoners who had been taken from Ravensbrück. We thought Ravensbrück was just about as bad as a camp could be, but from what they said the conditions under which these poor old sick creatures now vegetated were even worse: roll calls which lasted even longer than at Ravensbrück, less food and even worse food, no warm clothing, and no medical attention. Naturally, they were dying like flies.

In 1944, a second crematorium was built on the other side of the bunkers, and the black, stinking smoke which belched out of the two chimneys became one of the ordinary features of the Ravensbrück scene. The prisoners were on familiar terms with the idea of death, and it played a big role in their witticisms. "There goes poor So-and-so" was a constant joke when there was a sudden big belch of smoke, and the overseers and SS men were fond of telling us that the only way we should ever leave Ravensbrück would be "up the chimney."

On April 21, 1945, two days following Hitler's birthday, Cilly, a Block Senior, entered with a list of prisoners, all Germans and Czechs, who were to assemble "with their things."

My name was among them. There was immediately a babble of voices.

"You're going to be released."

"You're going off!"

"Lucky devils."

I could hardly believe it. I had already thought out what I was going to do if the Russians came: go with the Poles, if that worked, or slip away in the confusion on my own, if it didn't.

The one possibility I had never even considered was that I should be released before the Russians arrived. Anicka, Inka, and I embraced each other and did "Ring a ring of roses" for joy. They had been more worried about my fate than I had suspected.

Then I collected my things. We went through lines of cheering, waving prisoners to the office where about sixty German and Czech prisoners were lined up. They were all "old Ravensbrückers" who had been in the camp for five years or more.

It was April 21, 1945, but they had the effrontery to give us a chit stating that we were released from the concentration camp Ravensbrück and had to report to our local Gestapo office within three days under pain of arrest and punishment. We didn't know whether to laugh or to be angry.

Then, in our camp clothes, with different colored patches fore and aft, with a few loaves of bread to keep us going on the way, and the chit that served us as a transport warrant, we set off through the camp gates "in columns of five"—for the last time. SS Overseer Binz accompanied us until we were outside the camp precincts and on the way to Fürstenberg.

"Halt!" she bellowed. It was the last order she gave us and we obeyed it meekly.

"Frau SS Overseer Binz," someone piped up. "I live in Cologne. Can you give me the address of the local Gestapo there? I shouldn't like to be late in reporting."

Everybody laughed and Binz made an angry face.

"You can do what you like," she snorted, "and go where you like. From now on, regard yourselves as fugitives."

And with that she turned around and went back to the camp. We started off on our own toward Fürstenberg. So this is freedom, I thought. For the first time in seven years there's no one just behind me to tell me what to do and where to go. I could sit down by the roadside if I wanted to, or go across the fields, or go back.

Strangely, we were still in columns of five. Old habits die hard. One or two of the weaker ones dropped back. Gradually the idea seemed to spread that we were free. There was no need to march in rank. We could walk at our own pace. As though by common consent, the ranks broke. Then someone with a voice which sounded as though it had been used to command shouted, "We can't go into Fürstenberg like a straggling lot of sheep. Keep in columns of five."

But the deadly potion of freedom was beginning to have its effect. Those who had been slaves were now beginning to be free, and there was a chorus of indignation and one or two threats to the would-be commandant.

"You get yourself out of the habit of bellowing at us like that or you'll end up badly."

The bent spines straightened.

Now remarried, Mrs. Buber-Faust is a resident of Stockholm, Sweden.

Chapter 18

"The song rose
to a mighty roar . . ."

In the early morning hours of May 27, 1942, Reinhard Heydrich, an especially vicious sadist in the hierarchy of the Nazi secret police, was assassinated in Prague by Czechs who had been trained in England and parachuted back to their occupied country. Since at that time the thirty-eight-year-old Heydrich was Berlin's top emissary in Czechoslovakia, the "Protector of Bohemia and Moravia," Hitler could not be expected to overlook the murder.

And he did not do so.

More or less at random, the little coal-mining village of Lidice, twenty miles northwest of Prague, was picked for extermination. After midnight on June 10, nearly 200 men and boys were machine-gunned to death, 82 children were later gassed, and 195 women were removed to concentration camps.

Obviously, there were few survivors by the time of the surrender in May, 1945, to tell of Lidice's night of horror. However, before the war, Zdena Trinka of North Dakota, who as a child came to the United States with her parents, traveled throughout Czechoslovakia at that country's invitation. She knew Lidice and the people there. After the partial rebuilding of Lidice several years later, she revisited Czechoslovakia to interview one woman who had miraculously returned from her ordeal in prison.

This is the story of "Marie," as retold by Zdena Trinka:

Already, on June 7, they had virtually become prisoners of the Germans. For on that day the German Colonel General Kurt Daluege, who had succeeded Heydrich as "Protector of Czechoslovakia," had sent down ten truckloads of German Reich soldiers to set up six big guns on the hill above the village. These green-uniformed ones immediately set up sentries at every exit and entrance to the village.

By morning fifteen hundred German soldiers had surrounded the village. No one was let in except nine miners who had been away in Kladno on night shift duty, and who, despite all warnings, returned to be with their families. And no one was let out. A young lad, and later a woman, who in the growing uneasiness in the village tried to escape the ring of steel, were mercilessly shot to death.

After two nights and days of constant vigil, when it began to seem that for another night at least they would be safe from the guns on the hill, the worn-out people of the village—some disrobed and others fully dressed—fell into a broken sleep.

It was a sleep in which the least little noise brought the men to their feet, a sleep in which the pillows of the women were wet with the tears of a dim foreboding. Even the children slept fitfully, stirring restlessly in their sleep. The big guns outside and the presence of the regular German army boded nothing good.

It was in the wee hours of the night, just before the break of dawn, that it happened; five huge trucks loaded with the dread Gestapo and SS men roared into the village.

The scene enacted itself before her [Marie's] eyes. With horrible clearness she saw it all. Sirens screamed in the quiet and the trucks had scarcely come to a stop when men in green uniforms and men in boots and brown shirts began jumping out. She saw the troops pounding on doors with their gun butts, breaking into houses.

In a moment the village was on its feet. Lights and faces began to appear at windows—the grim faces of men who hadn't a gun between them with which to defend their lives, their homes—the pale, anxious faces of women—the faces of wide-eyed, frightened children. To all it meant the same thing—the Germans had come! The word "Germans" was enough to strike terror in every heart.

At one window a young mother was holding her firstborn to her, bundled up in its embroidered pillow; with the other hand she clutched together the nightdress at her throat. In her white face there was not a drop of blood, only the anguish written there. Behind her, pushing his hands into the sleeves of his coat, her husband was saying something to quiet her fears. In that brief interval his tense face seemed to have taken on years.

She saw the troops breaking into houses, seizing every living soul and telling everyone to take all their valuables, all their money, with them. She saw the men of the village being lined up on the village square under heavy guard. Among them she began to recognize the faces of the Rakos men, the Stribrnys, the Cermaks, the Horaks, Father Stemberk, the schoolmaster Otto-mansky. And good God, they were even lining up all boys of fifteen and over, on the square! What could it mean?

She saw groups of women, young and old, with their children, being driven at gunpoint toward the schoolhouse and locked in. She saw the men in boots and brown shirts running in and out of the houses, looting, despoiling, setting fire to them. She heard the cry of despair: "They are setting fire to our homes!"

She saw men and women break away and rush to save homes that for generations had been handed from father to son. She heard the single sharp fusillade aimed at these people, saw the spurt of flame as some bodies toppled and others reached their destination. She saw women return to the side of a felled husband and then rise. In their grief they threw themselves on the Germans, beating with their fists the stony breast of the German Wehrmacht until, mercilessly shot, they joined the pool of blood beside their beloveds.

There were other women living on the outskirts of the village who never knew what had happened to their husbands until the day of their liberation. When their husbands had armed themselves with picks and shovels and axes and had sped to the relief of the village, these women had remained in their cottages, to be later picked up in a truck with their children by the Germans.

She saw the dear men of Lidice, with pick and shovel and bare hands, fight the armed enemy until shot dead or over-powered and herded onto the square, where nearly two hundred men and boys were being held at gunpoint to prevent their escape.

Everywhere along the street named after an American president, the dead and dying were lying. She saw a figure crawl out of a burning home, hair singed, face seared by fire. He rose to his feet, tottered as another shot felled him to his knees, and cried out in the last strength of his death agony: "We shall arise, you shall witness soon. We do not die in vain—"

The sound of a shot was followed by a stunned silence. Then a quivering voice took up the words of the Czech national anthem, "Kde Domov Muj," followed by other voices on the village square until the song rose to a mighty roar.

Even as the song was swelling on the break of dawn, gun butts were descending on the heads of the singers, wielded by the infuriated Germans. Cringing, begging for mercy—that they could understand, for it was what they would have done had the tables been reversed. But men standing up to them, singing, holding on to their human dignity even in the face of waiting death—that they could not comprehend. It made them somehow feel cheated, as if the vaunted, self-imposed title of "supermen" had somehow been indelibly replaced by the unpretty epithet, "murdering gangsters!"

She was in the last group of women being driven to the schoolhouse. She was with them, but not of them. She moved like someone in a dream, conscious only of the straining grasp of her child's hand in hers. But her eyes were seeking, seeking. Then just as the men began the death march toward the church, she saw him—saw Josef. Their eyes met and in them all their love. Others of the marching men and youths were straining their heads, too, for a last look at a beloved face, a loved one—a mother, a wife, a sweetheart.

And then she was in the schoolhouse.

From the direction of the courtyard of the church could be heard the sound of marching feet coming to a standstill, the swearing of the guards, and a snarling German voice reading something amid a dead silence at first, then interrupted by loud howls, shrieks, protests. These were followed by the single sharp fusillade of shots, and the hearts of the women in the schoolhouse died within them. The children were too frightened to do more than whimper.

Beloved Father Stemberk was the first to die, to bear witness at the throne of God. For a moment he remained standing as if the shots had left him untouched. Then his knees doubled under him, and he fell at the foot of the old pear tree in the church courtyard, in whose shade the youth of Lidice had played for generations. His torn, rent cassock covered the ground about him like a shroud.

A shocked silence fell. Then voices of sheer horror were heard from outside, followed by the cursing and swearing of the Germans. Even as the women locked in the schoolhouse were dying by inches, the voices outside grew fainter and stopped, to be heard again from the direction of the old cemetery by the church, now no longer used, where slept their last sleep the generations of Lidice men and women.

It was here on the sacred ground of their forefathers that the good men and boys of Lidice were stood up against the cemetery wall, ten at a time, and shot dead before the anguished eyes of fathers and sons awaiting their own turn at the hands of the fiends who wanted to own the earth and stopped not at murder to gain it.

Always the single sharp fusillade of shots aimed at the ten stood up against the wall, stripped naked—for there is no dignity even in death in a German world—the spurt of flames, the bodies toppling. Then silence pierced with strange sounds, sometimes with a shriek; then again the single sharp fusillade, the spurt of flame, bodies toppling—over and over and over, fourteen times, fifteen times, until she lost count. She was conscious only of the ringing in her ears, the awful feeling—like the hand of death itself—creeping over her and choking her breath.

And then she heard her own child's voice crying with sheer terror.

"No, no! Let me be!" And, frantically: "Mamiko, don't let those horrid men take me—"

No wonder some of the mothers were on the verge of going mad, in the sheer agony of it all. An agony in which six pregnant women had to be taken from the convoy as it neared Prague and placed in the maternity home on Vinohrady, suffering from premature labor pains. These were to arrive later at the concentration camp at Ravensbrück, north of Berlin—without their babies, which had been torn from their arms shortly after birth to be placed for adoption into German families. All except a little girl born to Mrs. Kohlickova; it died shortly after birth. A seventh baby, born later at the Ravensbrück concentration camp to Mrs. Frantiska Hronikova, was likewise torn from its frantic mother's arms and was believed to have been done away with by the brutal SS guards at the camp.

As the trucks were being loaded, fire was set to the church, the school, and the buildings yet untouched by flames. She could see the demoniac Karl Hermann Frank, head of the Gestapo, shouting out orders and personally directing the booted, brown-shirted ones.

She could see the crazed German soldiers and the booted, brown-shirted ones running around among the flames like so many minions of hell, setting fire with their flaming torches to everything that was still standing and shooting at everything that still showed life.

The last she saw of Lidice, as the trucks were bearing them away, was the whole village aroar with flame and smoke, with the steeple of St. Martin's Church still untouched, towering above the ruin as if in sheer contempt of anything the German madmen could do.

Karl Hermann Frank, the deputy and minister to Heydrich, the Reichsprotector of Bohemia, also ordered the execution of seventeen hundred hostages in Prague and thirteen hundred in Brno. To become known as the "Butcher of Lidice," Frank at his postwar trial would confess to ordering approximately one-third of the seventy thousand executions in Czechoslovakia of which he was charged. Frank was hung in Prague.

Chapter 19

"The bodies were laid out in a row . . . "

Atrocities, the evil companions of war, were not peculiar to the Nazis alone. Since recorded time the passions of combat have spawned excesses quite beyond comprehension or adequate description.

On a scale involving millions, there has been nothing to compare historically with the Third Reich's extermination of the Jews, or with the execution, maltreatment, and starvation of other multitudes. However, the Russians were also capable of mass slaughter.

After the war, for example, it was proved to the satisfaction of a Select Committee of the United States House of Representatives that the Soviet Union had callously murdered approximately ten thousand officers of the Polish army in a wooded region known as Katyn Forest, twelve miles west of Smolensk and about two hundred miles west of Moscow.

The executions in Katyn Forest, by bullets in the backs of the officers' heads, had taken place, according to all evidence, during the first week in April, 1940, seven months after Poland had been overrun.

The Germans marched in from the west and the Russians from the east, each army capturing a great number of prisoners. Not until early in 1943, after the Nazi invaders advanced eastward over the plains of Soviet Russia, was the slaughter discovered. The references to Katyn here presented are not, however, intended primarily to describe or sift the evidence of a mass crime against humanity—almost genocide in capsule—but to narrate the bizarre and unusual experience of an American prisoner of war, the then Captain Donald B. Stewart, captured in North Africa and imprisoned in Oflag 9 [officers' prison camp] at Rotenburg, on the Fulda River. Along with Lieutenant Colonel John H. Van Vliet, Jr.—another American taken prisoner in Tunisia—a South African officer identified only as Colonel Stevenson, and two others, Stewart was asked in May, 1943, to visit the grave site, over nine hundred miles to the northeast, under guard, and act as a witness.

The following account is from hearings before the Select Committee, during the Eighty-second Congress. "Q" identifies questions by Congressmen or counsels during the investigation. This is Stewart's testimony (recorded in October, 1951, before the regular hearings began, as he was en route to an overseas post):

We gathered our stuff together and went down for our search. They issued our rations—cans of meat and a loaf of bread. We left in the evening. We went by train to Kassel, twenty-five to thirty miles north of our prison camp. When we reached Kassel, we looked around the railroad station and were surprised to find it had not been bombed.

We were supposed to meet General Fortune, a British officer from another prison camp, at Kassel. He was not there. The Germans put Colonel Van Vliet, Colonel Stevenson, and myself on the train, and we made an overnight trip to Berlin.

Q. How far is that, approximately?

About two hundred miles. We arrived at Berlin during the daylight hours of Monday [May] the eleventh. Upon our arrival there, we were taken to what the Germans called Arbeitskommando—a work camp, an apartment-house prison on the Spree River, not far from the Tiergarten in Berlin.

We stayed there that night and found that at this prison camp there were already some men gathered who were all supposed to make the trip. There were several American soldiers. One of them, Taussig, was from Colonel Van Vliet's unit. I did not know Corporal Taussig personally, but I had a number of my men captured at the same time. When I talked with him, I found that he knew one of my corporals, Corporal Benoit, and that these American prisoners had come from a POW camp east of Berlin.

They had been brought to Berlin to the same camp where we were. There were also British enlisted men present that had come from some camps in Germany that I do not remember. There was a British civilian who was an internee, not a prisoner of war. This British internee had lived on one of the Channel Islands, either the island of Guernsey or the Isle of Man. I do not recall which one. All these people had been ordered here to go to Katyn.

The fourth officer, Captain Stanley Gilder, a Scottish officer in the British Medical Corps, came in from a camp down at Rottweil-on-Neckar. We were a little suspicious of Captain Gilder. It turned out that he could speak German, and also he could speak a little Russian. As we checked on him, we had our confidence established, and we felt that he was really a British officer—as he turned out to be. In a prison camp you are always suspicious of everybody. We do not believe anyone is who he says he is until we can find positive proof that he is. We wanted to make sure nobody was planted on us to listen to what we might say.

Tuesday afternoon, so far as I can recall—and that would be the twelfth of May, 1943—the Germans held interviews with us in one of the downstairs rooms of the commando. Colonel Stevenson was the senior officer. The Germans usually dealt with the senior officer, and we felt that he should speak for all of us. We had agreed that we would not tell the Germans exactly how we felt, that we would not participate in a propaganda effort. However, the Germans wanted to speak to each of us, and from our conversations with each other later, we found that the Germans had about the same routine.

I was the junior officer and last to go down. As I walked into the room, there was a mixture of German officers and civilians sitting around a table about the size of the one in this room [three by nine feet] in a room twice this large; later we agreed it was probably a combination living-dining room, roughly fourteen by twenty-four feet. I gave my name and prisoner-of-war number, KGF 1581.

One of the Germans, who spoke English very well, said, "Captain Stewart, since you have volunteered to go to Katyn and investigate the massacre of those Polish officers, I am glad to see you."

I told him I had not volunteered; that I was under orders; that I felt the matter was a propaganda effort and, in any event, it was a political effort. He said it was not propaganda—"We just want to show you the facts." I repeated that I considered it to be a political affair, a political matter. I was in the Army and I had no desire to get mixed up in any international political complications.

Then the next thing he said was, "You are an officer of the regular army. Surely you must have an interest in what has happened to officers of the Polish army."

I told him that I had no desire to have anything to do with a propaganda effort or a political matter. They stopped talking and I saluted and went back to the room. Back in the room the people asked me what I had been asked and what I had said, and it jibed with what had happened to them.

The Germans apparently had asked Colonel Stevenson if he would give our parole for the trip, not to escape, from Berlin to Katyn.

Q. How far is it?

That must be around seven hundred miles. It is a daylight flight. The exact distance is six hundred to seven hundred miles, so that the total distance from Rotenburg to Katyn is probably nine hundred miles.

Since Colonel Stevenson convinced the Germans we would not give our parole, the Germans said that they would have to send some guards along; therefore, they sent the two American enlisted men back to their prison camp. I do not know why they sent the Americans back instead of the British enlisted men, but they did.

The party, as we finally left for the plane, and the party that visited the graves at Katyn, consisted of four officers: Lieutenant Colonel Stevenson of the British South African Forces; Lieutenant Colonel Van Vliet of our Army; Captain Stanley Gilder of the British Medical Corps; and myself. The names of the three British enlisted men and the British civilian, I do not remember. So, the total visiting party consisted of eight of us.

In addition to that, there were the German enlisted guards, German civilians from the Propaganda Ministry, and some German interpreters, plus a German officer or two. The total number in the plane was about twenty men.

Q. Do you know the name of the interpreter?

He said that his name was Von Johnson.

Q. Do you know anything about his background?

He was very pleasant, quiet-spoken, and spoke American, not English. He said that he had lived in the part of Germany that after World War I became Poland, and when Poland was established, he and his mother left and came to America. He said he spent nineteen years in Texas and that he came back to Germany in the late 1930's. I do not remember the reason he gave for saying he came back, but he spoke the American idiomatic language.

When we left the Arbeitskommando, we got into a bus and drove out to the airport. We stopped at the Ministry of Propaganda and Public Information. That is where the officials of that organization got on. One of them brought a little carton of cigarettes with him.

We drove to the Tempelhof airfield, got on the plane, and we flew, making a stop at Breslau, which is roughly in this vicinity [indicating on map]—apparently just a refueling stop—flew on and made a lunch stop in Poland, at a town called Bielsk-Podlaski. Lunch consisted of a hard-boiled egg, a bowl of soup, and a slice of bread. Then we continued on the flight, following the railroad tracks, and came into Smolensk—so our flight generally went in this direction [indicating northeasterly on map]. We got into Smolensk in the late afternoon.

The Germans did not black out the airplane. For instance, we flew by Warsaw from some miles distant so we could not identify any particular building, but we could see the built-up section of the town and see smoke rising from the chimneys.

As we got further along the old Polish-Russian border, flying along the railroad, every so often on each side we could see entrenchments, shell holes, and craters which had been put there, apparently, when the Germans drove in on their attack on Russia.

The plane did not seem to get more than two or three hundred feet above the ground. We were always very low. This country is flat. There were no hills over the area we went through and the plane was always low.

When we landed at the airfield at Smolensk, the Germans loaded us into the equivalent of one of our command cars and took us to an apartment building, which was still in fairly good shape. Apparently they were using it for barracks, and they put us four officers in one room and the civilian and the British enlisted men in another room with the guard in the hall. While we were in that room we of course could not talk because we felt it might be wired so that anything we would say would be overheard. As a matter of fact, we never talked to each other inside of any room about any matter except the weather.

We did not talk with the enlisted men except to tell them they were in a tight spot and they must never say anything among themselves or to the Germans that would get them into trouble.

Shortly after we had arrived there, we were put in the room where there was some singing taking place outside. I looked out the window and there seemed to be a company of German soldiers. Captain Gilder, the Scottish doctor, said they were Russians, prisoners in German uniforms. He had been at a prisoner-of-war hospital, and among his patients were some Russians, so he had learned some Russian.

The Germans came over and invited us to go to the officers' mess. As we left our room and went to the other room that was the officers' mess, they asked us if we would like to talk to the Russian soldiers. Nobody did, particularly, but Colonel Stevenson thought of a question, so Captain Gilder asked the Russians, "What will happen to you if you are captured by the Russians?" and he was told that they would be executed.

We went on to the officers' mess. There the room was about twice the size of this one. It had a couple of tables and a few chairs in it. It appeared to be the dining room of a service unit or supply unit.

At that time the east front was about forty miles beyond Smolensk. There were no combat troops to speak of in the Smolensk area that we could see. At first the Germans did not talk about Katyn at all. They were just passing the time of day, making themselves interesting and telling us about the Battle of Smolensk and how Smolensk had been captured.

Supper was very meager—a piece of cheese and a slice of rye bread and tea. That was it. They gave us the supper they themselves ate. Then after supper they brought out a couple of bottles of some sort of liquor (the bottles were labeled "Bols"), but we did not dare drink any more than a sip or so for fear we might say something that could be useful to them.

We returned to our room as soon as we could.

The next morning they loaded us into another command car and took us out to the woods of Katyn. This is about twelve miles from Smolensk itself. I did not see any built-up area around it, although there was a villa [a big country house on the river reportedly used by the Russian OGPU]. All there was, was a small knoll covered with pine woods. The pine woods were not very thick. There were some trees possibly six to eight inches in diameter and a number of smaller trees. It was more like a park land than a natural forest.

We drove into the area and got out of the vehicles. They took us over to the graves. All this time each one of us was trying to give absolutely no indication by expression that we were interested in what we were seeing.

The Germans were taking movies; they were taking still pictures, and if we looked at anything with too much interest, we felt they might make some propaganda out of it. If we indicated too much interest, we felt we would be playing into their hands. We felt this was a German propaganda effort and we did not want to be involved in it any more than we could be forced to do so.

We approached the grave site. The area was sand, a light yellow-colored sand, like we find on the beaches of Lake Michigan and South Carolina; the ground was rather high near the river, but just slightly rolling further away.

We walked over to the graves. There were three main graves open. The largest one was shaped like an L. We estimated individually the sizes of the graves—I have forgotten the exact dimensions now—but I know that they were approximately the size of a swimming pool. There were just three of them, and one was L-shaped, the size of a swimming pool.

As we walked along the edge of the graves, the Germans were giving us a certain amount of explanation.

Q. Pardon me, Colonel, I would like to ask you a question so that we could have an estimate of the size of the grave. It has been estimated by someone that this L-shaped grave was about thirty by fifty yards. Could you tell us whether, to your recollection, that would be close to what you thought the size of the grave was?

Yes, sir; that would be about as close as you could judge on it.

The Germans walked us along, showing us the various graves, giving us an explanation of their theories on the murders.

Then they took us down into one of the graves for a closer examination. We went down the side of the bank and walked across the bodies to see more closely what they were trying to make us look at. I tried to walk carefully on the backs and to avoid stepping on the heads, arms, or legs, while at the same time keeping my face expressionless.

Now, in general, in all the graves the bodies were laid out in a row across the narrow dimension of the grave. Practically all bodies were face down. There were layer after layer; they were practically all headed the same way.

It was obvious that they had not been tossed into the graves from the banks; they had been apparently thrown down in there after they were killed, and then packed in very tightly.

The grave in which we walked, the officers were mostly dressed in overcoats, overcoats of heavy material, a little darker and a little longer than our own. There were a few men in that grave dressed in the black robes of a Catholic priest.

Individually, we tried to form an estimate as to how many bodies were in those graves. From the surface of the ground to the top layer of the bodies exposed is roughly about my height, which would be five to six feet.

Then, since one of the graves had been dug all the way down in the ground to the bottom layer of the bodies, we were able to get an estimate as to how many layers there were; so we counted the number of men in each row, we counted the number of layers, and we counted the number of rows individually.

Later, when we confirmed, when we checked with each other, we found that we arrived at an estimate of about ten thousand bodies. That may or may not be correct, but our individual estimates were running about nine or ten thousand, based on the calculation of how many bodies in a row, how many rows in a grave, how many layers in a grave.

After we left that grave, I walked over toward the autopsy table. We went up to a little path where the Germans had already removed several hundred bodies for their examination and re-burial. Very few of those bodies had overcoats on, and all of them were tied. Their hands were tied behind their backs with strings, the equivalent of binder cord, sunk into the flesh so that it was obvious that it had been put on when they were alive; it was not a recent addition.

As we walked up the path to the autopsy table, it was not pointed out to us by the Germans, but each of the four officers noted that these men were very well dressed. They had boots on, black boots, of very good leather.

You can look at a piece of leather and you can tell whether it is good or not. Those boots were good. They had leather heels on their boots, and the leather heels were not worn down; the heels were in good shape.

Most of them were in breeches of elastique material similar to our prewar Army-officer breeches. That material was of very good quality and showed practically no wear.

The blouses were darker. Now, when I say that they showed no wear, the material did not look new, but it was not frayed or worn. They were dirty and stained from the graves and from the bodies themselves, but the material was not worn, and the boots were not worn. The clothing fitted; they looked like they were tailor-made clothes. That group of bodies along the path did not have overcoats on; the others in the grave did.

We passed those to go to the autopsy table. Now, the Germans had insisted that we point out a body at random in the grave, and Colonel Stevenson pointed to one. They pulled that body out of the grave and brought it to the autopsy table.

They performed the autopsy on it so that we could see what had caused the death, and to show us how they searched each body in order to identify it. The surgeon made a circular incision around the head and pulled the scalp off.

The body had in the back of the head—in the back of the head was a smaller bullet hole, and in front of the head was a larger bullet hole.

The Germans said that practically all the corpses had that same small bullet hole in the back, and larger bullet hole in the front.

Now, the Germans kept giving us a theory about this or a theory about that. We did not accept them because it would appear to me that we could not prove it. We could not prove anything.

Although the Germans told us that no papers or documents had been found on these prisoners dated later than April or May of 1940, there was no way we could check it. We felt that if they did find a document such as that it would be very easy for them just to destroy it.

There were a considerable number of newspapers lying around that they said had come from the grave, a lot of the prewar Polish money lying around. They asked us if we wanted some souvenirs, and we told them no.

The Germans said that practically all the bodies were killed by being shot, but that there were a few that they found with bayonet wounds. They showed us some material, overcoat material, that had a sort of triangular hole in it, as if it had been made by an old-fashioned bayonet on one of our muzzle-loading rifles, sort of a triangular hole, not a straight cut as our present bayonet makes, not a knife cut.

There was a tree there that had possibly a dozen rather small bullets embedded in it. The German officer went over and put his forehead against the tree and put his hand up behind it to indicate that very probably the persons who had done the killing had made a man lean his head against the tree and then shot him. One of the officers said it could very well have been just somebody doing target practice. However, it did appear to us that the men had been shot by a small-caliber weapon.

When we returned to the prison camp, we kept our notes to ourselves. Of course, we had written nothing down that the Germans might use, and we told nothing to our other prisoners. We agreed that at the end of the war, reports would be made to our own governments. That was in May, 1943, when we made our decision.

In June, 1943, we were moved with all of the American Army officers to Oflag 64 in Poland. Colonel Van Vliet and I stayed in the same camps. When the Russians took Warsaw in January, 1945, our prison camp of just under twelve hundred officers started out on foot, westward. It was quite cold and a number of the people could not make it, so as they could not walk, the Germans loaded them into boxcars and sent them off westward.

Colonel Van Vliet did not complete the march, and he wound up in a prison camp in Luckenwalde, south of Berlin. I completed the forty-day march and I eventually wound up in Hammelburg, down east of Frankfurt.

My notes on the Katyn trip had been censored by the Germans, marked "*Gepruft,*" but when I entered the Hammelburg camp and was searched there, they took away my notebook. They left me with pictures because each individual picture was stamped, and they left me with my orders because those read, "Do not take it." But the notebook they took. I believe they took the notebook because they thought I might have written something else in it and they wanted to check.

In March, 1945, the Fourth Armored Division sent a company of tanks and infantry on a raid and liberated the camp overnight, but we were prisoners again the next day. The Germans yanked us out of the camp suddenly and I never got the notebook back. The pictures and orders never left my possession.

Having lost my notes of the detailed names and individuals and times, I had to rely on my memory. I was liberated in April down near Munich and taken to Camp Lucky Strike near Le Havre. Here I found that Colonel Van Vliet had already checked in. He had gone to Paris, so I did not say anything about Katyn. I knew that he would want to make the report.

Q. Colonel Stewart, how long were you a prisoner of the Germans?

Two years, two months, and two weeks.

Colonel Van Vliet, who testified before the same committee in January, 1952, expressed Captain Stewart's conclusions as well as his own:

. . . we pursued every line of attack to weaken the German story and avoid the conclusion that the Russians had done the killing. It was only with great reluctance that I decided finally that it must be true; that for once the Germans weren't lying, that the facts were as claimed by the Germans. I have thought about this a lot in the past seven years and freely admit that there never was presented to me any single piece of evidence that could be taken as absolute proof. But the sum of circumstantial evidence, impressions formed at the time of looking at the graves, what I saw in peoples' faces, all proved the conclusion that Russia did it.

In a letter to the editor of this anthology, Colonel Stewart wrote:

"I accompanied Colonel Van Vliet to Katyn and my observations and conclusions were the same as his. I have not written any account of my POW years but I could say nothing that would differ from Colonel Van Vliet's ultimate decision about the Katyn affair. His summary is certainly as complete and accurate as could be."

Chapter 20

"The long purgatory of internment . . . "

*Allied prisoners in Germany totaled approximately some 1,800,-
000: 765,000 of these were French; 550,000, Italian; 200,000,
British subjects; 125,000, Yugoslavs; and 90,000, Americans. Because Russia was not party to the Geneva agreement requiring
that nations give complete, accurate lists of enemy soldiers taken
in battle, those held in Soviet camps or Russians held in Germany
were uncounted.*

*The responsibility of supervising the prison camps and reporting
on the enforcement of rules fell to the government of Switzerland and to the International Red Cross. Additionally, the Red
Cross handled food packages and other supplies for the internees,
as well as their incoming and outgoing mail.*

*The Prisoner of War, a monthly journal published for the Red
Cross in England, carried articles about the camps—first hand
stories and letters from the prisoners. While patently cheerful—
and surely censored—this news gave inklings of what went on
and, for this reason, appealed to families and friends of those
interned either as civilians or military prisoners of war.*

*This first sketch from the September, 1943, issue is by naval
gunner Norman H. Gould, at that time a prisoner in a German
stalag [prison camp for noncommissioned prisoners of war].*

British prisoners of war, from the very fact of being British, are
always grousing. Unless they are officers or of a rank higher than
lance corporals, they must work. This, of course, is perfect
grounds for a grouse—the hours are too long, the work is too

hard or too monotonous, nothing is ever right. Only on the score
of variety is there no complaint—not, of course, that this makes
any difference.

I have, since June, 1940, been employed at almost every
conceivable form of unskilled and some semiskilled work. I have
groomed horses, washed cars, dug holes, filled them in again,
loaded and unloaded every imaginable commodity, and a host
of other things. Now, in 1943, I have settled into a "nice little
job" for what remains of the duration. Or so I hope!

There are about a hundred of us—Englishmen, Scotsmen,
Irishmen, Australians, and New Zealanders—working in a large
agricultural machinery factory. The total number of employees
is well over a thousand, and we are all mixed up with the rest.

Our men work in all parts of the factory in all sorts of jobs.
Some are molders in the foundry, others are electric welders,
smiths, millwrights, or fitters, and a large number are employed
as laborers. We work under the supervision of the shop foremen
and change hands in the same way as the civilian employees.
Guards from the camp are formally in attendance, both to protect our interests and to insure that we don't do anything contrary to rules and regulations.

We are extremely fortunate in that our employers are most
reasonable. Any reasonable request is always granted, and any
man has access to the chief engineer for this purpose. It is quite
common for a man to ask for a change of job and to be granted
his transfer.

There is one great obstacle in the employment of prisoner-
of-war labor. We, the prisoners, have little or no interest in the
work we do. We are not working to keep ourselves, we are not
working in or for our own country. True, we are paid a few
shillings a week and receive a certain amount of extra food, but
neither of these provides for any great incentive to work. On
the other hand, the employers are interested only in their production figures. A solution to the difficulty has been found in
a compromise.

As many men as possible have been put on a piecework
basis, whereby they finish when a given amount of work has
been done. For example, the fitters contract to assemble thirty

plows a day. They and the firm regard this as a fair day's work of ten and a half hours. If the fitter can assemble this number in eight hours—and he does—then he can take two and a half hours' extra leisure instead of working on and earning more money as the civilians do.

Everyone is satisfied by this. The firm is satisfied because they get the work done more quickly and because men working for themselves on piecework require little or no supervision. We are satisfied to get the job done in the shortest possible time, knowing that we have done enough, but not too much, work. This very subject of how much work, what sort of work, and how long to take to do it, is the topic of endless arguments among ourselves.

My "nice little job" is in the tempering shop. This is non-repetitive, congenial work. (I had earned it previously with six months in the foundry.) My co-workers are civilians and, since they understand no English, I must speak German the whole time. I find this is stimulating and useful.

We "moan" about having to work, but it is at any rate a contact with the outside world and gives a semblance of normality to our queer "life within a life." I have purposely written about work because this, and most other camps, are work camps. We have our sports, our dance band, our stage shows—and our Red Cross parcels—but work takes up most of our time.

Lieutenant Commander S. H. Beattie was captured during the commando raid on St. Nazaire in March, 1942. Like the average married POW, Beattie consumed much of his leisure time in writing to his wife:

We are settling in well, and while away our time learning German and various things. There are lessons in shorthand, drawing, Shakespeare, and such, all given by our select staff of officers. I am with an awful nice lot of chaps here, and life would be very pleasant if it were not for the barbed wire.

We have our own little service every Sunday. We have a prayer book and a New Testament, but no hymnbook, so we have to try to remember the hymns. So far we have three for each service without repeating ourselves, but we usually manage to get a couple of verses out of each hymn; we write them in chalk on blackout paper. Everyone can remember the first line or two out of a dozen hymns, but the rest is difficult.

We have had a move to more commodious huts in a different part of camp, and it really is quite pleasant. Fir trees are fairly close with plenty of birds in them, and it is a treat to hear them sing; and we have a view of some pleasant country. Altogether we are really quite comfortable and are being well treated. I happen to be the second officer here, not that it entails any privileges except that I mess with the colonel, who is a damn fine chap, a man called Newman, for whom I have great admiration [Colonel Newman also took part in the St. Nazaire raid.]

One thing I like about our new huts is the washhouse; I can have my cold bath in the morning, a thing I have missed for the past few weeks. We have also been gardening; the cress is already up and the radishes are just showing.

You know, there is one thing I have been meaning to ask you to send and haven't mentioned yet. Some photographs of you. And, by the way, I can get a good selection of books to read, but should you send any, it is wise to send cheaply bound ones, as they are apt to get torn in transit.

We have arranged lectures and so forth on almost every subject and, really—what with that and gardening and other things, such as cooking the food we get in the Red Cross parcels —I hardly have a minute to spare.

I am learning an awful lot. We have experts in all sorts of things, from farming to ancient history. All most interesting, and the time passes so quickly, one can hardly believe it. By the way, I heard about my award [the Victoria Cross] on Sunday from the German officer in charge, who was very courteous about it. I can't believe it.

One or two letters have come in for people, about six of them, so we can all reckon it can't be long now until we hear. I am hoping for one this week; it is very nearly three months now. I am afraid I shall have to cut my beard off, as they (beards) are unpopular in these regions for some reason. I have almost forgotten what I look like underneath, and I am sure I have forgotten how to shave.

Great news. My first parcel has arrived. I haven't had it yet. I am told it looks like cigarettes, but I'll let you know. No letters for over a week.

I promised to tell you how we spend our time. There are some five hundred officers and men here (all naval) but the accommodation is reasonable. The huts, at any rate, are waterproof, and we have bunks to sleep in. Five chaps in my room, which is quite a spacious apartment. We have *Appel* [roll call] three times a day, but otherwise the day is entirely our own. I read a good deal, and do my Russian. Luckily, there is a chap who can help me. There are three others learning, but it's a hell of a language. Then they try to have some sort of show once a week. *Hay Fever* was to be shown this week, but has been put off till next.

In late 1940 an Englishwoman, Frieda Stewart, was interned in France by the Nazis. First held at Besançon camp, about thirty-five miles from the Swiss border, she was later transferred to Vittel. A former resort town of some three thousand people, Vittel had been taken over by the Germans and its several hotels commandeered for an internment camp, mainly for women. Ultimately, Miss Stewart escaped to England and wrote for the June, 1942, journal:

I was in Paris when the Nazis came in two years ago, working for a committee dealing with refugee children.

I tried to get away, but all my efforts to get a conveyance of any kind failed. So I had to stay. It wasn't a pleasant prospect for any of us Englishwomen, but we had to make the best of it.

Then one day—it was December 5, 1940—we were gathered up by the Nazis and taken—three thousand British subjects, the old, the sick, the children, even babies in arms—to Besançon, on the extreme eastern border of France.

We traveled all through the night under conditions of great discomfort. In my carriage was an old lady over eighty, who couldn't possibly have been a spy! There was an old man who was almost bedridden; there was a woman who had been taken out of a maternity hospital, where her baby had been born a few days previously. Poor woman! Her baby died shortly after we reached the barracks, where we were to be interned for five months.

Life in that camp was rather grim. The French doctors who looked after us did their best, but there was not much that could be done in view of the cold, the dreadful unsanitary conditions, and the bad food. They could only recommend that those who suffered most from the diet not touch the food—which meant that one would have to starve!

After a time we were moved to a camp where conditions were better, though food was still scanty. It can be imagined with what feelings we received the first batch of Red Cross parcels from England. I shall never forget the excitement when their arrival was announced—nor the pleasure at finding the marvelous variety of good things inside. We found it hard to believe there was a whole parcel for each one of us.

The Nazis had done their best to impress on us that English food went to the bottom of the sea, and that what was left to eat was of a very poor quality! The first sight of sausages, sardines, biscuits, and butter was an eye opener, both to us and to the Germans who saw the parcels. The meals of bacon and sausages and the good cups of tea which followed were the best possible advertisement for the Allies. They counteracted months of Nazi propaganda and enormously raised the morale of the camp.

Each day when the parcels were distributed, which happened frequently after this, was a festival. Swapping tins and bartering chocolate for cigarettes, biscuits and jam for sardines and pilchards, became a regular business.

The material for clothes and the knitting wool, which arrived later through the British and American Red Cross, were also a godsend; we recovered a good deal of self-respect when we were clad in decent garments again, instead of in the incongruous and shapeless French military coats and trousers which had been distributed by the authorities.

The French soldiers, prisoners of war like ourselves, who

were kept on at Besançon and Vittel to do the heavy work of the camps, also got a share in the distribution of parcels. We were very glad of this, as they were mostly splendid men who bitterly resented the German control of France, the betrayal of the French army by its leaders in 1940, and the surrender of Pétain. They were waiting with impatience, they said, for the next chance to fight by the side of the Allies for the freedom of France. In the camp they were friendly and helpful to us, and we were sorry when they left last summer.

We did our best during our internment not to lead an entirely aimless existence. People went to classes and concerts, played games, and worked in offices, in the garden, and in the hospital.

But it must be admitted that material things played a very important part in our lives. When I think with sorrow of my friends left behind in the camp, it is at least a consolation to realize that, thanks to the Red Cross, they have got enough to eat, to wear, and to smoke; the parcels, with their skillfully chosen contents, and the news from home make the long purgatory of internment bearable, if not pleasant.

Eventually my friend Rosemary Say and I climbed through a hole in the barbed wire surrounding the camp. I must not describe how we found our way to Marseilles, or how we were helped all the time by the French. Anyhow, we did win through and eventually we got across to Spain. From there we flew to England, freedom, and safety.

Vittel was 165 miles southeast of Paris. Originally for women only, the camp later added husbands to its number. In March, 1943, according to Red Cross reports, 277 internees were at Vittel; in June, 1944, there were 821.

Mrs. Ray Eddington, another British subject, also escaped and wrote about Vittel in December, 1943:

We were really very fortunate in our commandant. I believe he had been a prisoner in British hands in the last war, and he certainly did his best to be as lenient as possible with us, to try to make us comfortable, and to give us—within reason—what we asked for. We could have been very much less fortunate; we certainly would have been, had we had his second-in-command, a Gestapo official who had very little love for the British and was as harsh as he could be.

On festive occasions, such as Christmas, Easter, Empire Day, and Shrove Tuesday, we were allowed to have a dance in the big main hall, which was gaily decorated with greenery and paper hangings. The orchestra gamely played almost up to midnight without pause. The girls, and older women too, danced happily either with their own sex or with the men who were allowed over from the Continental for the evening and the doctors from the Vittel-Palace.

The post office was run by the women internees, under the head censor, but the parcels were entirely in the care of the German soldiers, who opened and censored each parcel in front of the recipient. Unfortunately, many of the personal parcels sent to the internees from their relatives and friends in this country had been pilfered on the way, and a great deal of the contents of some were missing when they finally left the parcel office in the arms of the internee.

In November of 1941, the first batch of husbands from Saint-Denis arrived at Vittel, and of course, the fortunate wives were overcome with joy at the reunion.

I have given to the last part of this article the title "Victory" because I look upon it as such, so far as I was concerned. For many months I had been planning to escape, but "the best laid plans of. . . ."

In my first attempt, my companion was unfortunate enough to run into the arms of the patrol, and they felt it their duty to report her. My second attempt was made some two months later with another girl, but we were seen leaving by a German civilian who promptly raised the alarm, and we were arrested some fifteen minutes away from the camp. This girl made her second try alone a fortnight later while the commandant was in Germany, celebrating Christmas and the New Year, and she succeeded in her bold attempt!

My third effort was crowned with success, taking place just three months and a week after the second fiasco. After a certain amount of hardship and difficulty, and a great deal of uncertainty as to whether we would win through in the end, my twenty-year-old companion and I reached unoccupied France. We parted at Lyon, I eventually making my way through France, Spain, and Portugal, to land in England in June.

In the sixteen months which had passed since our arrest—twenty-four others had tried and succeeded, although several of them had been caught and had tried again—Pamela Moore and I made the twenty-fifth and twenty-sixth successful evasions in sixteen months. Not a very high percentage in such a large camp.

Part 5
Liberation

Chapter 21

"For us
the game has just begun . . . "

The spread of Russian reconquest and revenge continued unchecked in Europe during the spring of 1945. Those who lived under Nazi terrorism were even more fearful of the advancing eastern hordes. As remnants of a defeated and disorganized Wehrmacht struggled westward, civilians in Estonia, Latvia, Lithuania, East Prussia, and Poland were close on their heels. Franz Wilhelm Müller, although no disciple of Hitler's, had reason for concern as eastern Germany was overrun. He had been chief forester of a large preserve on the peninsula of Darss, jutting into the Baltic some 140 miles north of Berlin. The fact that Reichsmarshal Hermann Göring's hunting lodge was located in the preserve was perhaps enough to send Müller before a firing squad. His wife Mona was dead, so he sent his two children to friends in Hamburg, then refused to leave the area himself despite repeated warnings from well-wishers.

Confident that he could safely hide until the worst was over, he built two bunkers—"foxholes," as he called them—one deep in the forest and the other nearer the Baltic shore. Wooden walls, floors, and roofs defined the cellar-like cavities, which were covered with several feet of dirt and camouflaged with growing grass, moss, and bushes. They were also well stocked with necessary supplies.

How Müller and his companion "foxes" (Cirstens, a refugee scientist; Pierre, an escaped French forced-labor prisoner; and Muske, Müller's longtime forestry worker and general handyman) sought to evade and escape the Russians is told in his diary. The account begins on the last day of April, 1945.

For a whole day I had had no home. The house, of course, was still there, only half an hour's horseback ride from the foxhole in the earth where I was sitting, hunched over a packing-box top, writing. But I had a home no more.

As I lay there on the sand thinking over what had happened, my dog, Horant, lifted his head and whined a warning. At the same moment the sky lighted up in the south. I rose to my knees slowly, for I was accustomed to move with caution; I didn't need to stand up because I recognized what the light was.

So it's happening at last, I thought. We had seen many flares in the south and out to sea. Now the enemy was really moving in our direction. Until that moment he had not dared set foot on our wooded peninsula.

Three days before we had watched from the Darss lighthouse and knew that our troops must be retreating from the east, blowing up the bridges one after another, and that the air force was setting afire the hangars on the airfields. Then we heard the coast artillery on the narrow neck of land joining the Darss peninsula with the mainland open fire, and we realized that from then on there was no barrier between us and the Russians. Smoke began to cover the heavens and the fiery ring grew nearer and nearer.

We had a conference. I explained to the other "foxes" how we should prepare for escape. If necessary we could go by boat —I had hidden a collapsible boat not far from the western shore of the Baltic—or we could cross the lagoon, south and east, to the mainland. Should any one of us get lost, he should explain that he was a refugee and had just come over from the mainland. I concluded emphatically that if anyone did not return, no one would try to look for him. He had to be considered gone for good. There was a deadly silence until I added that while we were together, no one was to leave another if he were wounded or ill. We must depend on each other absolutely. We would try to stay on Darss as long as it seemed wise; then, together, we would try to make the break for freedom.

Thus we agreed to stick together.

In mid afternoon Muske shook me awake. Pierre spoke in a tense whisper: "Ivan has come! At 2:00 P.M. I saw from our observation platform in that deserted eagle's aerie, a movement

on the drawbridge at Zingst [on the mainland across the lagoon
and to the east]. The reconnaissance cars rolled across first, then
the tanks with infantry. I counted twenty trucks and twenty
tanks. Some of the men must have been left in Přerov and Wieck.
Then I saw a cloud of dust as they entered Born. I heard
shots. Two shots. There's not a person there who would think
of resisting, is there?"

"No," I answered. "The last pistol there has long since been
thrown into the deepest pond. But for us the game has just begun. This evening we send out scouts. Muske and Pierre toward
Wieck. Cirstens and I will go to Born to see what has become
of the Forestry Administration headquarters."

About seven that evening we slipped out. I stood still a moment, lingering and listening. From high in a tall beech came a
blackbird's clear call and the yearning "oooh-yuuu" of a dove.
How often had my wife Mona and I, riding through the forest
together on just such a Maytime evening, listened to that song.

We went on. The first lights of the village appeared. I
posted Cirstens behind an oak and went on to a house I knew
well. I knocked on the bedroom window. As the curtain was
drawn aside, the head of my friend Leopold appeared.

"Get out of sight, quick!" he whispered. "A Russian officer is
asleep in the living room. I'll meet you in the meadow."

I left quickly. In a few moments Leopold joined me.

"The commandant is living in your *Forsthaus*. They control
the telephone service. All the men must report, but so far none
has been arrested. They searched the houses, and what they
went after first were schnapps, jewelry, clocks and watches . . ."

"Has there been any mention of me?"

"The Russians are asking about you, and a lot of other questions besides. 'Where is Göring? Where is Himmler?' And let me
tell you this—they have put a price of ten thousand marks on
your head."

"And what's happening at my house?" [Müller's Forsthaus
included dwellings, outbuildings, the headquarters, and other
structures of the Forestry Administration.]

"Hanna Drews, your old cook, is cooking from dawn to dark
and keeping the fellows in a good mood. They are comical char-
acters," Leopold laughed softly to himself.

He told how they seized every bicycle in the village but didn't know how to ride, fell off, and tried again until one corporal in a fit of rage smashed his machine to junk. Suddenly the rest followed him in an orgy of wheel smashing, and they left a mountain of wrecked bicycles in the street.

I took Cirstens by the hand and led him cautiously toward the Forsthaus. We went into the garden. There was a light in my room and my desk lamp was on. The window was open. I crept slowly across the rose garden and neared the house. There, sitting at my Louis XIV writing desk, was an officer with close-cropped blonde hair, a broad back, and a snub nose. He was reading some papers and had a bottle of my Napoleon brandy before him, and when I saw what was standing next to it, a surge of hatred came over me. It was the picture of Mona. I clenched my hands as if they were around a man's neck. I closed my eyes so tight that I saw green lights under my lids. I thought I was about to faint. The starter hummed in a nearby tank. The wireless telegraph began its "da-da-dit." Suddenly we heard a clock striking loudly. It seemed to come from outside the house.

A group of Russian soldiers were sitting around a wood fire at the side of the house, engrossed in a collection of clocks of all kinds. They would turn the hands of the clocks until all were striking at once. As the Russians grunted with pleasure, Cirstens tapped his forehead. I nodded and signaled that we had better leave.

My long struggle toward a goal had been in vain. The conqueror had seized my home. He had established dominion over the forest. He had bored into the heart of my preserves like a worm into the core of an apple. The fulfillment of my dream was the strongest motive for staying here—the real reason for my remaining, which until now I had not admitted. The whole reason for my existence was this sea-circled forest where I could rule as a prince without lands who had won a principality!

Then a bad night brought more than one disappointment. On a reconnaissance we found that our collapsible boat had been removed and a battery of artillery had been stationed on the neck of land joining the mainland. This meant that the Russians were here, not temporarily as we had first thought, but permanently.

We were hemmed in on all sides. The broad highway of the open sea had become a great blue wall. The dunes were patrolled. Cossack patrols, the wild commandos, were everywhere. We would have to keep close watch on the shore of the lagoon where the fishermen moored their boats, for we would then have some chance if we were forced to move.

News from the village warned that the hunt for the chief forester was being intensified. Raids by soldiers on foot, or in trucks and tanks, took place frequently, but the "foxes" remained safe in their burrow, ready to move to the second foxhole if they had to. Meanwhile, Müller had a surprise on his return from a foraging trip.

Having managed to catch a duck, I was returning in a cheerful mood and was mentally enjoying the smell of the duck while it roasted, when Cirstens appeared. Beckoning to me, he proceeded with his astonishing news. We had another member of the family. Pierre had been out picking berries near the bunker and had found a young girl, weak from hunger and exposure. He had taken her to the bunker.

"Come on," I said. "I'll give this damn Frenchman a piece of my mind. I'm not running a lost and found department, or a public waiting room either."

There on a pallet lay a blond wood nymph covered to her chin with blankets, her delicate features almost hidden in a tangle of hair. Her cheeks were the color of ivory, but her bright blue eyes sparkled. That is one of the peculiar effects of starvation—the cheeks turn pale and heighten the brightness of the eyes.

Shall I send her away? I thought. I cannot do it.

She was a Viennese girl named Lisle, who had worked in a dress shop before joining the Luftwaffe ground force. The outfit, mostly composed of women, had been camped on the Darss when the Russians came. They had taken the women and had probably killed the elderly ground officers in charge. Lisle had escaped and hidden in the forest.

With us, she soon recovered and, apt with a needle, made over some of the men's clothes. Pierre cut her hair.

A young page stood before us after this transformation. I admitted Lisle to our circle and turned over the kitchen to her. She cooked and served charmingly as only a Viennese can. I was thankful that she had come to us.

Almost a week later Muske returned from the village of Born.

"Up, up, everybody," he said, as he handed me a note which had been left in our secret drop. I read it aloud without comment.

"Big raid and search tomorrow, the seventeenth. The villagers are forced to join. They assemble at 7:00 A.M. If they start in your direction, I'll do all I can to divert them—will warn you with our signal. Tallyho—Leopold."

The hunt started at 9:00 A.M. I left the cover of our foxhole open two centimeters and soon heard the officers shouting commands. The crowd sounded like a boar hunt. A couple of times I could distinguish Leopold's voice, as he wished us to do. Then we heard the vehicles start to roll and the tramp of feet.

I remember thinking, What a relief my children aren't here. And just what must we do if they locate us, because there won't be a minute to spare. The narrow fox-burrow [secret exit] will be our only means of escape. We will come out in a thick pine undergrowth. We must push our way through this last cover before the wild shots into the thick pines become deadly shots under the tall birches. Perhaps we can reach the other bunker in safety by night.

Muske paused. I too heard something.

"Quiet," I commanded.

I put my ear to the air vent. I heard voices. Were they German or Russian? Muske's chin dropped. Sand sifted through the roof boards, and I imagined I heard the wind—or was it the rustle of the branches as men pushed their way through the underbrush? God! I could hear nothing but the pounding of my own heart!

Then I heard an unbelievable sound. I heard the whistled signal, Leopold's "All's well." It was as if a great wave about to engulf us had suddenly rolled away. Leopold! Rescue!

I dropped down at the table and picked up the playing cards: "All right. As you were, everybody."

Lisle sank back on the straw, Pierre dusted the sand from his knees, Muske stuck a cold pipe under his crooked nose and puffed energetically on nothing.

Things grew dangerous when Ivan began a systematic search for us. There was a constant commotion in the forest, with Cossacks riding patrols in every direction. Two armored cars and a Mercedes ran back and forth from the road to the lighthouse.

In a moment no one could possibly have foreseen, the unbelievable occurred. It was the last day in May and we were sitting in our tightly closed hiding place. It was afternoon. Cirstens was asleep. Lisle and Pierre were reading, and I was leafing through some of my private papers. Horant lay at my feet.

We heard a not unfamiliar sound. The muted noise probably came from a truck passing over the road. But unexpectedly, gears were shifted as if the truck had become stuck in loose soil. The light trucks usually had no trouble in the soft sand, although sometimes the drivers would turn out of the road onto the grass.

This happened then, as we could hear from the sound. Horant lifted his ears and then his head. He got up. I hand-signaled, "Lie down." He obeyed, but unwillingly. I myself was all ears.

The truck came nearer and it was obviously a heavy one. Then the wheels were right over our heads. The motor roared as sand, which now poured down on us—and on Horant, He sprang went into high gear and we could hear the tires grinding in the sand, which now poured down on us—and on Horant. He sprang up and gave an angry bark.

I hadn't time to think. I grabbed a hammer and struck him on the head.

The motor roared, the wheels ground, the roof shook, and the whole place trembled. Then the pressure was eased. The truck rolled away.

It was over. It had been a matter of about a minute, certainly no more. I had acted without thinking. I had killed the last true friend of my old life. He had scented a deathly danger and I had had to strike!

We were all crushed, and Lisle wept when she saw tears in my own eyes. I wasn't ashamed of my emotion and I cursed my hand as I ran into the forest.

The forest was surrounded. Our last bridge across the water, the fishing boats in the lagoon, seemed to have disappeared. We had to find out where the boats were tied up when they came in—or had the Russians commandeered the peaceful fishermen? Other alarming news: They were hunting us again. Another big raid would come tomorrow, but from what direction we did not know.

There was no other solution. We decided to sacrifice one of our bunkers in order to mislead the Russians and appease them. We planned to move to the "chicken bunker," leaving everything superfluous behind: the Gramophone, the records, and some conveniences we didn't need. But the statuette of our patron saint, the holy St. Francis, we would take with us.

We carried our last load to the chicken bunker in the night. I pushed things around to make it look like a hurried flight. Near the entrance I dropped an empty preserve can with a bright red label.

Pierre came back from Born with the news that for the first time the fishing boats were back.

"Get ready! Pack up—tomorrow we leave the Darss!"

But a note, also brought by Pierre, ended any thought of waiting even that long. A special force was already gathering in Zingst—a detachment of infantry with dogs. It was urgent that we charter a boat and cross the lagoon that night.

Shortly after midnight, with nothing more than what we wore or could carry, we managed to reach the shore of the lagoon and sever the moorings of a rowboat.

I took the lead and helped Lisle into the boat; next came Pierre, Cirstens, Muske. We kept close to the shore, then rowed into the open lagoon. We expected an alarm to go up at any moment, but nothing happened. It seemed to me that we had hardly moved from the shore. I let Pierre take my oars and, turning toward the village, I noticed Lisle as she sat there with her cap off, revealing her close-cropped hair. Her face seemed smaller and she looked extremely sad. I realized that never since we had all been together had we been stirred with such deep feeling as now. We were leaving a place where, for a few weeks at least, we had felt safe. Now we were being thrust into a new and perilous situation. We had been hunted, then tracked, and now forced to flee. We had come to feel that we belonged to each other.

We reached the mainland, tied up the boat where it could easily be found, and left cigarettes for its owner. We moved on, avoiding the main roads, sleeping in the woods or fields, and heading southward toward heavily wooded country with which I was thoroughly familiar. We passed villages and manor houses which the Russians had sacked, smashing what they couldn't carry off.

After three days we approached Buchenhof, the estate of my friends, the Count and Countess von Bohna. Here I expected news of my children, who were to have stopped there on their flight to Hamburg.

I remember my thoughts: Now we'll see the castle. The family will be in bed; the elderly parents always retire early. Ingeborg [the eldest daughter] will be worn out with her kindergarten work in the village, and Jutta [the younger, both war widows] will have spent a day in the saddle overseeing the farm hands or working on the estate accounts—a typical lady of the manor.

But what a picture I was painting! Was there still an estate, or even a village, where the old life did go on as it used to? As we shuffled along for half the night I tried to hearten my comrades with the hope of a green-tiled bathtub for Lisle, a wine cellar filled with bottles covered by a mouse-gray mantle of dust for Muske and Cirstens, and even a hint to Pierre of a Steinway on which he might play as long as he wished.

Suddenly Pierre, first to catch sight of Buchenhof, cried out in French, "Ooo, là, là! The dream-chateau!"

And then we heard the sound of Buchenhof—hardly what we had hoped for. Not magic music coming from a castle, but the snarl of a machine followed by the rattle and roar of a tractor.

Then I saw a strange light—a little, feeble light—then a second and a third, moving back and forth. Never had I seen such a light in the fields of Buchenhof. We came to the edge of the field. A tractor and a plow drawn by a team of horses moved across the field in opposite directions. They bore lanterns and behind them walked two women—bowed shadows, silent, submissive, humble, expressionless, scattering seed potatoes in the dark furrows.

I walked across the field and called to the boy driving the horses. He held up the lantern and looked me over.

"Man, get out of sight and be quick about it, or they'll put you to work until morning. Don't let them see you. They're after anyone they can find, like the devil after a lost soul."

I asked about the master and mistress.

"Master and Mistress! All that stuff is over. The Countess Jutta is out there with a basket following the plow. It's all bone and no meat around here. And the potatoes have to be in the ground by Sunday. That's the regular routine. Otherwise we get a visit from the commissar and then—*ach, du Lieber!*"

When Countess Jutta came over to refill her basket, I identified myself. She echoed the boy's warning.

"The commandant may come any minute," she whispered, "so stay where you're hidden. Your children were here. They went on. I'll tell you about it in the morning. I'll hide you in the village."

Next morning Jutta took us to a peasant's home. She told me, "The children arrived safely on foot after their horses and carriage had been seized by the Russians. They left with a friend who was also journeying westward and was glad to take them in his cart."

While I read letters left for me by the governess and the two children, Jutta dropped her head on her arms and immediately fell asleep.

The children were safe. I looked at Jutta, her golden hair partly covered with a peasant's handkerchief, her hands—a peasant's hands, a fieldworker's—with broken nails, black with soil. She awoke and told me her story—how the Russians came, looted the castle, shot the count and countess, spared the two daughters but forced them, along with the older boys, to replace the men in the fields who had been deported or killed.

I read the letters a second time and then a third time. Then the happiness began to melt and turn rancid like butter in the hot sun. What had happened to them since they left Buchenhof?

It is a long way to Hamburg—two hundred kilometers in a straight line and by their zigzag route perhaps twice as far. Did they need me? Yes, I thought they did. I had stayed too long in my foxhole.

Did I now belong to anyone? Not to myself, not to my fond memories, not to Mona, not to the dead. I had once thought that I belonged to the forest and the earth which had been entrusted to me. But I had been unable to protect the forest and I had even let my own flesh and blood leave without me, and now I was floundering like a fool in a high sea who had thrown away his rudder. I didn't even understand my own actions.

When we left I tried to persuade Jutta and her sister to join our party in an attempt to escape, but they refused to do so.

It was then the beginning of July. The farther we went, the more difficulties we encountered. So a fish must feel when it realizes the current is sweeping it into a weir. The country was crawling with soldiers, the roadside trees were gray with dust raised by the armor, and the back roads were so cut up by the hooves of the passing cavalry regiments that they looked as if they had been harrowed. Troops were bivouacked in field and forest, regardless of weather. And between the camps there was always movement.

We went on, avoiding the roads, sleeping in the woods, encountering other refugees occasionally. For weeks we moved westward, passing fewer and fewer people. Once we were arrested, but the Russian discipline was lax and we escaped their vodka-befuddled guards. After a month we entered a "dying land" of deserted farms and villages. As we neared the limits of the Russian occupied territory, we learned that most of the population had escaped across the border to the British zone. At last we were in the vicinity of the final Russian border guard.

We moved through the fog like shadows. A field of rye brushed our faces with damp dew. Then a whistle, a shot. A second shot. Those swine. Only a hundred meters more to the frontier. At last!

We sank to the ground and screamed. Safe—safe!

A milk truck came along and for a fare of five cigarettes took us aboard. The green steeples of Hamburg on the Elbe rose before us.

Chapter 22

" 'Have a good trip,'
the crowd jeered . . . "

After the Normandy invasion on June 6, 1944, Allied military leaders concentrated on the overall problem of totally defeating the Nazis. In their opinion, any attempts to recapture Paris would have slowed the Allied drive across France. Certainly they did no deliberate planning for such a liberation.

Hitler, on the other hand, dreaded the city's loss. Raging that "he who holds Paris, holds France," he decreed that the French capital city be held at all costs—or be destroyed. This order, incidentally, was never carried out by his Paris commander, General Dietrich von Choltitz.

Four years had passed since the Germans had occupied the city, and five million Parisians were hungry and without fuel and other necessities. They were ready to turn on their oppressors even as General Charles de Gaulle, Free French leader, called for a national liberation movement on August 14. Although his deputies were cautioned against instant revolt, Alexandre Parodi, Gaullist political chief in Paris, heard rumors four days later about a Communist take-over. He boldly seized the city's most important public building, the prefecture of police, and called a meeting of local French gendarmes. Their police strike on August 19 triggered a six-day citizens' uprising that literally pushed the Germans off the streets of Paris and ultimately out of France.

A member of the French resistance, Claude Roy, was in Paris on that Friday in August. His description of the uprising follows:

Later, much later, when the frenzy of anger and joy which has exalted us has faded from the horizons of memory, a writer will be able to speak of the events we have experienced and express everything properly. But at this time it is difficult to write in any way other than under the tumultuous dictation of history. Let us try to describe accurately and faithfully what we have seen, heard, and lived through during the past week—it is a great deal.

Saturday, August 19. That night Paris slept a feverish, breathless, interrupted sleep. Darkness had fallen over a city without police. The next morning we hastened to the doors of the closed stations to read the summons of the Police Committee of Liberation. On Rue Saussaises and Rue Laurent-Pichet, in the Bois de Boulogne, in front of Gestapo offices, there were flurries of black, burned paper ashes. "They" were burning their records. Wehrmacht trucks were patrolling the streets. On Place de la Concorde a truck passed, then another with boxes and a German soldier holding a sewing machine on his knees, seated on top. Where were the Allies? Where was [Free French General Jacques] Leclerc's army?

At Versailles, at Rambouillet, at Marly? Nobody knew. The paper ashes fluttered in the sun. A little black flake landed on the blond hair of my companion. Last night, on turning the corner of Rue de Buci to enter Rue de Seine on our way to the Senate, she had shouted, "Fireworks!" But as the red and blue rockets came toward us, making a buzzing sound about our ears, we saw that they were volleys of machine-gun fire, with stray bullets flying about everywhere. With all possible speed we took cover in a bistro, where the proprietor was waiting for the electricity to be turned on.

On Boulevard Saint-Michel the Germans fired on a crowd which had been watching them as they packed up. These militiamen had already moved out. They wore handsome uniforms and had fine machine guns.

"Have a good trip!" the crowd jeered, and the Germans fired. There were many wounded and killed.

There was shouting in the street, so I opened the restaurant window which was above the street on the second floor. In front of the café, people at all the windows were pointing to something I could not see. Then the proprietor shouted: "THE FLAG IS ON THE PREFECTURE!"

I hurried down into the street. It was true. On the roof of the prefecture was a small, black, moving speck—the fellow who had just run up the flag. It fluttered in the wind. Then another rose over the tower of Notre-Dame, and a third on the balcony, and another and another.

The square in front of Notre-Dame was black with people. Suddenly tricolor brassards were to be seen everywhere, and quick, choking emotion engulfed us as the leaders of the Police Liberation Committee gave rapid instructions to their men in plain clothes.

The great doors into the courtyard of the police headquarters swung open and in a few minutes the buildings were occupied. Telephone operators worked like mad. Orders flowed out. Thousands of ununiformed Paris policemen set off to reoccupy the stations they had abandoned during the occupation.

Opposite the city hall, where another flag was flying, they ran the colors up over the Poor Law Administration building. The first "Marseillaise" was heard—the wavering anthem of a yet hesitant insurrection—a hoarse, awkward, atrociously flat "Marseillaise."

A man showed me his papers. He was a political prisoner, only that morning freed by the FFI [Forces Françaises de l'Interieur, activated by Charles de Gaulle in March, 1944] from a German camp in the Paris region. He seemed haggard and bewildered. Liberty took his breath away, just like a swimmer's first moment after a plunge into cold water.

I entered the courtyard of the prefecture just as the new prefect of police of the provisional government was taking up his duties. The colors were hauled to the top of a flagpole. Then a second "Marseillaise" began—the "Marseillaise" of a thousand men's voices, exultant and free, thundering in the square courtyard which reverberated like an echoing well—a "Marseillaise" which was a signal to all Paris.

Then a big car drove up. In it were armed men wearing brassards and flying the tricolor flag of the FFI. I recognized two comrades, cinema operators. They had just come from the city hall which they and their men had occupied for the Parisian Committee of Liberation. Julien and Allard told me of the arrest of the prefect of the Seine and of Bouffet. With machine guns in their hands they had entered the ex-prefect's office. He welcomed them arrogantly until the guns were pointed at him. The ex-prefect stopped boasting at once. He was imprisoned in the police station, where others joined him later.

The French flag was raised on the Sorbonne, now freed from traitors and Nazi intellectuals. A student kissed his girl friend joyously. It was the finest day of his life. The old professor put on his glasses so he could see better. The crowd took up the swelling "Marseillaise." A girl threw her hands in the air, laughing and dancing. Yes, it was the finest day of our lives!

German trucks passed, firing as they went. But above the Saint-Vincent-de-Paul Hospital, on the School of Mines, on all the commissioner's offices, our flag was floating. Groups in the streets read the white notices of the National Council of Resistance—that longed-for appeal to national insurrection. In the streets, mere boys advanced toward strategic points; tricolor brassards came out of their pockets and were worn proudly. Violin cases, shopping bags, parcels opened to display concealed weapons.

The Nazis dashed about here and there, with hunted, dumbfounded looks on their faces. They shot at random, and passersby were killed. Gradually the streets were cleared. The only people moving now were the FFI with their coveted brassards on their arms, patriot liaison officers, and other officials. The leaders organized the defense, the plans of attack, and the resistance in official buildings occupied by our men. In front of cafés the chairs and tables were piled up into barricades. The iron shutters were closed. It was rumored that the distracted Germans would try to set the curfew for two o'clock.

The whole staff of the underground *Lettres Françaises* was entrenched at *Paris-Soir.* The FFI, with machine guns ready, guarded the entrance after having cleared the big building of collaborators the day before. At one-thirty a telephone call came through to the newsroom from the police station. The Germans were attacking the prefecture in full force.

Impressions were kaleidoscopic for the next few hours. In Rue de Rivoli, FFI first-aid stations were set up in the arcades under a Red Cross flag. On the Châtelet square, stray bullets whizzed about. Not a soul was to be seen. The sound of shooting came from Boulevard du Palais. A German truck rushed out and was stopped and seized by the defenders. Shooting died down. The truck seemed to be abandoned and its passengers powerless.

I started out again, and the shooting resumed as I dodged in and out toward the prefecture. Its doors opened before me as I sprinted forward, head lowered, like the winner in the famous cross-country race, the Tours de France.

In the courtyard of the prefecture, armed men were rushing back and forth. Already it was filled with German trucks, cars, ammunition, and light motor lorries captured from the enemy. The Ordnance Corps had difficulty in finding the necessary light ammunition for the volunteer combatants. One had a French machine gun, another an English weapon, still another a captured German rifle. The shooting reechoed strangely in the courtyards, hall, and stairways. During the rare lulls, the big doors would swing open to allow all ambulances and stretcher-bearers waving Red Cross flags to come and go.

There was a great deal of return fire from the defenders, patriot police, and FFI of the Latin Quarter who rushed through between lulls, across the bullet-swept square in front of Notre-Dame, the Boulevard du Palais, and the quays and bridges. At the first sign of a concerted attack by the SS, the outlying stations telephoned the prefecture. Policemen, thus warned, took the assailants in the rear, arriving by way of Rue Saint-Jacques and Boulevard Saint-Michel. They acted with remarkable daring. The besieged carried out counterattacks and sorties resulting in many prisoners and booty.

In the prefect's office where I went to telephone, one of the three secretaries who had come into the stronghold that morning smiled. She wore a white dress. Beside the telephone stood a bouquet of roses, somewhat faded. The liaison officers in khaki shirts, machine guns under their arms, came and went. She smiled. They brought in boxes of captured explosives, charges, and detonators with which the Germans had intended to blow up the Paris bridges. Still she smiled. The cannon fire made the windows rattle, and bullets whizzed over the roofs. She smiled.

"I guess I shan't go swimming at Deligny today," she said, between two telephone calls.

"I don't think so."

She spent the night at her post. The next morning, the little frock was still marvelously, gloriously white.

Men came in to telephone to their homes.

"Don't worry, dear, I already have five Boches to my credit. We'll get them all. We've got them," said one.

"Above all, don't go out," said another to his wife. "Watch the little one. No, I'm in no danger—none at all. Have you bread and provisions? Remember, don't go out."

At four o'clock, German tanks went into action. Their guns blasted holes in the entrance of the prefecture and in the square in front, causing damage and deaths. A barricade of sandbags and trucks was hurriedly thrown up. Young men calmly filled bottles with gasoline in case the tanks managed to get through. However, the gunfire of the defenders prevented the SS infantry from taking advantage of the partial gains made by the tanks. They fell back.

Five-thirty. The Germans were now trying to sprinkle the court with mines. Quickly reduced to silence, however, they next tried to penetrate the prefecture by means of the roofs. Going through a café, they had entered the building on the corner of Place du Palais and Boulevard Saint-Michel. Our men holding the street and those defending the inner courtyards fired at the roofs.

Six o'clock found me busily firing with a group of policemen from an office window on the Marché-Neuf quay facing the Saint-Michel quay. The panes had all been shattered. Splintered glass, munitions, and weapons littered the office desk, the blotter, the inkwell, the moleskin armchair. The violent jolts of the sten gun reverberated through the offices and halls, making a deafening din. By this time five enemy trucks had been destroyed on the Saint-Michel quay and a gasoline truck was burning at the Notre-Dame corner on Rue Saint-Jacques.

Flames from the burning truck had now caught the awnings of the sidewalk café and were licking the walls of the Notre-Dame Hotel. All fire from the windows of the prefecture ceased while, at the risk of their lives, the FFI and the police combatants who now held the Saint-Michel quay tried to move the blazing vehicle and save the building, which was already blackened by the smoky flames. Fire trucks arrived on the scene.

In the evening, the rumor spread that the Germans were asking for a truce. The order was given to cease fire, and an extraordinary and bewildering silence descended on the huge building which all day long had rocked and roared with the bursts of cannons, the incessant rat-tat-tat of automatic-gun fire, and the whine of rockets.

The truce was only a fiction. All night and for days afterward they went on fighting around the prefecture—Parisian stronghold of the national insurrection.

On Sunday, toward noon, I succeeded in getting out of the prefecture. The fighting continued, and by order of the FFI general staff, Paris was bristling with barricades. The most violent battles took place at the city hall in the Latin Quarter and in the vicinity of the Batignolles municipal buildings. The German flag still flew above the Senate, the Admiralty, and the Hotel Meurice, and the Germans were entrenching themselves in certain sectors.

From the doorways and windows, spectators followed the progress of the fight. But they too were mobilized. The home front must stand fast, the home front too must serve. In this case, the home front was the little square on Mont-Sainte-Geneviève where the whole population from the ages of three to twelve and from seventy to ninety sawed wood for the bakery, collected provisions for the FFI, cleaned weapons, and ripped up the pavement to build barricades.

To make these barricades, they first brought down the sandbags arranged according to civilian defense measures. Cobblestones were taken up, builders' supplies requisitioned, fences around trees removed, and the trees themselves sawed down. An overturned German tank propped up bedsprings and a cretonne-covered armchair. At the Halles market, wagons and pushcarts had been piled with vegetables. On Rue Mazarine, a truck obstructed the road. Cabbage stumps were rotting in the August sun.

German tanks patrolled the streets that were still open, firing haphazardly at windows and doorways. Occasionally, one met unexpected pedestrians, such as Father Bruckberger, a Dominican and also the author of the scenario of *Anges du Péché*. He walked about the streets in his white robes, visiting the hospitals in his capacity as FFI chaplain.

Hour by hour, by means of infinite patience, ingenuity, and the great victorious rage of insurgent Paris, the barricades methodically closed their traps upon the Germans.

Tuesday, August 22. The battle raged in the whole of Paris.

To get about the streets, you only had to have an FFI pass, slow up at the crossings, watch out for tanks, stoop while crossing bridges, avoid gaping pavements and still-smoldering fires, and keep a wary eye out for bits of flying glass and stray bullets from the guns of isolated German snipers or militiamen. With luck, you might for instance arrive at the town hall of the Seventeenth Arrondissement, in the heart of insurgent Batignolles.

Armed with six revolvers and a few machine guns, the FFI and patriotic militiamen of the arrondissement had succeeded three days before in occupying the town hall. Thanks to weapons seized from the enemy, we were able to arm more than four hundred fifty combatants.

The new municipal council was in session. The men were staid, methodical, clear-minded, and honest—order reigned behind the strongly defended barricades. Battle was one thing, administration another. The district had to live, eat, defend itself. The mayor thought of everything: wood for the baker, milk for the children, repression of pillage. While I was in his office, which was guarded, the telephone rang. The Germans were attacking on Rue Boursault and Boulevard des Batignolles.

I accompanied a detachment which went single file along the walls to take up its combat duty and reinforce the FFI outposts. We were preceded by a tank—a Somua tank—which still bore the registration number of the Wehrmacht. The workmen in the Somua factories had hastily finished assembling this tank for the FFI, who had succeeded in getting it off the premises in spite of heavy German resistance. Now, driven by the FFI, it crossed Paris from Saint-Ouen to Batignolles to assist in the defense of the town hall of the Seventeenth Arrondissement.

Unarmed except for the single German hand grenade tucked in his belt, and under heavy enemy fire, a young FFI lieutenant directed the setting-up of combat equipment and tank movements in the very center of Batignolles. The firing went on, the Germans taking shelter on the roof of 58 Boulevard des Batignolles. From this vantage point they sprayed us with machinegun fire and hurled grenades which burst a few yards from us. A cameraman friend of mine, Georges Mejat, darted about among the bullets taking pictures—what a splendid document of French street fighting that will be. The tank moved about in front of the shops.

Meanwhile, in the center of Paris, the Germans had been hurling their Tiger tanks and automatic machine guns into a furious attack on the city hall and the police station. But the vital centers of resistance were holding out. The Allied armies were tightening their grip upon the city.

Wednesday, August 23. I came out of 92 Champs-Elysées, the offices of the Cinema Liberation Committee. More shooting at the Rond-Point of the Champs-Elysées. I ran toward Victor-Emmanuel III Avenue. Two Tiger tanks and two Goliath tanks were maneuvering among the clumps of trees on the avenue, which was swept with machine-gun fire. The asphalt had been torn up by Caterpillars. People were running for cover, taking shelter in doorways. I just had time to fall in front of the American bar, l'Escargot.

The Germans attacked the police station at the Grand Palais. The FFI retrenched in the post were seriously outnumbered, but were defending themselves fiercely.

Smoke belched from the Grand Palais. A moment or two later the clang-clanging of trucks announced the arrival of the fire brigade. I saw them conferring with the Germans, who refused to let them put out the fires started by incendiary bombs. The firemen persisted, and the Germans opened fire on them. Bullets pierced the hoses which they had feverishly unwound. In Victor-Emmanuel Avenue, ten little fountains played, bullets whistled. Ridiculously, I thought of the sideshows at country fairs where you shoot at eggs, dancing on fountains of water.

Blinded with smoke, the besieged sought refuge in the cellars. All this time, German armored cars were shooting down passersby on the Champs-Elysées. The desperate defenders now had no ammunition but grenades. Some of them escaped. Others were captured and, with the civilians who had been driven into the Grand Palais by the bullets, were marched off in columns of three.

The fire spread. The firemen brought their hoses into position. Amid the smoke, the spouting water, and the noise, there was still sniping going on under the huge stained-glass windows. Stretcher-bearers darted about in the hubbub, bringing in the wounded.

Volunteers made a chain to clear the booths of the Ame des Prisonniers exposition at the Palais de la Découverte. Firemen, Germans, rescuers, and prisoners all milled about together. The Germans didn't seem to know whether they should arrest the rescuers or help them. We floundered about in the debris of papers, rubbish, charred wood, water, and cartridge cases. The people looked in through the windows at this mad spectacle, and watched the lunch cooking on a small paper stove. It was noon. The firemen had the fire under control.

Thursday, August 24. With the Hygiene Section. I wanted to spend the morning at the Hôtel-Dieu Hospital with those young men and women whom for five days I had seen darting about in the heavy fighting, waving their little Red Cross flags to divert the flying bullets, and picking up wounded Frenchmen or Germans.

Not one of the professors, surgeons, doctors, interns, nurses, stretcher-bearers, or blood donors had slept for five days. Lives saved, suffering spared or assuaged—these had been the only things that counted.

I confess that at times I have doubted my comrades, doubted the youth of France. But that day I knew that I had been wrong. Anyone who saw those joyful and weary looks knows what faces show hope—those of the combatants and the stretcher-bearers of the Parisian uprising, the heroes wearing brassards and the heroes in white working side by side. We will not forget them.

At noon two cars raced up to the Hôtel-Dieu Hospital. The president of the National Resistance Council and the prefect of the Seine came to greet the wounded.

It was not an anonymous and official face, nor was it a

solemn and inscrutable mask which came to meet the feverish
looks of our wounded fighting men. Two fiery eyes, black and
steady, those of the president of the National Resistance Council, M. Georges Bidault. The prefect of the Seine, thin, graying,
attentive, silent M. Flouret, accompanied him. The latter was
welcomed by the stretcher-bearers, to whom he spoke briefly,
sincerely:

"With minute-to-minute heroism, you rescued our soldiers,
and those of the enemy. In the name of the nation already liberated, already victorious, I thank you."

Then he, who had been one of the leaders of the daily combat, during four years of struggle, went the rounds.

"Combatants, you are already victors!"

The wounded man lying on one bed was little Maurice N.
of the National Teams, motorcyclist of the Fourth Motorized Aid
Service. He had first been wounded by a militiaman's bullet on
the Quai de la Tournelle, and then by a German bullet on
Avenue Daumesnil. He made a feeble attempt to get up.

"Don't, my good fellow. Let me embrace you."

We had scarcely entered the building when heavy firing
broke out. Shots rang through the corridors and rattled the windows. They were fighting on the square in front of Notre-Dame.
Thanks to Dr. A., I was able to obtain a Red Cross armband. I
left the little official group and accompanied Odette D., philoso-
phy student, and her team of voluntary stretcher-bearers on their
duties.

With all communications cut off, a German convoy of six
trucks carrying heavy loads had got caught in the barricades on
the quays between the prefecture and Notre-Dame. One of the
trucks was already ablaze. The trapped Germans put up a strong
defense and some fierce fighting ensued. There was still shooting
going on near the Notre-Dame bridge, toward which Odette D.
and I were speeding with our stretcher mounted on rubber
wheels.

Near one of the trucks was a wounded man. His FFI captor
was loath to release his prisoner in the heat of the battle and we
almost had to take the German away from him by force. Some of
the gasoline tanks on the truck had been pierced with bullets
and the gasoline was now mixed with the blood and dirty rain-

water on the ground. We took charge of one wounded man whose abdomen and shoulder were bleeding profusely. My hands were covered with blood. We ran up with the stretcher.

In the hospital yard, he was transferred to a hand stretcher and taken to the first-aid station. Doctors and nurses bustled about. French and German wounded were undressed. One of the men that they were tending groaned. There was the smell of perspiration, disinfectant, and blood. However, it was not ten minutes before these naked, blood-spattered men had been washed, had had their wounds dressed, and had been evacuated —some to the operating room, others to the room for shock victims, and still others to the room for those suffering light wounds.

The members of the National Resistance Council were very restless. It was in this office that the waiting—the interminable, dull, painful waiting—would come to an end.

In the prefect's big office the telephone rang. The leaders of the resistance, men of long patience, nervously tapped the arms of their chairs, paced about, went to the windows. Night fell. On a pedestal was the bust of the Republic; on the high mantelpiece, a poor photograph of General de Gaulle wearing a tricolor tie. Bullets had starred the mirror above it. On the sills of the big windows were sandbags, machine guns. The FFI, with several days' growth of beard, dusty and black, kept watch.

In the courtyard—among the enemy trucks, the captured German antiaircraft batteries, German Caterpillars, and FFI cars —Allied flags were being taken out, ready for the welcome.

The Allies were at Sceaux, at Bagneux, at the Porte d'Italie. The advance guards of Leclerc's division had taken the Lakamal Lycée a moment before. French mechanized forces rushed the Italian front.

At eight o'clock, everyone except the men on guard went into the dining hall. The prefect and members of the National Resistance Council ate noodles and bread from the trestles.

Suddenly, Georges Bidault rose, and his voice stuck in his throat as he announced, "The first French army tanks have crossed the Seine into the center of Paris."

There was tumultuous applause. Standing on the tables, a thousand united men, the FFI of the prefecture, sang the "Marseillaise" of the deliverance.

Then there was a rush outside. The Romilly car stopped at the corner of the Hôtel-de-Ville quay and the square. It was 9:22 P.M.

Carried along by a crowd of weeping, laughing, shouting armed men, two soldiers entered the prefect's office.

"Captain Dronne and Private Pirlian of the Chad Regiment de Marché."

The president of the National Resistance Council embraced the bearded captain.

"Captain, in the name of the soldiers of France without uniform, I embrace you as the first French soldier in uniform to enter Paris."

I also embraced the captain, with his face covered with perspiration, his kepi soiled and broken.

He said only, "But I am so dirty, disgustingly dirty—it was such a long road."

Captain Dronne had come to Paris from the Cameroon, by way of Mersa Matruh—Tobruk—Bengasi—Bir-Hakeim—the Chad —London—Cherbourg. It had taken him forty-eight months.

Private Pirlian had a Nice accent and wore an odd little round cap, so surprising over a French face—an American cap.

Rockets streaked the night. There was a thunder of guns. They shouted.

"They are firing a salute!"

But tiles broke, glass chandeliers shattered to bits, and plaster fell from the ceiling. The Germans were attacking the city hall. We turned out the lights. The FFI at the windows returned the fire.

"All unarmed men lie flat!" shouted Commandant Stephane, leader of the City Hall FFI.

Lying flat, with the battle raging furiously around, the members of the National Resistance Council, the officials, and the prefect lived through the first moment of French liberation.

I tried to leave the city hall. It was impossible by the doors, where there was hard fighting going on. A single exit left—the metro. Accompanying an FFI patrol which was going to relieve guards at the Châtelet station, I emerged into a sudden silence and made my way along the faintly lighted passageways, on the tracks where our daily metro trains no longer sped their noisy way. We paused at the different stations. Approaching footsteps. Had the enemy succeeded in getting in? We shouted:

"The password?"

"Verdun!"

Our steps resounded as we progressed slowly along the labyrinth of tracks and passageways.

A gateway was ajar. Suddenly I came out into the darkness of Paris. At the end of the Rue de Rivoli, a huge fire reddened the sky. Church bells were ringing in the night, and around the square, Paris was singing of its deliverance and its victory in the triumphant strains of the "Marseillaise":

"Allons enfants de la Patrie,
Le jour de gloire est arrivé."

Friday morning, August 25. Eight o'clock. A steady stream of mechanized troops, jeeps, and tanks flowed down Rue Saint-Jacques. The tanks bore names marvelous to read after four years of Nazi parades: Valmy, d'Artagnan, Porte de la Chapelle, Le Mort Homme.

The crowds cheered and threw flowers, cigarettes, and kisses to the dusty, tanned, unkempt men. That morning was an extraordinary mixture of triumphant parades and street fighting.

From the roofs of the Sorbonne, militiamen shot at the crowds acclaiming the Leclerc Division. In Rue des Ecoles, women and children were killed. There was blood on the asphalt.

As if by a miracle, the barricades were wide open.

All day long, French tanks went to the aid of the FFI in mopping-up operations. At the Republic, at the Senate, at the Kommandantur, and on Rue de Rivoli, the last islands of enemy resistance were attacked, pounded, and soon forced to surrender. As our mechanized forces advanced on the German entrenchments, shouts of joy burst forth behind them from the pavements. Silk stockings, tobacco, and bread taken from enemy trucks, stocks amassed by enemy pillage and rapine, were distributed. Girls walked arm in arm with soldiers. Young lads played with the mysterious gadgets on the automatic machine guns.

People pressed about the fighting men with questions about their amazing adventures. They told about their escape from

France, the Spanish Fascist prisons, the march to Chad with the Leclerc column. They told about Tobruk, Mersa Matruh, Bengasi, Bir-Hakeim, the battles of Tunis, the landing and the battle of Normandy, the war in France. The Parisians listened eagerly.

Frenchmen were talking to Frenchmen.

Epilogue

The war did not end with the liberation of Paris. Many more lives would be sacrificed; much more destruction would be visited heavily upon the continent. However, even as the fall of Paris had symbolized the completion of a Nazi victory in western Europe, so did the return of the French capital to its inhabitants signify a body blow to Hitler's *Festung Europa* [Fortress of Europe].

But the milestones continued to be passed on the road to the defeat and oblivion of the Third Reich. These included:

The fall of Antwerp, the second largest port in Europe, on September 4, 1944.

The capture of the Ludendorff Bridge at Remagen on the Rhine by the Ninth Armored Division on March 7, 1945.

The execution on April 28 of Benito Mussolini by Italian partisans. Two days later, the Nazi dictator who had started World War II died by his own hand in his Führer bunker in Berlin.

The surrender on May 2 of the remaining German troops in Italy.

The arrival of Seventh and Third Army troops in Austria and western Czechoslovakia during the same first week in May.

VE Day on May 8 signaled, at long last, the end of the war in Europe.

Now the grand scale of human wretchedness, of the destruction and disruption of Europe's economy, was apparent; it was far greater than that of the first world war. In October, 1945, the trials of German war criminals began at Nuremberg, Germany.

And in July, 1947, sixteen nations met in Paris to discuss a unified reconstruction program, the so-called Marshall Plan.

Yet for the millions who had survived the hell of those six war years, their experiences would remain with them as long as they lived, with the vividness of yesterday's nightmare.

Sources

Permission has been granted to reprint and publish the excerpts in this book, which are from the following sources.

Introduction. Dominik Wegierski (pseudonym for Professor Karel Estreicher), *September, 1939*, Minerva Publishers (London, 1940).

Prologue. *Arbeiter Zeitung* (Basle, Switzerland, July 31, 1942).

Chapter 1. Robert W. Bean, "An American Student in Norway," *Scandinavian Review* (New York, September, 1940).

Chapter 2. Liesje van Someren, *Escape from Holland*, Barrie and Rockliff/ Herbert Jenkins Ltd. (London, 1946).

Chapter 3. Roger Langeron, *Paris, Juin '40*, Flammarion & Cie (Paris, 1946).

Chapter 4. Ruth Parmelee and Emilie Willms, "Three Times 'No,' " *Greece Fights; The People Behind the Front*, Homer W. Davis, ed., American Friends of Greece (New York, 1942).

Chapter 5. Chris Jecchinis, *Beyond Olympus*, George G. Harrap & Co., Ltd. (London, 1960).

Chapter 6. Eugene Weinstock, *Beyond the Last Path*, Boni & Gear (New York, 1947).

Chapter 7. 1) Ivan Ivanovich Isakov, *Partisan Bonfires* (Leningrad, 1966). 2) Yelizaveta Prokofyevna Stanishevskaya, *From the History of the Partisan Movement in Byelorussia over 1941–44* (Minsk, 1961).

Chapter 8. T. Bor-Komorowski, *The Secret Army*, Victor Gollancz Ltd. (London, 1950).

Chapter 9. Carlo Christensen, *Under Jorden i Borgergade*, Nyt Nordisk Forlag (Copenhagen, 1945).

Chapter 10. Jean de Vos, *I Was Hitler's Slave*, Quality Press, Ltd. (London, 1942).

Chapter 11. Maria Brzeska, *Through a Woman's Eyes*, Maxlove Publishing Co., Ltd. (London, 1944).

Chapter 12. Catherine Klein, *Escape from Berlin*, Victor Gollancz Ltd. (London, 1944).

Chapter 13. Lena Yovitchitch, *Within Closed Frontiers*, W. and R. Chambers Ltd. (London, 1956).

Chapter 14. 1) Reginald C. F. Maugham, *Jersey Under the Jackboot*, W. H. Allen and Co. (London, 1947).
2) Horace M. Wyatt, *Jersey in Jail*, Alba Press, Ltd. (London, 1945).

Chapter 15. Hans Dibold, *Doctor at Stalingrad*, Hutchinson & Co., Ltd. (London, 1958).

Chapter 16. Dr. A. V. Borosini, trans., "Escape from Hell," *South Atlantic Quarterly*, Duke University Press (North Carolina, January, 1947).

Chapter 17. Margarete Buber-Neumann, *Under Two Dictators*, Victor Gollancz, Ltd. (London, 1949).

Chapter 18. Zdena Trinka, *A Little Village Called Lidice* (Lidgerwood, North Dakota, 1947).

Chapter 19. U.S. Congress, House of Representatives Special Committee on the Katyn Forest Massacre, October 11, 1951, and November 14, 1952; Washington, Chicago, London, and Frankfurt, United States Government Printing Office (1952).

Chapter 20. *The Prisoner of War*, H. Marshall and Sons for the British Red Cross and the Order of St. John of Jerusalem (London, 1942–45).

Chapter 21. Franz Wilhelm Müller, *Kein Ort zu Bleiben*, Interverlag A. G. (Zurich, 1949).

Chapter 22. Claude Roy, *Paris Uprising*, French Information Service (Ottawa, 1944).

Bibliography

Blumenson, Martin. *Breakout and Pursuit*. Washington: U.S. Army in World War II, Office of the Chief of Military History, Department of Army, 1961.

Collins, Larry, and Lapierre, Dominique. *Is Paris Burning?* New York: Simon and Schuster, 1965.

Eisenhower, Dwight D. *Crusade in Europe*. New York: Doubleday & Company, Inc., 1945.

Font, M.R.D. *S.O.E. in France, an Account of the Works of the British Special Operations Executive in France, 1940–44*. London: Her Majesty's Stationery Office, 1966.

Guderian, Heinz. *Panzer Leader*. Translated by Constantine Fitzgibbon. New York: E. P. Dutton and Co., Inc., 1952.

MacDonald, Charles B. *The Siegfried Line*. Washington: U.S. Army in World War II, Office of the Chief of Military History, Department of Army, 1963.

Shirer, William L. *The Rise and Fall of the Third Reich*. New York: Simon and Schuster, 1960.

Toland, John. *The Last 100 Days*. New York: Random House, 1966.

Werstein, Irving. *That Denmark Might Live*. Philadelphia: Macrae Smith Company, 1967.

Young, Peter. *World War 1939–1945: A Short History*. New York: Thomas Y. Crowell Company, 1966.

Zotos, Stephanos. *Greece: The Struggle for Freedom*. New York: Thomas Y. Crowell Company, 1967.

PRINTED IN THE U.S.A.